HERO OF KUMAON

The life of Jim Corbett

In memory of
Billy Arjan Singh

HERO OF KUMAON

The life of Jim Corbett

DUFF HART-DAVIS

Merlin Unwin Books

Contents

Glossary

atta wholemeal flour

ayah nurse

bandobast festivity

bhago! run!

bhalu bear

chital spotted deer

chota hazri small breakfast

churail mysterious bird, witch

dak bungalow rest house for touring officials

dal dried pulses

flehmen grimace made by tigers

Garhwali a regiment of the Bengal Army

gharial fish-eating crocodile

ghat sloping riverbank

ghoral mountain goat

gur unrefined sugar

haldu flowering tree

havildar sergeant

howdah platform on elephant

jaggery unrefined sugar

jangias pants

jarao hill name for sambar

jemadar sergeant

kakar barking deer, also called muntjac

langur monkey

machan raised platform, on stilts or in a tree

mahout elephant driver

mahseer freshwater fish

nullah small ravine

patwari village headman

pundit learned man, priest

puja prayer

sal *shorea robusta,* hardwood tree

ringal hill bamboo

sadhu holy man

sahib mister, master

sambar large deer

semul silk cotton tree

sher tiger

shikar hunting

shikari hunter

tahsildar local tax collector

Foreword

For much of his life Jim Corbett was hardly known outside Kumaon, the area of northern India where he lived. He grew up in a poor Irish-Indian family, one of 15 children: a born hunter, equipped (as he himself said) 'with a pair of eyes that few are blessed with', he went barefoot and alone in the jungles round his home. He learnt to imitate birds and animals so accurately that he could call them to him, and he shot his first leopard at the age of ten.

His working life, as a manager on the railways, was far from glamorous, but in his own territory during the 1920s and 1930s he acquired a god-like reputation as a destroyer of the man-eating big cats which terrorised the native population, killing hundreds of country people. The hill-folk worshipped him, and the Government decorated him for his humanitarian outlook.

Then, in the 1940s, with the publication of *Man-Eaters of Kumaon* – his narrative of days and nights in the jungle – he suddenly acquired international fame. First published by the Oxford University Press in Bombay, then in America and England, the book quickly sold 250,000 copies. Never since has it been out of print. The most recent British biography of the author came out in 1986, but it included little of Corbett's own writing, and only a brief mention of the Corbett

National Park and Project Tiger, the Indian Government's last-ditch attempt to save the species. This new life describes the progress of the Park, the efforts being made to minimise conflict between its animals and the villagers living round it, and the overall success of Project Tiger to date.

My aim is to take the reader into the jungle, as far as possible in Corbett's own words. To keep the book to a reasonable length, I have abbreviated some of his topographical descriptions, but all the exciting action is here in his own narrative, for he was a marvellous story-teller. The book also emphasises his gradual conversion from killer to preserver, and the change in the general attitude to big game animals – tigers, leopards, elephants, rhinos – which he helped bring about.

Duff Hart-Davis
September 2021

Introduction

When, as a boy of fourteen, I won a form prize at school, I was lucky enough to be presented with a copy of *Man-Eaters of Kumaon*. Immediately gripped by Jim Corbett's life-and-death encounters with tigers and leopards in the Indian jungle, I read the book from end to end, again and again. Its magic has never faded.

Half a century later, on a glorious winter's day in Chitwan, the great forested wilderness south of the Himalayas in Nepal, I was decanted from elephant-back into the branches of a tree, along with Hemanta Mishra, then Head of the country's Wildlife Department. Half a mile away, ten more elephants had lined out, ready to drive a huge block of ten-foot grass towards us. The aim of the operation was to anaesthetise a particular tigress and fit her with a radio collar which would reveal the pattern of her movements.

Although the objective was research, the manoeuvre was strikingly similar to the Victorian and Edwardian shoots in which tigers were driven to riflemen safely mounted on machans (raised platforms) or elephants. The difference was that Hemanta had no lethal weapon – only a dart gun with an effective range of about forty yards, with which he hoped to anaesthetise the tigress as she crossed the open glade beneath us.

Perched in our tree, we waited breathlessly. At first only the harsh calls of hornbills broke the silence. Then, in the distance, an amazing cacophony started. Each driving elephant bore a cargo of four or five men, and at a signal all began to yell, howl, hoot, whistle and rattle tin cans full of stones. The moving wall of noise, faint at first, gradually drew closer. Soon we could hear the swish and crash as the heavyweight beaters cleared passages for themselves by swatting down the coarse grass with their trunks. Then, to our left front, an elephant screamed. Seconds later, another let fly from the middle of the beat, then one to our right. Our quarry was there, sure enough, ranging along the line, trying to break back.

Swish, crash went the elephants. The closer the beaters came, the greater the pressure on the tigress, the higher the tension up our tree. We hoped that she would come forward slowly and pause to get her bearings in the open space beneath us – but no: when at last she came, she came all-out, a lithe streak the colour of apricot jam, covering the ground in great bounds, and was gone in a flash, giving Hemanta no time to aim or pull the trigger. The drive had failed – but by heaven it had been exciting.

That experience, along with other tiger close-encounters, made me feel that, although I never met Jim, I had caught glimpses of the world that he had known, and they left me eager to help perpetuate his memory. In this book I have quoted his own narratives at length, because it is his skill with words, combined with his extraordinary prowess as naturalist and hunter, that has enthralled many million readers.

CHAPTER ONE

Barefoot Boy

He was born on 25 July 1875 in Nainital, a lovely hill-station in north-west India, 6,500 feet above sea-level, on the southern fringes of the Himalayas, in the district of Kumaon*. The fourteenth child in a family of Irish immigrants, he was christened Edward James, and always known as Jim. By the time of his birth, his family was well established in India: his grandfather Joseph Corbett had sailed from Dublin in July 1814, and although he was only 5' 4" tall, had served in the artillery until his death in 1830. He and his wife Harriet had seven children, the last of whom, Thomas, was tied to a tree and burned to death by insurgents during the siege of Delhi in 1857.

Christopher, Jim's father, was the third child. He had served in the first Afghan War, the Sikh wars of the 1840s, and the Mutiny, perhaps as an Army doctor. He then set up as an apothecary, or assistant surgeon, in Mussoorie, and later became the postmaster in Nainital – not, one would guess, a very demanding position. With his first wife, Mary Anne Morrow, he had three children, and after her death in 1859 he married Mary Jane Doyle, a widow with three children of her own (another had died in infancy). She had first been married when only fourteen, and during the Mutiny she and her young family had joined other whites in the safety of

* Kumaon is now within the state of Uttarakhand, which was created in 2000 from part of the former United Provinces.

11

the fort at Agra; but in 1858 her husband Charles was killed fighting the mutineers with the local conscripts at the battle of Harchandpore.

Thus Mary Jane had been widowed at twenty-one. With her Christopher proceeded to father nine more children, of whom Jim was the last but one. The siblings with whom he identified most closely were his step-brother Tom, fifteen years his senior, and his sister Margaret, always known as Maggie, eighteen months older than him. She was short, dumpy and snub-nosed, and rarely left home, but she and Jim remained devoted to each other throughout their lives, neither marrying, and she supported all his ventures with unstinting devotion.

A grant of ten acres of land from Sir Henry Ramsay, the Commissioner of Kumaon (known as the King of Kumaon), enabled Christopher to build a spacious house, made of locally-fired bricks and stone retrieved from the river. Known as Arundel, the house stood on a south-facing slope in the village of Kaladhungi, thirteen miles south of Nainital and 3,000 feet lower, at the base of the hills, in a modest community sustained by an open-cast iron ore working and a charcoal-burning business. Water for the house came from the river Boar, via a canal which ran along the northern boundary of the plot. A keen gardener, Christopher surrounded the dwelling with shrubs and an orchard of mango and other fruit trees, and there the family lived during the winter. In a lovely passage written late in life Jim described the scene:

The white line at the foot of the village is the boundary wall, which took ten years to build, and beyond the wall the forest stretches in an unbroken line until it merges into the horizon. To the east and to the west as far as the eye can see is limitless forest, and behind us the hills rise ridge upon ridge to the eternal snows.

Wildlife abounded in the jungle all round, and the variety of birds was phenomenal, especially when, in spring and autumn, migrants passed through on their way to and from the high mountains. In summer, from April to November, the family also migrated, and moved up to Nainital, to escape the burning heat of the plains. In the early days there was no motor road between the two: women were conveyed for most of the way in a contraption called a *doolie dak* – a large box suspended from poles borne by eight men – but for the final ascent they transferred to a *dandy*, a hammock slung from a single pole. Men and boys had to walk a steep, stony track through jungle, travelling at night as well as by day, lighting fires to scare off tigers and leopards.

Nainital was, and is, a beautiful place. Tree-covered hills slope down to the shores of a pear-shaped lake, two miles long, half a mile across at its widest, and sacred to Hindus. Legend related that the first Europeans who found it resolved to keep the secret of its existence to themselves, so attractive did it seem. 'Forests came sweeping down to its shores, and deer drank fearlessly from its edge,' wrote Audrey Baylis, whose family came to live there in 1912; and in the far distance, sixty miles beyond the head of the valley to the north, the snow-summits of Trisuli and Nanda Devi gleam among other giants on the horizon.

The first European settler had reached the valley in 1841, and more houses, built on plinths, with roofs of corrugated iron painted bright red, had quickly gone up as British soldiers and colonial officials discovered the beauty of the place and its climate. Then on 18 September 1880 the little town was hit by a natural disaster, as heavy rain – over fifty inches in two days – set off a mud-slide which swept away many of the houses and buried most of the shops, a hotel, a Hindu temple and the Assembly Rooms, killing 151 people, including forty-three Europeans.

Undeterred, the survivors dug in, but only six months later Christopher Corbett was struck down by a heart attack, and after a few days died, aged 58. His widow Mary Jane had already bought a plot of land on Ayaparta Hill, opposite the scene of the disaster, and now supervised the construction of a dwelling there. A two-storey structure with four bedrooms, it was called Gurney House, and it became the family's summer home.

Nainital was then the summer capital for the British administration of the United Provinces. The Governor would arrive by the end of April, and remain in residence until the end of September. Government House was perched on the summit of Ayaparta hill, and residential houses clung to the surrounding slopes. The whole place had a strongly English air, and society was strongly colour-conscious: only privileged Indians were allowed to use the Upper Mall, which connected the ends of the lake. In contrast, Kalahundi had only two white families, and Jim – who at first was looked after by an *ayah* (or nurse) – grew up with the village boys, speaking Hindi and learning country dialects, so that he became able to communicate with illiterate folk at work and in the hills – an indispensable asset when he went after the man-eating tigers and leopards which were the curse of rural communities.

He loved his mother, and was fascinated to hear how, as a girl of six or seven, she had travelled by bullock cart and boat from Calcutta to the Punjab – a journey of more than 1,000 miles that took several months. In one of his few descriptions of her Jim wrote that 'she had the courage of Joan of Arc and Nurse Cavell combined,' and that she was also 'as gentle and timid as a dove.'

His sister Maggie (known in the family as 'Maggs') gave a fuller account:

In appearance she was very small, with delicate features, lovely colouring and beautiful blue eyes. She was utterly unselfish, and never felt that any self-denial or self-sacrifice on her part was too great where her children were concerned. I have often thought that Jim inherited many of her characteristics: bravery, courage, generosity and kindness combined with a strong sense of duty.

In a room set aside for the purpose, she taught the children basic spelling, arithmetic and singing. Jim had a clear treble voice, which later developed into a tenor – a gift which helped him imitate the calls of birds and animals. Maggie became an accomplished musician, and later taught piano to hundreds of pupils in Nainital. In Kalahundi she ministered tirelessly to the sick, no matter whether they were Christian, Hindu or Moslem; she treated ten or a dozen patients a day for injuries and ailments ranging from malaria to hiccoughs, from ear-ache caused by ticks to gore wounds inflicted by bullocks. She also grew into a botanist of considerable fame in the Kumaon hills, and she loved birds, particularly those of the jungle round the village.

Over a period of ten years Jim went to three different schools in Nainital, among them the Philander Smith College; but the one he liked best was run by the American Methodist Mission, whose teachers introduced him to the adventure stories of James Fenimore Cooper. He read *The Last of the Mohicans* again and again – and maybe the American's easy, natural style influenced his own writing later in life. He was often buried in a book, and in the dormitory at boarding school the boys would cluster round his bed while he read aloud to them.

School was tolerable; but he far preferred to be out of doors, for from his earliest days a powerful hunting instinct burned inside him – so much so that he was constantly wandering off into the jungle that surrounded Kaladhungi, often going barefoot to make sure that he could move silently, and to facilitate the climbing of trees – a skill rendered difficult by leather shoes. Later he remarked that being brought up in the hills made him as sure-footed as a goat.

His first weapon was a catapult, given him by his brother Tom, to help him recover from a dangerous bout of pneumonia; and with this primitive equipment he became a deadly shot, killing dozens of small birds which he skinned to mount and add to his collection, or to give to his cousin Stephen Dease, who was writing a book about the birds of Kumaon. He then graduated to a pellet bow, which had a small square of webbing fixed between its twin strings. This weapon was more powerful than a catapult, but less accurate, and Jim never really liked it. All the same, he became proficient enough with it to defeat the *havildar* (sergeant) of the Gurkha detachment that guarded the Nainital treasury, in a contest aiming at a match box set on a post twenty yards away. When the deficiencies of the pellet bow became too annoying, he made himself a bow and two arrows, basing their design on hints picked up from reading the Fenimore Cooper novels, and setting out to emulate the Red Indian warriors depicted in the books. Conceiving an ambition to be a lumber-man in Canada, he became so skilled with an axe that (it was said) he could split a match-stick.

He was also a gifted mimic, and learnt to imitate the birds that lived in or passed through the forests – crow pheasants, golden orioles, bulbuls, rosy pastors, scimitar babblers, drongos, parrakeets, laughing thrushes, kingfishers, jungle fowl, hoopoes and peacocks, among many others. He would go off into the jungle for days at a time, accompanied by an old gardener to carry his bedding roll and a small bag of *atta* (wholemeal flour) with which to make chapattis. At night they would keep a fire burning, for warmth and as a deterrent to tigers.

Soon, from bird calls, from the alarm cries of deer and monkeys, from the way vultures were circling in the sky, he could divine the movements of predators, and in time he became so skilled that he could call leopards and tigers up to him. Later in his life a legend grew up that he could converse with animals – and even if they never answered in words, they certainly responded to his overtures. 'Animals who live day and night with fear can pinpoint sounds with exactitude,' he wrote, 'and fear can teach human beings to do the same'.

> *Sounds that are repeated – as for instance a langur [monkey] seeing a suspicious movement, or a peafowl calling at a tiger – are not difficult to locate, nor do they indicate immediate danger calling for instant action. It is the sound that is heard only once, like the snapping of a twig, a low growl or the single warning call of bird or animal... that is of immediate danger and calls for instant action. Having acquired the ability – through fear – of being able to pinpoint sound, I was able to follow the movement of unseen leopards and tigers, whether in the jungle by daylight or in bed at night.*

He later reckoned that from his experience he 'absorbed' jungle lore, rather than 'learnt' it, and he went on doing so for the whole of his life. One key skill which he gradually mastered was that of tracking. At first he found it hard to distinguish between the pug-marks of a tiger cub and those of a leopard, which were much the same size; then experience showed him that he could differentiate by concentrating on the imprint of the toes, for those of a young tiger are larger, and out of proportion to those of a leopard. In the same way, he learnt the difference between the prints of a wild pig and the similar indentations left by a young *sambar* deer. An even more arcane skill was his ability to deduce, from its track, the identity of a snake and the direction in which it had been moving. 'When you see the track that shows excessive wriggling,' he wrote, 'you can be reasonably sure it is the track of a poisonous snake.'

At the age of eight one of his duties was to chaperone the girls of the family when they went swimming in the canal which formed one boundary of the Corbetts' land in Kaladhungi. They went every day of the week except Sunday, and he found the task intensely embarrassing, for decorum obliged the young women, between nine and eighteen, to wear their nightdresses while they swam, and as they entered the water, the flimsy cotton garments were liable to float up round their heads – to the edification of villagers walking along the far bank of the canal to collect firewood from the forest. 'When this happened, as it very frequently did,' Jim wrote later, 'I was under strict orders to look the other way.' Some commentators have suggested that glimpses of pubescent girls' bodies may have left him with inhibitions about women which made him a lifelong bachelor.

His earliest experience with a gun was nearly his last. One day Dansay Fleming, a burly young Irishman who had been disinherited by his father (a general) for refusing to join the army, took him into the jungle to shoot a tiger, carrying not only a muzzle-loading rifle, but also a muzzle-loading shotgun slung on his shoulder. Luckily they found no tiger, but on the way home Dansay suggested that Jim should try the shotgun on a flock of white-capped laughing thrushes which were scratching up dead leaves in search of ants. Obeying instructions, he took aim, gently squeezed the trigger of the ancient weapon – and was blown backwards, heels over head, not injured but severely shocked.

Soon he had a weapon of his own – a double-barrelled, muzzle-loading shotgun that had seen better days. Someone had split the right-hand barrel by over-loading it, and the hand-grip, cracked in the explosion, was held together by lapping of brass wire. The budding hunter formed a close association with Magog, a liver-and-white spaniel, who doted on him. While he was still small, the dog was strong enough to carry him about, and later he took the boy for walks in the jungle. From this useful companion Jim learnt a great deal – not least that it was unwise to pass close to thick cover in which animals might be asleep. Magog also taught him how to walk noiselessly – and they had some stirring adventures together.

Once, when they were out after peacock, the spaniel followed a covey of the birds into thick cover, out of which there suddenly erupted the angry roar of a disturbed tiger. 'Magog, after his first yelp of fear, was barking furiously and running,' Jim remembered:

> The tiger was emitting roar upon roar and chasing him, and both were coming towards me. In the general confusion a peacock, giving its alarm call, came sailing through the trees and alighted on a branch just above my head, but for the time being I had lost all interest in birds, and my only desire was to go somewhere, far away, where there were no tigers. Magog had four legs to carry him over the ground, whereas I had only two; so, without any feeling of shame – for deserting a faithful companion – I picked up my feet and ran as I had never run before.

Another day, stalking a cock jungle fowl, he got another bad fright. As he put a bare foot down into some long grass that grew in a hollow, he trod on the coils of a python. That made him jump 'as no boy had ever jumped.' Clearing the depression, he whipped round, fired a shot 'into the writhing mass' and ran – for pythons, he knew, could reach a length of eighteen feet, and a diameter of over two feet, and if this one had caught him, it could easily have crushed him.

Many years later he recalled the fear that accompanied his early forays into the forest:

After a lifelong acquaintance with wild life, I am no less afraid of a tiger's teeth and claws today than I was the day that a tiger shooed Magog and me out of the jungle in which he wanted to sleep. But to counter that fear and hold it in check, I now have the experience that I lacked in those early days. Where formerly I looked for danger all around me and was afraid of every sound I heard, I now knew where to look for danger, and what sounds to ignore or pay special attention to. And, further, where there was uncertainty where a bullet would go, there was now a measure of certainty that it would go in the direction I wanted it to. Experience engenders confidence, and without these two very important assets, the hunting of a man-eating tiger on foot, and alone, would be a very unpleasant way of committing suicide.

Among the skills which he gradually perfected was that of sleeping up trees – an expedient to which he frequently resorted when sitting over a man-eater's kill. As a boy he would often go up a tree with a book, and sit happily on a branch, reading. Also, by constant practice, he became a skilled fisherman. Maggie told how he once caught a 60lb mahseer in the lake at Nainital: 'It was so big we felt it should go to an institution where there were a lot of people to eat it, so took it to the YWCA, and they said it was one of the best they had ever eaten. I took it up with two men carrying it slung from a pole.'

After the death of their father in 1881, when Jim was only six, his stepbrother Tom, whom Jim hero-worshipped, took over as head of the family and looked after his tribe. It was he who fostered his young brother's hunting instincts most keenly – but was it not dreadfully irresponsible of Tom to initiate a bear hunt when Jim was only ten? In spite of protests from their mother, off they went together, with Tom carrying two weapons – his own rifle and a double-barrelled shotgun. When they came to what Jim described as 'a deep, dark and evil-looking ravine', Tom left his young companion sitting on a rock with the shotgun while he himself went off to perch in a solitary oak tree on the side of a mountain half-a-mile away. If Jim saw a bear approaching his brother's position, he was to go and tell him. As Jim recalled,

A wind was blowing, rustling the dry grass and dead leaves, and my imagination filled the jungle round me with hungry bears... That I would presently be eaten, I had no doubt whatever, and I was quite sure the meal would prove a very painful one for me. Time dragged on leaden feet, each moment adding to my terror, and when the glow from the setting sun was bathing the mountainside in red, I saw a bear slowly making its way along the skyline a few hundred yards above Tom's tree... The opportunity I had been praying for to get away from that terrifying spot had come... So, shouldering the gun, which after my experience with Dansay's muzzle-loader I had been too frightened to load, I set off to tell Tom about the bear and to re-attach myself to him.

Jim soon became more proficient with weapons, for, still at the age of ten, he joined the school cadet company of the Nainital Volunteer Rifles, and on the range began firing a .450 Martini carbine – a heavy rifle with a notoriously vicious kick, quite unsuitable for a boy of his age. Then the sergeant-major in charge, seeing his eagerness, lent him a muzzle-loading .450. Armed with this clumsy weapon, he would go off on solo hunting expeditions into the dense jungle round Kaladhungi, shooting birds for the pot. This required no mean skill, for the rifle had only iron sights – no telescope – and unless he managed to decapitate a jungle fowl or partridge, rather than hitting it amidships with one of his heavy bullets, there would be nothing left for his mother to cook. As he himself wrote later, he 'revelled in the beauty of the jungle,' and rejoiced whenever he gained access to ground that he 'loved and understood.' Time spent in the jungles 'held unalloyed happiness for me.'

His own reminiscences reveal this as a slight exaggeration, for he also had moments of sheer terror – not least when he shot his first leopard. He was out after jungle fowl with his .450, and was sitting on a rock on the edge of a steep little ravine when he saw a leopard bounding towards him. Seconds later it appeared on the lip of the gully, only fifteen feet away. Taking careful aim, he fired at its chest. A cloud of smoke from the black powder cartridge blocked his view, and he caught only a fleeting glimpse of the animal as it sailed over his head, leaving splashes of blood on his clothes. Following up, he made his way along a steep hillside dotted with rocks and bushes, behind any of which the wounded animal might be sheltering.

Moving with the utmost caution, and scanning every foot of ground, I had gone half-way down the hillside when from behind a rock, some twenty yards away, I saw the leopard's tail and one hind leg projecting. Not knowing whether he was alive or dead, I stood still until presently the leg was withdrawn. Having already hit the leopard in the body, and not killed him, I now decided to try his head, so, inch by inch, I crept to the left until the head came into view. He was lying with his back to the rock, looking away from me. I had not made a sound, but he appeared to sense that I was near, and as he was turning his head to look at me, I put a bullet into his ear.

It is not possible to describe my feelings as I stood looking down at my first leopard. My hands had been steady from the moment I first saw him bounding down the steep hillside and until I pulled him aside to prevent the blood from staining his skin. But now not only my hands but my whole body was trembling with fear at the thought of what might have happened if, instead of landing on the bank behind me, the leopard had landed on my head. Trembling with joy at the beautiful animal I had shot, and trembling most of all with anticipation of the pleasure I would have in carrying the news of my great success to those at home who I knew would be as pleased and as proud of my achievement as I was. I could have screamed, shouted, danced and sung, all at one and the same time. But I did none of these things. I only stood and trembled, for my feelings were too intense to be given expression in the jungle, and could only be relieved by being shared with others.

At that date – around 1890 – ideas about big-game hunting were totally different from those of a century later. Indian potentates, their guests, their sons and relations, as well as British officers and officials, all went out on *shikar* – hunting – as a matter of course. Of all trophies, tigers and leopards were the most highly-prized: because they were so powerful, and quite capable of killing a human aggressor, the pursuit of them was exciting and dangerous. A big male tiger might weigh 500 lbs, could move as fast as a racehorse, and was armed with formidable teeth and claws. A leopard, though much smaller, was equally well armed, and very fast and agile. Even if the rifleman was mounted on an elephant or sitting on a machan, the element of risk was high.

Until well into the 20th century local governments looked on big cats as vermin, and offered farmers rewards for their destruction – but, 5,000 miles away in London, someone thought he knew better. On 10 July 1906 a suggestion was made in the House of Commons that the bounty should be discontinued, on the grounds that the carnivores were performing a useful function – that of keeping 'down the head of deer and the sounder of pig, which destroy the crops of the cultivators.' The idea drew a dusty answer.

The Secretary of State does not consider that the discontinuance of these awards is advisable. Any indirect advantage to crops that might result from the multiplication of tigers and leopards would be more than counterbalanced by the increased danger to human beings, cattle and domestic animals.

In any case, prodigious numbers of tigers were shot. The Maharaja of Sargujah, though only one-eyed, killed 1,157. The Maharaj Kumar of Vizianagram – known as Fizzy Vizzy from his predilection for champagne – claimed a personal total of 383, and lined the entrance compound of his palace with mounted victims set in ornamental niches. During King George V's visit to India in 1911 the monarch and his retinue shot thirty-nine tigers, eighteen rhinos and four bears. *Shikaris* had no qualms about such slaughter, for, especially in the north of India, the supply of tigers seemed endless: no matter how many were killed, more kept coming down from the vast forests in Nepal to replace them, and occupy the territories left empty by their predecessors.

Grandfather Joseph Corbett had been tiny, but Jim grew up into a wiry six-footer with sturdy legs and formidable endurance, easily able to walk 20 miles a day, sometimes on earth roads, sometimes on the zig-zag tracks, worn by bare human feet, that wound up, down and around the steep, densely forested hills of Kumaon. By the age of seventeen he was sporting a moustache, and he kept it, thick but neatly trimmed, for the rest of his life. His voice was engagingly soft, his manner attractively modest. For preference he wore shorts (ridiculed by one Indian colleague as *jangias* – panties) and knee-length woollen stockings, as the combination was cooler and less restricting than long trousers, and had the extra advantage of not brushing noisily through grass or other vegetation when he was moving in thick cover. Sometimes, when caught up in the tension of a man-eater hunt, he would go without food for days. He was naturally abstemious, and hardly ever drank alcohol; for refreshment after hard work or a marathon trek he relied mainly on tea, which he liked made with warm cows' milk and brought to him in bowls. For him, 'a dish of tea' was the great reviver. His worst weakness was that he smoked heavily – a habit that must have exacerbated the bouts of malaria from which he suffered later in life.

Smoking may have accounted for – or at least contributed to – one strange gap in his otherwise-prodigious knowledge of wildlife. Tigers, he repeatedly wrote, have no sense of smell. This is not true. Tigers have a good sense of smell, and rely on it for marking their territories. By spraying urine on the trunks of trees, they delineate the boundaries of their domain and seek to warn off intruders; they pick up essential information by sniffing deposits left by rivals, especially by using the grimace known as *flehmen*, in which they lift their head and wrinkle their upper lip while inhaling. It seems very odd that, in all his accounts, Jim never mentions this essential element of tiger behaviour. He believed, on the other hand, that leopards do have a sense of smell – for he recalled that, when he was trying to poison the man-eating leopard of Rudraprayag, he was afraid the killer would detect the doses of cyanide which he had hidden in the body of a human victim.

Even in later life, when he came to write his books, and he had turned firmly in the direction of conservation, he showed no shame in describing his blood-lust as a youth.

On countless forays he was accompanied by Robin, a cocker spaniel whom he bought as a three-month old puppy, and who for almost thirteen years became his constant companion when after big game, often detecting the presence of tigers or leopards before his master.

In an affectionate chapter describing their partnership Jim told how one evening, out on his own in the jungle without the dog, he fired his rifle at an outsized male leopard which emerged from the undergrowth only fifteen yards away. At the shot, the animal rose high in the air, turned a somersault, and went crashing off through thick cover. The sudden silence that followed could mean one of two things: either the leopard had died, or it had reached open ground. Because the sun was setting, and Jim was four miles from home, he decided to leave it for the time being, and resume the hunt in the morning.

Before sunrise he was back on the scene, this time with Robin leading – and in the hunt that followed, the spaniel played a leading role, guiding his master with his nose. After much further manoeuvring, Jim set out to circle a fallen tree, in which the wounded animal had taken refuge. Gradually closing in until he could see under its branches, he and Robin had gone about two thirds of the way round when the dog stopped.

There was a succession of deep, angry grunts, and the leopard made straight for us. All I could see was the undergrowth being violently agitated in a direct line towards us, and I only just had time to swing half-right, and bring the rifle up, when the head and shoulders of the leopard appeared out of the bushes a few feet away. The leopard's spring and my shot were simultaneous, and stepping to the left and leaning as far back as I could, I fired the second barrel from my hip into his side as he passed me.

I had side-stepped to the left to avoid crushing Robin, and when I looked down for him now, he was nowhere to be seen. For the first time in all the years we had hunted together we had parted company in a tight corner. It was therefore with very great misgivings that I turned about to go in search of him. As I did so, I caught sight of his head projecting from behind a tree trunk on the edge of a small clearing only a hundred yards away. When I raised my hand and beckoned, he disappeared into the undergrowth, but a little later, with drooped eyes and drooped ears, he crept silently to my feet. Laying down the rifle, I picked him up in my arms and, for the second time in his life, he licked my face – telling me as he did so, with little throaty sounds, how glad he was to find me unhurt, and how terribly ashamed he was of himself for having parted company from me.

Our reactions to the sudden and quite unexpected danger that had confronted us were typical of how a canine and a human being act in an emergency, when the danger that threatens is heard and not seen. In Robin's case it had impelled him to seek safety in silent and rapid retreat – whereas in my case it had the effect of glueing my feet to the ground and making retreat – rapid or otherwise – impossible.

When I had satisfied Robin that he was not to blame for our temporary separation, and his small body had stopped trembling, I put him down and together we walked up to where the leopard, who had put up such a game fight, and had so nearly won the last round, was lying dead.

In 1893, at seventeen, Jim went straight from school into his first job, as a fuel inspector on the Bengal & North Western Railway. His beat was a long way from home, but the only area in which he could find worthwhile employment. For eighteen months he lived in a tent in the forests, in charge of felling 500,000 tons of timber to provide fuel for the engines, most of which still ran on wood. The trees had to be cut into three-foot billets and hauled on carts to the nearest point of the track, maybe ten miles off. There they were weighed and measured, then loaded onto trains for dispatch to distant fuel depots. As he himself recalled, it was strenuous work, but it kept him fit, and gave him unlimited sport, for the jungle was alive with *chital* (spotted deer), *muntjac* (barking deer), four-horned antelope, wild boar and peafowl. Because his job filled every hour of the working day, he had to do his shooting at night – and at this he became expert.

> *Shooting by moonlight is very different from shooting in daylight, for though it is easier to stalk a deer or a rooting pig at night, it is difficult to shoot accurately unless the moon can be got to shine on the foresight. The pea fowl had to be shot while they were roosting, and I am not ashamed to say that I occasionally indulged in this form of murder, for the only meat I ate during that year and a half was what I shot on moonlight nights; during the dark period of the moon I had perforce to be a vegetarian.*

After his stint in the jungle he spent a year working up and down the railway in a variety of jobs. By then many engines had been converted from wood to coal, and he rode on the footplates to report on consumption. This he enjoyed, for he was sometimes allowed to drive the engines; but he was bored by acting as the guard on goods trains – especially whenever he had to remain on duty for forty-eight hours at a stretch. Occasionally he also stood-in as assistant station-master.

Then one day in 1896, he received orders to go to Mokameh Ghat, an immense depot on the right (southern) bank of the Ganges (a ghat, pronounced *gort*, is a sloping river-bank or a series of wide steps going down to water; a landing-place). Mokameh Ghat was an important railway centre: not only was it a point at which the metre-gauge and broad-gauge systems converged, it was also one terminal of a ferry across the mighty river, which during the monsoon floods could swell to a torrent four or five miles wide. In the absence of a bridge, steamers and barges carried goods and passengers across the stream to Samaria Ghat on the opposite bank.

Appointed Trans-shipment Inspector at Mokameh Ghat, Jim arrived there to find a scene of daunting chaos. The Ferry Superintendent told him that not only were the sheds stacked to the roof with goods; outside in the yard 400 wagons were waiting to be unloaded, and on the far side of the river there were 1,000 more wagons lined up to be ferried across. A tour of the depot next day revealed that the congestion was even worse than the newcomer had been told: the goods sheds and sidings were a mile-and-a-half long, and beside the 400 metre-gauge wagons, the same number of broad-gauge wagons needed unloading. Altogether Jim reckoned that there were fifteen thousand tons of goods waiting to be shifted.

He was not quite 21 years old, and the hot weather was setting in – a season, he remarked, 'when all of us are a little bit mad.' Perhaps that was what made him take the job – but he was much encouraged by meeting Ram Saran, the black-bearded station master at Mokameh Ghat, who had been advised by telegram of his arrival, but did not know that he was to take over the handling contract. 'When I gave him this bit of news,' Jim recalled, 'his face beamed all over, and he said, "Good, Sir. Very good. We will manage." My heart warmed to Ram Saran on hearing that "we", and up to his death 35 years later, it never cooled.'

Some 500,000 tons of goods had been passing through Mokameh Ghat every year, and it was Jim's task to set the traffic moving. It took him two days to get acquainted with his staff, who included sixty-five clerks and a hundred shunters, pointsmen and watchmen. Across the river at Samaria Ghat were another hundred 'clerical and menial staff'. All these formed what might be called his private army; but the main workforce came from the Labour Company, from which he found several hundred 'very discontented men' sitting about the sheds.

Moving swiftly, he chose twelve men and appointed them Headmen, eleven of whom undertook to recruit ten men apiece. The twelfth agreed to provide a gang of sixty men and women for the handling of coal. As only one of the twelve was literate, Jim also took on one Hindu and one Mohammedan clerk to keep the accounts.

To shift the tremendous traffic block, he resorted to drastic action, and took the risk of unloading 1,000 tons of wheat onto the ground in the open, so that the same amount of salt and sugar could be transferred from broad-gauge into narrow-gauge wagons, thus freeing space in the sheds. Luckily no rain fell while the grain lay out, and within ten days the whole mass of transport had been shifted. Looking back, Jim reckoned that men had never worked harder than his. They began at 4am every morning, Sundays included, and laboured through until 8pm, eating their food – brought to them by wives, mothers and daughters – in the sheds. To transfer loads from the broad-gauge trucks to the narrow-gauge wagons, coal had to be shovelled or carried in baskets across a sloping, four-foot platform. In winter, men and women worked in bitter cold, often soaked by rain for days on end, and in summer the brick platform and the iron floors of the wagons became so hot that they blistered bare feet.

Jim shared their labours, and so won their undying loyalty. For the first three months neither he nor Ram Saran slept for more than four hours a night. He recorded how, for one particularly exhausting day, he had struggled to deal with an engine which had been three times de-railed and three times hoisted back on to the track with hand-jacks:

Tired and worn out, and with eyes swollen and sore from wind and sand, I had just sat down to my first meal of the day when my twelve headmen filed into the room, and seeing my servant placing a plate in front of me, with the innate courtesy of Indians filed out again. I then, as I ate my dinner, heard the following conversation taking place on the verandah:

One of the Headmen. 'What was on the plate you put in front of the Sahib?'
My servant. 'A chapatti and a little dal.'
One of the Headmen. 'Why only one chapatti and a little dal?'
My servant. 'Because there is no money to buy more.'
One of the Headmen. 'What else does the sahib eat?'
My servant. 'Nothing.'

Later the old Headman requested permission to enter the room, and told Jim that his men had so little food that they were scarcely able to work. 'But,' he concluded, 'we have seen tonight that your case is as bad as ours, and we will carry on as long as we have strength to stand.'

That was one of Jim's great assets, both on the railway and in the jungle: his readiness to share whatever hardships his men were suffering. 'As I could understand and speak their language as well as they could,' he once wrote, 'I was able to take part in their light-hearted banter and appreciate all their jokes.' No less important was his achievement in securing them regular pay, and his scrupulous honesty in sharing out any bonuses that the railway granted.

For someone whose home was in Nainital, Mokameh Ghat was no convenient or congenial workplace. Some 700 miles to the south-east as a vulture might fly, but a thousand by rail and road, the depot lay in dreary surroundings and a far less salubrious environment, where cholera was rife, and the only medical man within ten miles was 'a brute of a doctor, as callous as he was inefficient,' whose 'fat, oily throat' Jim hoped one day to have the pleasure of cutting. He himself, with his father's medical training, treated many of the small ailments suffered by his workers.

It seems extraordinary that a man of his intelligence could stick at the job for as long as he did – twenty-six years. At least he lived in a comfortable house, with a dining room, a sitting room and a bedroom opening on to a verandah, some 200 yards from the river. When he came home from work – usually at about 8pm – his house servant, waiting on the verandah, would call to the waterman to lay his bath in the little room next to his bedroom (for he always had a hot bath, winter or summer). The bath was made of wood, and long enough to sit in – but one evening he got a severe fright when, as he opened his eyes after soaping his hair, he saw a big cobra with its hood expanded looking over the rim, within inches of his toes. In his struggle to get out of the bath he extinguished the flame in his lamp, plunging the little room into darkness. 'Here I was (he recalled later) shut in a small, dark room with one of the deadliest snakes in India,' – and he had an agonising wait before a servant came to his rescue. Freed at last, he burst out onto the verandah stark naked.

Soon after he arrived at Mokameh Ghat he began making innovations to improve the community. The first was to start a school for the sons of his workmen and the lower-paid railway staff. Together with the station-master Ram Saran, he rented a hut, installed a master and started with a class of twenty boys. At once the organisers ran up against caste prejudices, for high- and low-caste boys were not allowed to sit together in the same hut. But since there was no objection to them sitting in the same shed, the master solved the problem by removing the hut's walls. The enterprise flourished: the school grew rapidly, and when it reached 200 pupils and eight masters, it was taken over by the Government, who rewarded Ram Saran by conferring on him the title Ri Sahib.

Together with Tom Kelly, the stout superintendent of the broad-gauge railway, Jim started a recreation club, cleared a plot of ground, marked out football and hockey pitches, bought a football and primitive hockey sticks. These were made of naked wood, as were the balls – with the result that painful injuries were common. Jim, being fairly nimble, played as a forward, and his status in the community was revealed one day when he tripped and fell over:

All the players... abandoned the game to set me on my feet and dust my clothes. While I was receiving these attentions, one of the opposing team dribbled the ball down the field and was prevented from scoring a goal by the spectators, who impounded the ball and arrested the player!

Soon after the start of the recreation club, the Railway built a club house and laid out a tennis court for the European staff, who, including Jim, numbered four. In the evenings he and Tom Kelly would play billiards – but a more exciting pastime was shooting. At dusk in the winter, when the moon was at or near full, thousands of bar-headed and grey-lag geese would come flighting in from their daytime roost on islands in the Ganges, to graze on ripening wheat in the fields or weeds in a cluster of tanks and pools some nine miles down the line. To reach their feeding grounds, the gunners rolled down on a trolley which had been provided, along with four men to push it, for the corpulent Tom, to save him walking great distances back and forth along the sidings during his work. The geese made easy targets, for as they drew near their feeding grounds, they started to lose height, and passed overhead quite low. Looking back, Jim remembered:

Those winter evenings, when the full moon was rising over the palm trees that fringed the river, and the cold, brittle air throbbed and reverberated with the honking of geese and the swish of their wings as they passed overhead in flights of ten to a hundred, are among the happiest of my recollections of the years I spent at Mokameh Ghat.

Later in life he claimed that his work there was never dull, and that time 'never hung heavy' on his hands. Besides handling a million tons of goods a year, he was responsible for the running of the steamers that ferried people and trains across the river, and he enjoyed the short voyages, as they gave him a chance to sit down, have a smoke and observe his fellow passengers. Occasionally a special train brought exotic travellers, and a touch of light relief, as when the Nepalese Prime Minister arrived from Kathmandu with twenty ladies of his household, a secretary and a large retinue of servants.

As the train came to a standstill, a blond-headed giant in Nepalese dress jumped down and went to the carriage in which the Prime Minister was travelling. Here the man opened a big umbrella, put his back to the door of the carriage, lifted his right arm and placed his hand on his hip. Presently the door behind him opened and the Prime Minister appeared, carrying a gold-headed cane. With practised ease the Prime Minister took his seat on the man's arm, and when he had made himself comfortable, the man raised the umbrella over the Prime Minister's head and set off. He carried his burden as effortlessly as another would have carried a celluloid doll on his 300-yard walk, over loose sand, to the steamer.

CHAPTER TWO

The Champawat Man-Eater
1907

The poverty and filth of Indian villages distressed any European who witnessed them, and the misery of country people was vividly brought to light by a Government survey conducted early in the 20th century in the district of Gurgaon, south-west of Delhi. In *The Remaking of Village India*, a small book which reported the findings, the author, F.L. Brayne, pulled no punches. 'The terrible lot of the women is the worst feature of Gurgaon village life,' he wrote:

For the average woman there are no latrine arrangements: she must wait, in discomfort and possibly pain, till nightfall, and then wander like a pariah on the outskirts of the village in the dark. The arrangements for her child-bearing are too revolting to describe... The filthy habits of the villagers make what should be the children's playground a combination of dustbin and latrine, so that the condition of the children is unbelievably bad.

Why is the villager in such a state?
His methods of farming are bad.
His village is filthy; he lives in dirt, squalor, disease and suffering.
He is the prey of endemic diseases.
He wastes all his wealth.
He keeps his womenfolk in degradation and slavery.
He pays no attention to his home or his village.
He resists all change: he is illiterate and ignorant.

In places of this kind, whenever a man-eating tiger or leopard began to haunt a particular community, the inhabitants' privations were horribly intensified by the presence of a killer. Nobody dared go outside at night – which meant that sanitary problems became still more acute – and even indoors people were by no means safe, for many houses were so flimsily built that a leopard could push its head through the wall or tear down the door and carry off a dog, a baby or a full-grown woman. Even in daylight men became too frightened to walk out and work on their crops in the fields, or to guard them from the depredations of deer: terror would grip the community and bring the place to a standstill.

Such was the situation in the village of Pali, some forty-five miles east of Nainital, when Jim arrived there one day in the summer of 1907. By then the tigress known as the Champawat man-eater was notorious, for in six years she had killed 200 people in Nepal and 234 in Kumaon. So dangerous was she that parties of Gurkas had been sent out after her; the Government had offered rewards for her extermination, and leading *shikaris* had been encouraged to pursue her – all in vain.

Jim was still working at Mokameh Ghat, but soon after he had come home on leave he got a call from the Deputy Commissioner of Nainital, who besought him to try for the tigress. He already had a reputation as an outstanding hunter of big cats: he had never killed a man-eater, but in 1900 he had shot an animal known as the Pipal Pani tiger, which had caused much distress by killing buffaloes, cattle and pigs, and living uncomfortably close to human settlements.

Now, seven years later, he agreed on two conditions: first, that all Government awards should be withdrawn, and second, that all other *shikaris* should be stood-down. He gave two reasons for making these stipulations: he did not want to be classed as a reward-hunter, and still less did he want to be shot by some nervous, trigger-happy competitor.

As he grew older, Jim had developed a high regard for tigers. Unlike other Edwardian hunters, he never referred to a tiger as a 'brute'. On the contrary, he admired the creature's physique and ferocity, and described it as 'a large-hearted gentleman with boundless courage.' Only when a tiger turned to killing humans or preying excessively on farm animals did he consider it an enemy.

So it was when, early one morning, word came in that a woman had been killed in Pali. Having engaged six men to carry his camp kit, Jim set off with his party after breakfast. They walked seventeen miles across country that day, and after two night-stops, camping out, they reached their objective on the third evening, five days after the woman's death. Jim later wrote:

> *The people of the village, numbering some fifty men, women and children, were in a state of abject terror, and though the sun was still up when I arrived, I found the entire population inside their homes behind locked doors, and it was not until my men had made a fire in the courtyard and I was sitting down to a cup of tea that a door here and there was cautiously opened, and the frightened inmates emerged. I was informed that for five days no one had gone beyond their own doorsteps — the insanitary condition of the courtyard testified to the truth of this statement — that food was running short, and that the people would starve if the tiger was not killed or driven away.*

For the past three nights the man-eater had been heard calling on the road only a hundred yards from the houses; so Jim, having installed his own men in a single room offered by the Headman of the village, opted to spend the night sitting beside the road with his back against a tree, hoping that the tiger would walk past. 'The length of road immediately in front of me was brilliantly lit by the moon,' he recalled, 'but to right and left the overhanging trees cast dark shadows, and when the night wind agitated the branches, I saw a dozen tigers advancing on me.'

In fact he saw none – but he sat out the night, and when his men came to collect him in the morning, they found him fast asleep, with his head on his drawn-up knees. Back in the village, locals were very surprised to find that he had survived the hours of darkness. After breakfast he spent the morning searching for tracks of the killer, and then in the afternoon stood guard with a rifle while the entire population of the village harvested their wheat. His presence had begun 'to put new heart into the people', and next day three of them agreed to lead him to a place where he could shoot a *ghoral*, or mountain goat, to provide food for his own men. In the event, on a steep hill, he shot three goats in quick succession, and by chance the bodies rolled down almost to where he stood, to the astonishment of his companions, who had never seen a rifle fired before. Back in the village he was hailed as a magician:

> *From where I sat in the open, having breakfast, I could hear the exclamations of the assembled crowd, when they were told that the ghoral had been shot at a range of over a mile, and that the magic bullets used had not only killed the animals – like that – but had also drawn them to the sahib's feet.*

His next move, escorted by two men, was to visit the spot on which the woman had been killed. There, in some soft earth, he found pug-marks which confirmed that the villain was a tigress, 'a little past her prime'. He also found a patch of dried blood, and signs of a struggle, including strips of skin torn off the victim's hands as she clung desperately to branches when the killer caught her and dragged her down out of the tree in which she had been harvesting oak leaves for cattle. Further on, the party found her clothes and a few pieces of bone, which they carefully collected and took home, so that her family would have at least part of her body for the essential Hindu rite of cremation, and her ashes would reach Mother Ganges.

For the next three days he searched the surrounding jungle, 'from sunrise to sunset', but, having found no more traces, he decided to move on to the village of Champawat, fifteen miles to the east. There he heard another terrible story, of how a party of men on their way to the bazaar had met a tiger carrying a naked woman, still alive, but covered in blood. Too frightened to take any action, they had simply continued on their way; but another party, fifty or sixty strong and armed with primitive guns, had gone out to search, and found the girl's body lying on a slab of rock.

Two days later the *tahsildar* (local revenue collector) of Champawat took Jim to a bungalow in which (he twice said) they would both spend the night; but then, after dark had fallen, he suddenly announced that he had a long journey to make, and must start at once. Jim was astonished that he proposed to walk four miles through an area 'in which men only moved in large parties in daylight' – yet off he went, followed by a man with a feeble lantern.

Jim could never bring himself to describe what happened next. All he recorded about the night was one short, uncharacteristically evasive paragraph: 'I have a tale to tell of that bungalow, but I will not tell it here, for this is a book of jungle stories, and tales 'beyond the laws of nature' do not consort well with such stories.' Clearly, he had been frightened by some apparently supernatural event or visitation.

In the morning the *tahsildar* returned safely, but then a villager came running up with the news that the man-eater had killed a young girl under some scattered trees on the shoulder of a nearby hill. Snatching up his double-barrelled rifle and some cartridges, Jim hurried to investigate. Soon he came on a pool of blood, where the girl had died. Splashes of blood led him on a trail, past her sari, past her skirt. Once again the tigress was carrying a naked woman, but mercifully on this occasion her burden was dead.

On went the trail, through blackthorn and nettles, then down a steep hill into a ravine, with a pool at the bottom. Beside the water lay part of a human leg. 'In all the subsequent years I have hunted man-eaters,' he wrote, 'I have not seen anything as pitiful as that young comely leg, bitten off a little below the knee as clean as though severed by the stroke of an axe.' Patches of blood and splinters of bone showed that he had disturbed the tigress at her meal. Then suddenly – although he had heard nothing and seen no movement – his sixth sense told him he was in danger.

Hurriedly grounding the butt of the rifle, I put two fingers on the triggers, raising my head as I did so, and saw a little earth from the fifteen-foot bank in front of me come rolling down the steep side and plop into the pool. I was new to this game of man-eater hunting, or I should not have exposed myself to attack in the way I had done. My prompt action in pointing the rifle upwards had possibly saved my life, and in stopping her spring, or in turning to get away, the tigress had dislodged the earth from the top of the bank.

Jim took up the trail through a wilderness of big rocks and hollows masked by ferns and blackberry vines – treacherous ground, dangerous to move over fast. A dozen times he found a place where the tigress had stopped to continue her meal. This, he recorded, was her 436th human kill, and she was quite accustomed to being disturbed by rescue parties.

But this, I think, was the first time she had been followed up so persistently, and she now began to show her resentment by growling. The sound of the growling and the expectation of an attack terrified me, at the same time as it gave me hope. If the tigress lost her temper sufficiently to launch an attack, it would not only give me an opportunity of accomplishing the objective for which I had come, but it would enable me to get even with her for all the pain and suffering she had caused.

The growling, it turned out, was only a threat. The tigress kept moving – and as evening was already coming on, Jim decided to abandon the hunt for the day. On his way back, knowing that the girl's severed leg would be needed for her cremation ceremony, he buried it in a hole by the pool, whence it could be collected, and made his way down to the village. There, with the *tahsildar*, he planned a tremendous beat for the next day.

The local men were reluctant to take part in such a dangerous operation, but by midday 298 had assembled, equipped with unlicensed firearms that (Jim remarked) 'would have stocked a museum.' Their instructions were to line out along the ridge on one side of a valley, while he went round and climbed the hill opposite. When they saw him signal by waving a handkerchief from under a solitary blasted pine tree, they were to fire their guns, shout, beat drums and roll rocks down the hill.

Taking the *tahsildar* with him, he set off on his circuit, but before they could reach the spot he wanted, the beaters lost their nerve.

Pandemonium had broken loose on the ridge. Added to the fusillade of guns was the wild beating of drums and the shouting of hundreds of men, and when the din was at its worst, I caught sight of the tigress bounding down a grassy slope between two ridges to my right front, and about 300 yards away. She had only gone a short distance when the tahsildar, from his position under the pine, let off both barrels of his shotgun. On hearing the shots the tigress whipped round and went straight back the way she had come, and as she disappeared into thick cover I threw up my rifle and sent a despairing bullet after her.

The men on the ridge, hearing the three shots, not unnaturally concluded that the tigress had been killed. They emptied all their guns and gave a final yell, and I was listening for the screams that would herald her arrival on the ridge when she suddenly broke cover to my left front and, taking the stream at a bound, came straight for the gorge. The .500 modified cordite rifle, sighted at sea level, shot high at this altitude, and when the tigress stopped dead, I thought the bullet had gone over her back, and that she had pulled up on finding her retreat cut off; as a matter of fact I had hit her all right, but a little far back.

Lowering her head, she half-turned towards me, giving me a beautiful shot at the point of her shoulder at a range of no more than thirty yards. She flinched at this second shot but continued, with her ears laid flat and bared teeth, to stand her ground, while I sat with rifle to shoulder trying to think what it would be best for me to do when she charged, for the rifle was empty and I had no more cartridges.

Fortunately the wounded animal most unaccountably decided against a charge. Very slowly she turned, crossed the stream to her right, climbed over some rocks and found a narrow ledge that went diagonally up and across the face of the precipitous hill, to a great, flat projecting rock. At the point where the rock joined the cliff a small bush had found root-hold, and going up to it the tigress started to strip its branches.

Throwing caution to the winds, I shouted to the tahsildar to bring me his gun. A long reply was shouted back, the only word of which I caught was 'feet'. Laying down my rifle, I took the hill at a run, grabbed the gun out of the tahsildar's hands

*and raced back. As I approached the stream, the tigress came out
on the projecting rock towards me. When I was within twenty
feet of her I raised the gun and found to my horror that there
was a gap of about three-eighths of an inch between the barrels
and the breech-block. The gun had not burst when both barrels
were fired, and would probably not burst now, but there was the
danger of being blinded by a blow-back. However, the risk would
have to be taken, and, aligning the great blob of a bead that did
duty as a sight on the tigress's open mouth, I fired.*

*Maybe I bobbed, or maybe the gun was not capable of
throwing the cylindrical bullet accurately for more than twenty
feet; anyway the missile missed the tigress's mouth and struck her
on the right paw, from where I removed it later with my finger-
nails. Fortunately she was at her last gasp, and the tap on the
foot was sufficient to make her lurch forward. She came to rest
with her head projecting over the side of the rock.*

Released from tension, the beaters rushed forward screaming
with rage and excitement, brandishing guns, axes, rusty
swords and spears, with which they proposed to hack their
arch-enemy to pieces. Jim, anxious to preserve the skin,
managed to calm them, and in due course they carried the
body up a 1,000-foot climb and then down to the village
on an improvised stretcher made from two saplings lashed
together, arriving after dark.

The cause of the tigress's man-eating was immediately
apparent. The upper and lower canine teeth on the right side
of her mouth had broken off, making her unable to kill her
natural prey. That evening he skinned her, and next day he
cut the body into small pieces, to fill the lockets which hill
children wore round their necks to give them courage and
immunity from attacks by wild animals.

The *tahsildar* and other village notables planned a
magnificent feast to celebrate their release from fear, but

Jim had a seventy-five mile journey ahead of him, so he excused himself and slipped away early next morning with the tiger skin strapped to the saddle of a pony. He paused in the villages of Pali and Dabidhura, and on the last day, by holding the horse's tail on the up-grades, riding him on the flat and running on the down-grades, covered the last forty-five miles home to Nainital.

> '*I was young and inexperienced in those far-off Champawat days [he wrote later], but even so the conviction I came to after a brief sojourn in that stricken land – that there is no more terrible thing than to live and have one's being under the shadow of a man-eater – has been strengthened by thirty-two years' subsequent experience.*'

Already his outstanding skill as a *shikari* was recognised by the Government, which awarded him a rare privilege – the Freedom of Forests, which gave him unlimited licence to patrol the reserved forests whenever he wanted. A more concrete souvenir, given him at a durbar in Nainital, was a .275 Rigby rifle – the finest medium-gauge rifle of the day – with a small oval plate fitted on the stock, engraved with the inscription:

Presented to
Mr. J.G.Corbett

By Sir J.P.Hewett K.C.S.I
Lieutenant Governor of the United Provinces
in recognition of his having killed a man-eating tigress
at Champawat in 1907

As Jim's friend and mentor Sir Malcolm (later Lord) Hailey once remarked of the despair that gripped whole villages, 'There was indeed here something that passed the ordinary bounds of human fear, for the ways of the ancient gods of the hills are unpredictable, and who could tell that the terror was not a visitation from them?'

Hailey was much the same age as Jim. Governor of the Punjab from 1924 to 1928, and then Governor of the United Provinces, he one of the Raj's most astute officials, and also a keen *shikari*. Numerous outings in Jim's company made him a fervent admirer:

> *I have more than once been with him when villagers have come to complain of the ravages of a marauder. And let me add, they have shown a fitting sense of our respective values. The governor of a province of 50 million people was entitled to some respect; but their allegiance was clearly for Jim Corbett, for it was he who could relieve them of the terror that walked by night.*

CHAPTER THREE

Beyond Nature

In the middle of his account of the hunt for the Champawat tiger Jim wrote one strange and uncharacteristic short paragraph describing how he had been forced, by some deeply unpleasant sensation or happening, to vacate his quarters in the middle of the night. What was it that gave him such a fright? Normally fearless, he seems for once to have lost his nerve – to the extent that he had no wish to say what happened. Nor was this the only time he was driven into the open at night: he had a similar experience in another bungalow, and, rather than remain indoors, slept outside wrapped in a blanket.

The hill people among whom he moved were extremely suspicious. 'Every hilltop, valley and gorge (he wrote) is credited with possessing a spirit in one form or another, all of the evil and malignant kind most to be feared during the hours of darkness.' He would happily recall how his boyhood friend Dansay Fleming used to delight in telling ghost stories set in ancestral Irish halls, but how he changed his tune when he began to talk of the banshees that lived in the jungle.

According to Dansay, a banshee was an evil female spirit that resided in dense forests and was so malignant that the mere hearing of it brought calamity to the hearer and his family, and the seeing of it death to the unfortunate beholder. Dansay described the call of a banshee as a long drawn-out scream, which was heard most frequently on dark and stormy nights. These banshee stories had a fearful fascination for me, for they had their setting in the jungles in which I use to roam.

One of these banshees is known to all the people who live along the foothills of the Himalayas, and in many other parts of India, as the churail. The churail, the most feared of evil spirits, appears in the form of a woman. Having cast her eyes on a human being, this woman, whose feet are turned the wrong way, mesmerises her victims, as a snake does a bird, and walking backward lures them to their doom. When danger of seeing the woman threatens, the only defence against her wiles is to shield the eyes with the hands, any piece of cloth which is handy, or, if indoors, to pull a blanket over the head.

During all the years I have lived in Kumaon, and the many hundreds of nights I have spent in the jungle, I have heard the churail only three times – always at night – and I have seen it only once. It was the month of March. A bumper mustard crop had just been harvested, and the village was alive with happy sounds. Men and women were singing and children were calling to each other. The moon was a night or two from the full, and visibility was nearly as good as in daylight.

Maggie and I were on the point of calling for dinner – the time was close on 8pm – when clear and piercing on the night air came the call of the churail, and instantly every sound in the village was hushed. Opening our front door, Maggie and I stepped out onto the verandah, and as we did so the churail called again. The call came from the haldu tree in the right-hand corner of the compound, and there, sitting on the topmost branch in brilliant moonlight was the maker of the call, the churail.

No words of mine can describe the call of the churail. If I said it resembled the cry of a soul in torment, or of a human being in agony, it would convey no meaning to you, for neither you nor I have heard either of these sounds. Nor can I liken the call to any other sounds heard in the jungles, for it is something apart, something that does not appear to have any connection with our world and that has the effect of curdling the hearer's blood and arresting his heart-beats.

Jim's natural impulse was to shoot the bird, so that he could establish its identity beyond doubt; but he had no suitable weapon to hand, and, as he pointed out, if he had fired and missed, everyone within hearing distance would have been more convinced than ever that the call was being made by an evil spirit, against which even a rifle bullet would be of no avail. He therefore went back into the house and brought out a pair of binoculars, through which he carefully examined the unwelcome visitor. He reported:

(a) In size the bird was a little smaller than a golden eagle.

(b) It stood upright on its rather long legs.

(c) Its tail was short, but not as short as an owl's tail.

(d) Its head was not round and big like the head of an owl, nor did it have a short neck.

(e) On its head there was no crest of 'horns'.

(f) When it called– which it did at regular intervals of about half a minute – it put its head up facing the heavens, and opened its beak wide.

(g) In colour it was an overall black, or possibly a dark brown which looked black by moonlight.

What was it? Jim never discovered. As he wrote many years later, 'I know every bird in Kumaon, and its call, and this was no bird of our jungles.' He suspected it was a migrant, but he was never certain. Other experts have suggested that it was a crested hawk or a forest eagle owl, but for Jim and all his readers the *churail* remained a mystery.

There is no doubt that he was extraordinarily brave. Often in his stories he admitted to being terrified by the proximity of a man-eater, to the extent that he was shaking violently; but when menaced by a tiger or a leopard, he never lost his nerve. Had he done so, he would not have survived to tell the tale. On the other hand, there were two or three occasions when he was severely frightened by some force which he could not analyse. He once declared that 'superstition is a mental complaint similar to measles, in that it attacks an individual or a community while leaving others immune' – and he added that simple folk living high in the mountains were naturally more susceptible to superstitious beliefs than more sophisticated people lower down. He himself would never start a journey on a Friday, and whenever he began a hunt for a man-eater, he felt more confident if he could open his campaign by killing a snake. He also had a few nerve-racking experiences which defied rational explanation.

One had come when he set up a month's hunting expedition with his friend Major Robert Bellairs, whom he had met Flanders, in command of another company of Kumaon volunteers. By the time of the story, Bellairs had become a Settlement Officer at Kauasni, near Almora. Together he and Jim trekked into the hills at the foot of Trisul, the 23,000-foot mountain ten days' hard walk north of Nainital. Supporting them they had 'fifteen of the keenest and the most cheerful hillmen' Jim had ever been associated with on *shikar*, and outstanding among them was Bala Singh, a Garhwali who had accompanied him on many expeditions. Jim described him as 'a perfect specimen of a man of about thirty years of age,' who 'left Nainital full of the joy of life. It was his pride and pleasure when on *shikar* to select and carry the heaviest of my loads and, striding at the head of the other men, enliven the march with snatches of song.'

One morning Jim found the men making unscheduled preparations to move camp: when asked why, they offered various unconvincing reasons, but the real cause was the sudden decline of Bala Singh, who sat by the fire not speaking, with a blanket over his head and shoulders. When Jim asked him what the trouble was, he would not reply, except to say that he was not ill – and it was Mothi Singh, Jim's Garhwali servant, who revealed the truth: that while the men were sitting round the camp fire and singing the night before, 'the demon of Trisul entered Bala Singh's mouth, and he swallowed him.'

When Jim himself questioned Bala Singh, the story was the same. 'While I was singing a verse of one of our songs, the demon of Trisul jumped into my mouth, and though I tried to eject him, he slipped down my throat into my stomach.' When Jim asked 'Where is the demon now?' the sick man placed a hand on the pit of his stomach and replied with great conviction, 'He is here, *Sahib*, here. I can feel him moving about.'

All the porters were shaken by their colleague's decline: they had suddenly become frightened of him, and shunned his company. The collapse of morale in the party was so severe that Jim reluctantly decided he must abandon the hunt and take Bala Singh home, leaving Bellairs to shoot on his own. Back in Nainital, after another ten-day trek – which must have been a nightmare for Jim – the patient appeared to have lost all interest in life, sitting at the door of his house and never speaking unless spoken to.

In the town at the time was a distinguished Indian doctor – a friend of the Corbett family – who went at their request to examine him. Jim did not tell the doctor about the demon, but hoped that, being a Hindu and also a hill-man, he would be able to get through to the patient and cure him. The plan misfired. As soon as the doctor saw Bala Singh, he became suspicious; and after he had elicited the story of the demon, he 'stepped away from him hurriedly' and turned to

Jim saying, 'I am sorry you sent for me, for I can do nothing for this man.'

Jim's only recourse seemed to be to send Bala Singh home, to his own village eight days' walk away. With him went two men from the same community, and they completed the journey without trouble; but on the night they arrived Bala Singh suddenly announced to his relatives and friends that the demon wanted to be released, to return to Trisul, and that the only way this could be accomplished was for him to die. So he just lay down and died, and in the morning his travelling companions assisted at his cremation.

Robert Bellairs was also in trouble – though of a less desperate kind. His father, who owned two tea plantations north of Almora, was intent on disinheriting him, and sold one of the properties without offering it to him. When the second came up for sale, Jim stepped in and bought it for him.

CHAPTER FOUR

The Muktesar Man-Eater

1910

Three years after dealing with the Champawat man-eater, Jim began to hear reports of people being killed at Muktesar, a village on a high ridge eighteen miles north north-east of Nainital, said by some to be the most beautiful place in Kumaon, with wonderful views of the Himalayas and its foothills. At first, because there were 'a number of sportsmen at Muktesar, all of whom were keen on bagging the tigress', he considered 'it would be unsporting for an outsider to meddle in the matter'. But when the number of deaths rose to twenty-four, the Government solicited his help.

Accompanied by a servant and two men carrying a roll of bedding and a suitcase, he left home at midday and walked ten miles to the Ramgarh *dak* bungalow, where he spent the night. At 4am next morning he set off alone in the dark, armed with a double-barrelled .500 express rifle, and arrived in Muktesar to find that no-one dared to move about alone, even in daylight, and that after dark everyone had to remain behind locked doors.

Outside the post office he was joined by the post-master and several officials, all of whom offered advice; but his eye fell on a patch of cultivation a thousand feet below and two miles away. This, he learnt, was an apple orchard and market garden belonging to Badri Sah, son of an old friend who had visited him in Nainital and had offered to put him up, should he come in pursuit of the man-eater.

Deciding to call on Badri, Jim set off, again alone, and on the way fell in with a small girl of about eight, leading a recalcitrant black bullock. It took him some time to overcome her shyness, but gradually he got her to talk and found she was taking the bullock to her uncle, to make a ploughing pair. Why, he asked, had her uncle only one bullock? 'The tiger killed the other one yesterday,' she replied. As they plodded on Jim asked, 'Don't you know that the tiger is a man-eater?'

'Oh yes,' she said. 'It ate Kunthi's father and Bonshi Singh's mother, and lots of other people.'

Impressed by the coolness of his little companion, Jim escorted her safely home – but not before she had told him where the latest buffalo had been killed. By following a drag-mark, he soon found the body, lying at the foot of a high bank, some forty feet from the lip of a ravine. Since only a small proportion of its hindquarters had been eaten, he was sure that the tiger would return, and he immediately planned an ambush. Unfortunately there was only one stunted tree, smothered by a wild rose, within range of the kill, but he decided he would climb into it at sundown and wait.

Meanwhile, he walked down to call on Badri, who welcomed him with food and tea – 'of which I was in need, for I had done a lot of walking since leaving Ramgarh at four o'clock that morning.' Badri tried to persuade him not to go through with his plan for the night, but, insisting, Jim returned to the site, and climbed into the tree.

I was facing the hill, with the ravine behind me. I was in clear view of any animal coming down from above, but if the tiger came from below, as I expected, it would not see me until it got to the kill. The bullock, which was white, was lying on its right side with its legs towards me, at a distance of about fifteen feet.

I had taken my seat at 4pm, and an hour later a kakar started barking on the side of the ravine 200 yards below me. The tiger was on the move, and having seen it the kakar was standing still and barking. For a long time it barked, and then it started to move away, the bark growing fainter and fainter until the sound died away round the shoulder of the hill. This indicated that, after coming within sight of the kill, the tiger had lain down.

Minute succeeded long minute; dusk came; objects on the hill in front of me became indistinct and then faded out. I could still see the kill as a white blur when a stick snapped at the head of the ravine and stealthy steps came towards me, and then stopped immediately below. For a minute or two there was dead silence, and then the tiger lay down on the dry leaves at the foot of the tree.

Heavy clouds rolled up near sunset, and there was now a black canopy overhead blotting out the stars. When the tiger eventually got up and went back to the kill, the night could best be described as pitch black. Strain my eyes as I would, I could see nothing of the white bullock, and still less of the tiger. On reaching the kill the tiger started blowing on it. In the Himalayas, and especially in the summer, kills attract hornets... and a tiger – possibly after bitter experience – blows off the hornets adhering to the exposed portion of flesh before starting to feed.

There was no need for me to hurry over my shot, for, close though it was, the tiger would not see me unless I attracted its attention by some movement or sound. I can see reasonably well on a dark night by the light of the stars, but there were no stars visible that night, nor was there a flicker of lightning in the heavy clouds.

The tiger had not moved the kill before starting to eat, so I knew he was lying broadside on to me, on the right-hand side *of the kill. It had been my intention to take what aim I could – by the light of the stars – and then move the muzzle of my rifle sufficiently for my bullet to go a foot or two to the right of the kill. But now that the clouds had rendered my eyes useless, I would have to depend on my ears. Raising the rifle and resting my elbows on my knees, I took careful aim at the sound the tiger was making, and while holding the rifle steady, turned my right ear to the sound and then back again. My aim was a little too high, so, lowering the muzzle a fraction of an inch, I turned my head again and listened. After I had done this a few times, and satisfied myself that I was pointing at the sound, I moved the muzzle a little to the right and pressed the trigger.*

In two bounds the tiger was up the twenty-foot bank. At the top there was a small bit of flat ground, beyond which the hill went up steeply. I heard the tiger on the dry leaves as far as the flat ground, and then there was silence. This silence could be interpreted to mean either that the tiger had died on reaching the flat ground, or that it was unwounded.

Keeping the rifle to my shoulder, I listened intently for three or four minutes, and as there was no further sound, I lowered the rifle. This movement was greeted by a deep growl from the top of the bank. So the tiger was unwounded, and had seen me.

Because there was enough meat on the bullock to keep the tiger going for several days, Jim reckoned that 'there was no necessity for it to kill me.' So he allowed himself the luxury of smoking three cigarettes. Yet he had no option but to hang on to his precarious perch in the tree, and when heavy rain came on at 11pm, he was soon soaked to the skin. At 4am a cold wind got up, further increasing his discomfort, and by the time the faithful Badri reappeared at first light, with a companion bearing hot tea, his legs were so cramped that they would not function, and the two men caught him as he slid down out of the branches.

Revived, he planned a beat for the afternoon, and Badri, who was preoccupied with the task of getting his record pea-crop off to market, put his head gardener, Govind Singh, in charge of the operation. The first manoeuvre, with a force of thirty men, failed to produce anything; but as Jim and Govind stood facing each other discussing the possibility of another beat on the morrow, the gardener suddenly stopped talking and stared over Jim's shoulder. There was the tigress, quietly walking along the edge of a field about 400 yards away.

The tigress was coming towards us at a slight angle and would see any movement we made, so there was nothing I could do but watch her; and no tigress has ever moved more slowly. She was known to the people of Muktesar as the lame tiger, but I could see no sign of her being lame. The plan that was forming in my head as I watched her was to wait until she entered the scrub jungle and then run forward and try to get a shot at her.

Telling the men not to move or make a sound until I returned, I set off at a run as the tigress disappeared from view. The hill was steep, and as I ran along the contour I came to a wild rose bush which extended up and down the hill for many yards. Through the middle of the bush there was a tunnel, and as I bent down to run through it, my hat was knocked off, and, raising my head too soon, I was nearly dragged off my feet by the thorns that entered my head.

With little trickles of blood running down my face I continued to run until I reached a hollow, some forty yards long and thirty yards wide, into which I had earlier rolled a partially-eaten kill. As I reached the edge of the hollow and peered over, I heard a bone crack. The tigress had reached the hollow before me and, on finding the old kill, was trying to make up for the meal she had been deprived of the previous night.

I was considering the possibility of driving her out of the brushwood on to the open ground by throwing a stone on to the hill above her, when I heard a sound behind me. On looking round I saw Govind standing with my hat in his hand. At that time no European in India went about without a hat, and, having seen mine knocked off by the rose bush, Govind had brought it to me.

Near us was a hole in the hill. Putting my finger to my lips, I got Govind by the arm and pressed him into the hole. Sitting on his hunkers, with his chin resting on his drawn-up knees, hugging my hat, he just fitted into the hole and looked a very miserable object, for he could hear the tigress crunching bones a few yards away. As I straightened up and resumed my position on top of the bank, she stopped eating. She had either seen me, or, what was more probable, she had not found the old kill to her liking.

For a long minute there was no movement or sound, and then I caught sight of her. She had climbed up the opposite bank, and was now going along the top of it towards the hill. At this point there were a number of six-inch-thick poplar saplings, and I could only see the outline of the tigress as she went through them. With the forlorn hope that my bullet would miss the saplings and find the tigress, I threw up my rifle and took a hurried shot.

At my shot the tigress whipped round, came down the bank, across the hollow and up the path on my side, as hard as she could go. I did not know, at the time, that my bullet had struck a sapling by her head, and that she was blind of one eye. So what looked like a very determined charge might only have been a frightened animal running away from danger. Be that as it may, what I took to be a wounded and very angry tigress was coming straight at me. So, waiting till she was two yards away, I leant forward and with great good luck managed to put the remaining bullet in the rifle into the hollow where the neck joined the shoulder. The impact of the heavy .500 bullet deflected her just sufficiently for her to miss my left shoulder, and her impetus *carried her over the fifty-foot drop into the stream below, where she landed with a great splash.*

That evening, before a huge crowd outside the guest-house in Muktesar, Jim skinned the tigress, and found that in an encounter with a porcupine she had lost an eye and got some fifty quills, from one to nine inches long, embedded in her arm and under the pad of her right foreleg. Some of the quills had doubled back in the form of a U, and suppurating sores had formed where she tried to extract them. No wonder she had turned to easier targets than her normal wild prey.

At midnight Jim lay down to sleep in the *dak* bungalow reserved for the public, but at 4am he was on the move again, and by midday he was home in Nainital, after an absence of only 72 hours.

He claimed that his success was 'due entirely to luck' – and indeed he had been fortunate in that the tigress's death spring had carried her just wide of him. But courage and sheer physical endurance had also played a major part in his survival. As he remarked, the shooting of the man-eater gave him satisfaction at 'having done a job that badly needed doing, and having out-manoeuvred, on her own ground, a very worthy antagonist.' But the greatest satisfaction of all was that he had 'made a small portion of the earth safe for a brave little girl to walk on.'

CHAPTER FIVE

The Panar Man-Eater
1910

While hunting the Champawat tigress, Jim heard rumours of a leopard that was terrorising villages on the eastern border of Almora, a district some twenty-five miles east of Nainital. This animal, credited with the deaths of over 400 human beings, became so notorious that it was mentioned in the House of Commons in London; and in 1910, when no individual sportsmen had come forward offering to deal with it, the Government in Delhi again asked Jim to go into action.

At the time he was extremely busy in the depot at Mokameh Ghat: he and his workmen set up an all-time record by handling, without any mechanical means, 5,500 tons of goods in a single day, and several weeks passed before he could react to the Government's request; but then one day in September, he went to call on the Deputy Commissioner of Almora. Having walked fourteen miles accompanied by a servant and four men that morning, he was glad to be invited to lunch, but then got 'a bit of a jolt' when his host asked if he had made a will.

Moving on, the hunting party arrived by moonlight at a deserted school. As the door of the building was locked, Jim decided to spend the night in the courtyard – a proceeding he reckoned perfectly safe, as they were still many miles from the man-eater's territory. His men soon had a fire burning in a corner of the yard, and as Jim sat smoking with his back to the door, his servant laid a leg of lamb on the low wall along the road. Moments later, the head of a leopard appeared over the wall. Fascinated, Jim sat motionless and watched – until, as his man moved away, the raider grabbed the meat and bounded off into the jungle. Jim's reaction was to burst out laughing, but his servant was terrified and said in a very aggrieved voice: 'It was your dinner that the leopard carried away, and I have nothing else for you to eat.' In spite of the theft, the servant apparently conjured up a perfectly adequate meal.

Next day the party reached the Dol *dak* bungalow on the edge of the man-eater's domain, and on the following morning Jim set off alone in search of news, walking from village to village on the network of footpaths that wound among the steep, forested hills. Late in the evening he came on the pug-marks of a big male leopard on the track to an isolated homestead – a single, stone-built, slate-roofed house, surrounded by a few acres of cultivated land, in the middle of jungle. As he arrived, a young man in his twenties ran across the courtyard and threw himself sobbing at Jim's feet.

It appeared that the previous night, while he and his wife were sleeping on the floor, with the door open – for it was April and very hot – the man-eater climbed on to the balcony, and, getting a grip of his wife's throat, started to pull her head-first out of the room. With a strangled scream the woman flung an arm round her husband, who, realising in a flash what was happening, seized her arm with one hand and, placing the other against the door for leverage, jerked her away from the leopard and closed the door. For the rest of the night he and his wife cowered in a corner of the room, while the leopard tried to tear the door down. In the hot, unventilated room the woman's wounds started to turn septic, and by morning her suffering and fear had rendered her unconscious.

Throughout the day the man remained with his wife, too frightened to leave her, for fear the leopard should return and carry her away, and too frightened to face the mile of scrub that lay between him and his nearest neighbour. As day was closing and the unfortunate man was facing another night of terror, he saw Jim coming towards the house.

Jim was in severe difficulty. There was no medical aid nearer than Almora, twenty-five miles away. He was sure that if he himself went for help, the young man would go mad from fear of another attack by the leopard. He felt, in any case, that the young woman was going to die from her injuries: the leopard had clamped its teeth into her throat and left four-deep claw-marks down her breast, and the wounds were already turning septic. 'I very sincerely hope,' he wrote later, 'that no one who reads this story will ever be condemned to seeing and hearing the sufferings of a human being, or of an animal, that has had the misfortune of being caught by either a leopard or a tiger and not having the means – other than a bullet – of alleviating or ending the suffering.'

He decided to stay, but refused the man's pleas to remain in the single room, for the smell in there was more than he could stand. Instead, he chose to spend the night on the ground, in the space beneath the balcony, with his back to the house wall.

The moon was two nights off full, and there would be a short period of darkness. It was this period of darkness that was worrying me. If the leopard had remained scratching at the door until daylight, as the man said it had, it would not have gone far, and even now might be lurking in the bushes watching me. I had been in position for half an hour, straining my eyes into the darkening night and praying for the moon to top the hills to the east when a jackal gave its alarm call.

This call, which is given with the full force of the animal's lungs, can be heard for a very long distance, and can be described as pheaon, pheaon, repeated over and over again, as long as the danger that has alarmed the jackal is in sight. Leopards, when hunting or approaching a kill, move very slowly, and it would be many minutes before this one – assuming it was the man-eater – covered the half-mile between us, and even if in the meantime the moon had not risen, it would be giving sufficient light to shoot by – so I was able to relax and breathe more freely.

Minutes dragged by. The jackal stopped calling. The moon rose over the hills, flooding the ground in front of me with brilliant light. No movement to be seen anywhere, and the only sound to be heard in all the world was the agonised fight for breath of the unfortunate girl above me. Minutes gave way to hours. The moon climbed the heavens and then started to go down in the west, casting the shadow of the house on the ground I was watching. Another period of danger, for if the leopard had seen me, he would, with a leopard's patience, be waiting for these lengthening shadows to mask his movements. Nothing happened, and one of the longest nights I have ever watched through came to an end.

A day or two later the poor girl died. So Jim's first attempt on the Panar man-eater ended in failure, and six months passed before he had the time to try again. Once more he was accompanied by four men and a servant as he set out from Nainital at 4am on 10 September 1910. A twenty-eight-mile march brought them to Almora; after a night there, another all-day trek and a second night in a *dak* bungalow, they were back in the leopard's territory.

Here there were no roads – only footpaths running from village to village – and progress was slow, as Jim questioned local people and searched for the man-eater's characteristic pug-marks. One night, when the headman of a hamlet offered him the use of a room, he had a particularly unnerving experience. The room was filthy, but after Jim had got his men to sweep out all the rubbish, he slept well – only to wake at sunrise and see, sitting on the floor near his bed, a man who was clearly in the last stage of leprosy. Because the disease was prevalent throughout Kumaon, and particularly bad in Almora district, the headman had not thought it necessary to warn him that the room had for years been the home of a leper. 'It did not take me long to dress that morning,' Jim wrote later, 'and as soon as our guide was ready we left the village.'

I have never felt as unclean as I did after my night in that poor unfortunate's room. At the first stream we came to I called a halt, for my servant to get breakfast ready for me and for my men to have their food. Then, telling my men to wash my groundsheet and lay my bedding out in the sun, I took a bar of carbolic soap and went down the stream to where there was a little pool, surrounded by great slabs of rock. Taking off every stitch of clothing I had worn in that room, I washed it all in the pool and, after laying it out on the slabs of rock, I used the remainder of the soap to scrub myself as I had never scrubbed myself before. Two hours later, in garments that had shrunk a little from the rough treatment they had received, I returned to my men feeling clean once again, and with a hunter's appetite for breakfast.

After some exceedingly strenuous climbs, and the hazardous fording of a river in spate, Jim's party reached Sanouli, where four human kills had taken place earlier in the year. The small village, built on the side of a hill, looked out across a valley to cultivated terraces on the opposite slope and – a feature which immediately took Jim's eye – a patch of dense brushwood surrounded by farmed land. All four recent victims had been killed at night and carried some 500 yards into the brushwood, where the leopard had eaten them at his leisure – for, having no firearms, the people had been too frightened to make any attempt to recover the bodies, and they were convinced that the leopard was still lurking in the cover.

Earlier that day Jim had bought two young male goats, and now, in the evening, he staked the smaller one out on the edge of the brushwood. He did not sit up over it, because there was no suitable tree nearby, but he tethered the second goat to the roofed platform in the village which the headman had offered him as a base. After dark he listened to the goats calling each other, and the fact that they continued long into the night convinced him that the leopard was not within hearing distance.

Next morning – when 'the sun rose in a cloudless sky, every leaf and blade of grass was sparkling with raindrops, and every bird that had a song to sing was singing a joyful welcome to the day' – the smaller goat had fallen silent. Crossing the valley to investigate, Jim soon found that it had been killed and carried away. From the size of the pugmarks, he had no doubt that the culprit was the leopard he had hunted earlier in the year.

He could, as he later remarked, have assembled a force of local men and got them to drive the animal into the open, so that he could get a shot at it; but he decided that this was not an option, as he knew that the leopard, finding he was being driven towards open ground, might turn back and attack anyone who got in the way. Instead, he spent several hours trying in vain to stalk the killer in the brushwood, 'helped by bulbuls, drongos, thrushes and scimitar babblers, all of whom kept me informed of the leopard's every movement.'

Back in the village, he went down with one of his recurrent attacks of malaria, and for twenty-four hours lay on his platform in a stupor. Next evening, recovering swiftly, he resumed the chase. By then the villagers had tethered the second goat outside the brushwood, about 100 yards from where its partner had been killed. Close to this new site was an old oak tree growing out of a bank between terraced fields. The trunk was leaning away from the hill at such an angle that Jim was able to walk up it, but the only branch substantial enough to offer him a seat jutted out over the lower field, some fifteen feet from the ground.

On this he took up position – and to protect his back from attack he got his men to cut a number of blackthorn shoots, ten or twenty feet long, and lash them in bundles round the trunk with strong rope. 'To the efficient carrying out of these small details,' he wrote later, 'I am convinced I owe my life.'

By five o'clock my preparations were complete. I was firmly seated on the branch, with my collar pulled up well in front to protect my throat, and my soft hat pulled down well behind to protect the back of my neck. The goat was tied to a stake driven into the ground about thirty yards in front of me, and my men were sitting out in the field, smoking and talking loudly. Up to this point all had been quiet in the patch of brushwood, but now a scimitar babbler gave its alarm call, followed a minute or two later by the chattering of several white-throated laughing thrushes. These two birds are the most reliable informants in the hills, and on hearing them I signalled to my men to return to the village. This they appeared very glad to do, and as they walked away, still talking loudly, the goat started bleating.

Nothing happened for the next half-hour, and then, as the sun was fading off the hill above the village, two drongos that had been sitting in the tree above me flew off and started to bait some animal on the open ground between me and the patch of brushwood. The goat, while calling, had been facing in the direction of the village, and now it turned round, facing me, and stopped calling. By watching the goat I could follow the movements of the animal that the drongos were baiting, and that the goat was interested in, and this animal could only be a leopard.

The moon was in her third quarter, and there would be several hours of darkness. In anticipation of the leopard's coming when light conditions were not favourable, I had armed myself with a 12-bore double-barrelled shotgun loaded with slugs – for there was a better chance of my hitting the leopard with eight slugs than with a single rifle bullet. Again nothing happened for many minutes – and then I felt a gentle pull on the blackthorn shoots I was holding, and blessed my forethought in having had the shoots tied to the leaning tree, for I could not turn round to defend myself, and at best the collar of my coat and my hat were poor protection.

No question now that I was dealing with a man-eater, and a very determined man-eater at that. Finding that he could not climb over the thorns, the leopard, after his initial pull, had now got the butt ends of the shoots between his teeth and was jerking them violently, pulling me hard against the trunk of the tree. And now the last of the daylight faded out of the sky, and the leopard, who did all his killing in the dark, was in his element, and I was out of mine – for in the dark the human being is the most helpless of animals, and – speaking for myself – his courage is at its lowest.

Having killed 400 human beings at night, the leopard was quite unafraid of me, as was evident from the fact that, while tugging at the shoots, he was growling loud enough to be heard by the men waiting anxiously in the village. While this growling terrified the men (as they told me later) it had the opposite effect on me, for it let me know where the leopard was and what he was

*doing. It was when he was silent that I was most terrified, for I
did not know what his next move might be.*

*After one of these nerve-racking periods of silence, the
leopard jumped down off the high bank and dashed towards the
goat. I had tied the goat thirty yards from the tree, in the hope
that it would give me time to kill the leopard before it got to the
goat. But now, in the dark, I could not save the goat, which,
being white, I could only just see as an indistinct blur. So I
waited until it had stopped struggling and then aimed where I
thought the leopard would be and pressed the trigger. My shot
was greeted with an angry grunt, and I saw a white flash as the
leopard went over backwards and disappeared down another high
bank into the field beyond.*

For ten minutes Jim listened for further sounds. Then his
men called out, asking if they should come to him. He told
them to light their pine torches, made from long splinters of
resined wood cut from a living tree, and after a lot of running
about, some twenty of them left the village. Following his
instructions, they circled round above the terraced fields and
approached his tree from behind. The torches lit up the field
in which the dead goat was lying, but the field below was in
shadow.

When cigarettes had been handed round, Jim told the
men that he had wounded the leopard, but he did not know
how badly, and announced that everyone would now return
to the village, leaving any search for the animal until the
morning. This provoked such disappointment, and so much
argument, that after a while he relented, and agreed to go as
far as the edge of the field, to look down over the terrace.

*I made the men promise that they would walk in line behind
me, hold their torches high and not run away and leave me in
the dark if the leopard charged. This promise they very willingly*

gave, and after the torches had been replenished and were burning brightly, we set off, I walking in front and the men following five yards behind.

Thirty yards to the goat, and another twenty yards to the edge of the field. Very slowly, and in silence, we moved forward. When we reached the goat – no time now to look for a blood trail – the farther end of the lower field came into view. The nearer we approached the edge, the more of this field became visible, and then, when only a narrow strip remained in shadow from the torches, the leopard, with a succession of angry grunts, sprang up the bank and into full view.

There is something very terrifying in the angry grunt of charging leopard, and I have seen a line of elephants that were staunch to tiger turn and stampede from a charging leopard; so I was not surprised when my companions, all of whom were unarmed, turned as one man and bolted. Fortunately for me, in their anxiety to get away they collided with each other, and some of the splinters of burning pine – held loosely in their hands – fell to the ground and continued to flicker, giving me sufficient light to put a charge of slugs into the leopard's chest.

That night, for the first time in years, the people of Sanouli slept, and have continued to sleep, free from fear.

CHAPTER SIX

The Temple Tiger

Considering how often Jim deliberately put himself in mortal danger, he seems to have been extraordinarily careless about the weapons on which his life depended. One morning on a visit to Calcutta he walked into Manton, the gunsmith, and saw a rifle lying on a glass case near the door. The manager, an old friend, came up and told him that it was a Westley Richards .275, a new model which the makers were keen to launch on the Indian market. 'The rifle was a beauty,' Jim reported, 'and the manager had little difficulty in persuading me to buy it, on the understanding that if it did not suit me, I would be at liberty to return it.'

A few months later, while on the track of a man-eating leopard near Dabidhura, he fell into conversation with the aged *pundit* who officiated at the little temple 'nestling in the shadow of the great rock,' which had made the village a place of pilgrimage. When he asked if there was any shooting to be had in the neighbourhood, the old man replied, 'Yes – there is the temple tiger,' but he added with a laugh, 'I have no objection, *Sahib*, to your trying to shoot this tiger, but neither you nor anyone else will ever succeed in killing it.'

Jim was intrigued, but his first objective was to shoot a *jarao* – the hillman's name for *sambar* – to provide meat for his own men and for the villagers, and when someone told him he knew of a *jarao* 'with horns as big as the branches of an

69

oak tree', he set out in search of it, taking his new rifle, which would be ideal for the job. On his way to the open, grassy space on which the animal was wont to feed, he was intercepted by a farmer, who told him that a tiger had killed one of his cows the night before, and took him to see the carcase. Vultures had already eaten most of it, but a quick reconnaissance established that the tiger had made off up a water channel, and when Jim found a stunted oak tree into which he could climb in ambush, he decided to go back to the rest house for his heavy rifle, a double-barrelled .500 express.

His guide 'very sportingly' offered to save him the trouble, and went off to fetch it with one of Jim's best regular porters, Bala Singh. He himself settled down to chat with a villager at the door of his hut. But as the sun was setting the two men returned without any weapon, explaining that the cartridges for the heavy rifle were locked in a suitcase, and Jim had forgotten to give them the key. 'Well,' he remarked later, 'the tiger would have to be shot with my new rifle, and it could not have a better christening.' Leaving Bala Singh at the hut, with its owner, he returned to his perch in the oak.

The vesper songs of the multitude of birds in the valley were hushed as the red glow from the setting sun died off the hills. Twilight deepened, and a horned owl hooted on the hill above me. There would be a short period of semi-darkness before the moon rose. The time had now come, and the inmates of the hut were as silent as the dead. I was gripping the rifle and straining my eyes on the ground under me when the tiger, who had avoided passing under my tree, arrived at his kill and was angry at what he found. In a low, muttering voice he cursed the vultures who, though they had departed two hours earlier, had left their musky smell on the ground they had fouled.

For two, three, possibly four minutes, he continued to mutter to himself, and then there was silence. Another few minutes, and the moon rose over the brow of the hill, flooding my world with light. The bones picked clean by the vultures were showing white in the moonlight, and nowhere was the tiger to be seen. Moistening my lips, which excitement had dried, I gave a low whistle. Bala Singh was on the alert, and I heard him ask the owner of the hut for a light from the fire. Through the crevices of the grass hut I saw a glimmer of light, which grew stronger as the lantern was lit. The light moved across the hut, and Bala Singh pulled open the door and stood on the threshold awaiting my further orders.

With the exception of that one low whistle, I had made no sound or movement from the time I had taken my seat on the tree. And now, when I looked down, there was the tiger standing below me in brilliant moonlight, looking over his right shoulder at Bala Singh. The distance between the muzzle of my rifle and the tiger's head was about five feet, and the thought flashed through my mind that the cordite would probably singe his hair. The ivory sight of the rifle was on the exact spot of the tiger's heart − where I knew my bullet would kill him instantaneously − when I gently pressed the trigger.

The trigger gave under the pressure, and nothing happened.

Heavens! How incredibly careless I had been. I distinctly remembered having put a clip of five cartridges in the magazine when I took my seat on the tree, but quite evidently when I pushed the bolt home it had failed to convey a cartridge from the magazine into the chamber, and this I had omitted to observe. Had the rifle been old and worn, it might still have been possible to rectify my mistake. But the rifle was new, and as I raised the lever to draw back the bolt, there was a loud metallic click, and in one bound the tiger was up the bank and out of sight.

Jim had indeed been incredibly careless. It seems not only that he was unfamiliar with the .275, but that although he had owned it for several months, he had never fired it, even in practice. Too late, he remembered that the manufacturers had introduced 'a so-called improvement' in the form of a double trigger-pull: the first pull took up the slack, and the second released the striker.

Undaunted, he continued his hunt for the man-eater, now armed with his big double-barrelled .500. He did not have to wait long for another chance. Next morning the tiger again killed a cow and dragged the body away into a ravine, but left it uneaten in a hollow. Finding pug marks that led down the ravine, Jim felt sure that the tiger would return by the same route, and so, at about 4pm, he took up position in a small holly tree some thirty yards from the kill. He could not see the body of the cow, which lay behind by a thick growth of saplings, but he was confident that, on its way to the kill, the tiger would show up on the open ground in front of him, offering an easy shot. Expecting that alarm calls from deer, monkeys and birds would herald the carnivore's approach, he was surprised when he suddenly heard the tiger already on the kill, tearing at chunks of flesh; but he was even more surprised when he saw 'a great big Himalayan black bear' advancing on the scene.

Suddenly he [the bear] stopped, turned facing downhill and lay flat. The wind, as always in daylight in the hills, was blowing uphill, and the bear had got the scent of flesh and blood, mingled with the scent of tiger. Presently he got to his feet and, with bent legs and body held close to the ground, started to stalk the tiger.

It was a revelation to me in animal stalking to see that bear coming down the hill. He had possibly 200 yards to go, and though he was not built for stalking, as tigers and leopards are, he covered the distance as smoothly as a snake and as silently as a shadow. The nearer he got, the more cautious he became. I could see the lip of the fifteen-foot drop into the hole, and when the bear got to within a few feet of this spot he drew himself along with belly to ground. *Waiting until the tiger was eating with great gusto, the bear very slowly projected his head over the lip of the hole and looked down, and then as slowly drew his head back.*

Excitement with me had now reached the stage when the whole of my body was trembling, and my mouth and throat were dry. At the back of my mind was the thought that surely this bear would not be so foolish as to try to dispossess the king of the jungle of his kill. But that was just what the bear appeared to intend doing, and his opportunity came when the tiger was cracking a bone. The bear drew himself up to the edge, and, gathering his feet under him, launched himself into the hole with a mighty scream.

The object of the scream, I imagine, was to intimidate the tiger, but so far from having this effect, it seemed to infuriate him, for the bear's mighty scream was answered by an even mightier roar. I did not see the fight, but I heard every detail of it. Waged in a hollow of restricted area, the sound was terrifying. The fight may have lasted three minutes, or it may have lasted longer. Anyway, when the tiger considered he had administered sufficient chastisement, he broke off the engagement and came along the open ground in front of me at a fast gallop, closely followed by the still-screaming bear.

Just as I was aligning the sights of my rifle on the tiger's left shoulder, he turned sharp to the left and, leaping the twenty-foot-wide ravine, landed at my feet. While he was still in the air I depressed the muzzle of my rifle and fired, as I thought, straight into his back. My shot was greeted with an angry grunt as the tiger crashed into the ringals behind me. For a few yards he carried on, and then there was silence: shot through the heart, and died in his tracks, I thought.

A .500 modified cordite rifle fired anywhere makes a considerable noise, but here in the ravine it sounded like a cannon. The detonation, had not the least effect on the maddened bear. Storming down one bank, he came up the other straight towards me. I had no wish to shoot an animal that had the courage to drive a tiger off his kill, but to have let that screaming fury come any nearer would have been madness, so, when he was a few feet from me, I put the bullet of the left barrel into his broad forehead. Slowly he slid down the bank on his stomach, until his haunches met the opposite bank.

Confident that he had despatched both antagonists. Jim relaxed and looked forward to a soothing smoke; but as he was feeling in his pocket for his cigarette case, he suddenly saw the tiger cantering back across the open ground in front. He only had time to load one barrel and fire a single shot – and he saw the bullet strike a rock a few inches below his target's face.

Describing the sequence of events years later, he confessed that he had 'no defence to make against the accusation of bad shooting.' He had had three chances at the tiger – and the prophecy of the old priest – that he would never shoot the temple tiger – seemed to be coming true. His only compensation was that when he skinned the bear – the biggest and fattest he had ever seen – the villagers were delighted when he shared out its fat, which they valued highly as a cure for rheumatism.

In fewer than twenty-four hours he was in action again. Once more a tiger had killed a cow. Going to investigate in the company of a forest guard, he walked down a beautiful, park-like valley dotted with giant oak trees and soon found a large heap of twigs and dead leaves raked together – a sure sign that the kill had been hidden beneath it. As he searched the opposite slope he spotted the tiger lying on a small bit of flat ground with its feet towards him. Presently it turned over so that he could see part of its head and a strip of its back, but the target was too small for him to risk a shot – and in any case the chance was blown away by the arrival of a bear with two cubs. Seeing them, the forest guard exclaimed in loud voice *'Dekho, Sahib, bhalu, bhalu!'*

The tiger was up and away in a flash, but he had some twenty yards of open ground to cover, and as I aligned my sights on him and pressed the trigger, the forest guard, under the impression that I was facing in the wrong direction, grabbed my arm and gave it a jerk, with the result that my bullet struck a tree a few yards from where I was standing.

Losing one's temper anywhere does no good, least of all in a jungle. The forest guard, who did not know what the piled-up leaves implied, and who had not seen the tiger, was under the impression that he had saved my life by drawing my attention to the dreaded bears, so there was nothing to be said.

Next day an early reconnaissance confirmed that the tiger had not returned to his kill, and that bears had finished it, all but a few bones; but when Jim went back to the Rest House at midday, he immediately heard that a white cow had been killed, some five miles from the first. After a combined breakfast and lunch, he set out on foot to find the site, and soon was following the drag. He was moving carefully down a steep ravine when he suddenly spotted the tiger lying on a strip of sand beside a pool of water, with only its hind legs showing. Half an hour later it shifted slightly, then stood up and walked off out of sight. Jim was not daunted, for he knew the animal would return to its kill. He did the same, and made himself comfortable in an oak tree ten yards from the remains of the cow.

When the setting sun, showing as a great ball of fire, was resting on the rim of the earth, bathing the world in red, a sambar belled in the valley below me. The tiger was on the move. The ball of fire dipped below the horizon; the red glow died off the earth; twilight gave place to darkness, and all was silent in the jungle.

75

The moon was in its third quarter, but the stars – nowhere more brilliant than in the Himalayas – were giving enough light for me to see the kill. The head was towards me, and if the tiger came now and started to eat at the hindquarters, I would not be able to see him; but by aligning my sights on the white kill, and then raising the rifle and pressing the trigger, there was a fifty-fifty chance of hitting the tiger.

But here was no man-eater to be fired at under any conditions. Here was a 'temple' tiger who had never molested human beings, and who, though he had killed four head of cattle in four consecutive days, had committed no crime against the jungle code. To kill him outright would benefit those who were suffering from his depredations, but to take an uncertain shot at night, with the possibility of only wounding him and leaving him to suffer for hours, or if unrecovered to become a man-eater, was not justifiable in any circumstances.

Light was coming in the east, for the boles of the trees were beginning to cast vague shadows, and then the moon rose, flooding the open patches of the jungle with light. It was then that the tiger came. I could not see him, but I knew he had come, for I could feel and sense his presence. Was he crouching on the far side of the kill with just his eyes and the top of his head raised over the brow of the hill, watching me? No, that was not possible, for from the time I had made myself comfortable on my seat, I had become part of the tree, and tigers do not go through a jungle scanning, without a reason, every tree they approach. And yet, the tiger was here, and he was looking at me.

There was sufficient light now for me to see clearly, and very carefully I scanned the ground in front of me. Then, as I turned my head to look behind, I saw the tiger. He was sitting on his hunkers in a patch of moonlight, facing the kill, with his head turned looking up at me. When he saw me looking down on him, he flattened his ears, and as I made no further movement, his ears regained their upright position. I could imagine him

saying to himself, 'Well, you have now seen me, and what are
you going to do about it?'

There was little I could do about it, for in order to get a shot
I would have to turn a half-circle, and it would not be possible to
do this without alarming the tiger, who was looking at me from
a range of fifteen feet. There was, however, just a possibility of
my getting a shot from my left shoulder, and this I decided to
try to do. The rifle was resting on my knees, with the muzzle
pointing to the left, and as I lifted it and started turning to the
right, the tiger lowered his head and again flattened his ears. In
this position he remained as long as I was motionless, but the
moment I started to move the rifle again, he was up and away
into the shadows behind.

The tiger 'had definitely won another round.' The question
now was how Jim himself should spend the rest of the night.
Anywhere else, he would simply have slept on the ground;
but as he was in the territory of a man-eater, he did not
fancy the idea. Nor – as he had already walked twenty miles
that day – did he feel like trekking another eight miles to
the Rest House. Instead, he made his way to a cattle station,
whose inmates' bells he had heard earlier in the day.

There he found a hundred head of cattle in a large
open shed, surrounded by a stockade; and, having addressed
them with a few words of soothing cow language, which
he had learnt as a boy, he climbed the stockade, found an
open space between two recumbent cows, settled into it,
and, lulled by the 'honey-sweet smell of healthy cattle, slept
as one at peace with all the world, tigers and man-eating
leopards included.'

In the morning, back at the Rest House, after a hearty
breakfast of porridge, scrambled eggs, hot chapatis, honey
and a dish of tea, Jim decided to concede that the temple
tiger had won the day. Having failed to shoot it four times,

he felt that his pursuit was inducing it to kill more cattle than it would if he left it alone; so he decided he would have a day off, and in the morning make an early start for home. But scarcely had he taken this decision when a voice behind him said, 'Salaam, Sahib. I have come to tell you that a tiger has killed one of my cows.'

This new kill was on the eastern face of the Dabidhura mountain, several miles from where Jim had sat up the night before. The body of the cow lay in an open glade, and some ten yards down the slope below it stood a single mature oak. Excessive lopping for cattle fodder had left a crop of small branches sprouting all up the trunk, which made the tree easy to climb, but meant that when Jim took up position on a single, solid branch higher up, he could not see straight below him.

He had been sitting there for an hour, watching some red-whiskered bulbuls feeding on a raspberry bush, when he turned his eyes and saw the tiger's head projecting beyond a clump of bushes.

He was evidently lying down, for his head was close to the ground, and his eyes were fixed on me. Presently a paw was advanced, then another, and then very slowly and with belly to ground the tiger drew himself up to his kill. Here he lay for several minutes without movement. Then, feeling with his mouth, and with his eyes still fixed on me, he bit off the cow's tail, laid it on one side and started to eat. Having eaten nothing since his fight with the bear three days before, he was hungry, and he ate just as a man would eat an apple, ignoring the skin and taking great bites of flesh from the hindquarters.

The rifle was across my knees, pointing in the direction of the tiger, and all I had to do was to raise it to my shoulder. I would get an opportunity of doing this when he turned his eyes away from me for a brief moment. But the tiger appeared to know his danger, for without taking his eyes off me he ate on steadily and unhurriedly. When he had consumed about fifteen or twenty pounds of flesh, I thought it was time for me to act. If I raised the rifle very slowly, he probably would not notice the movement, so I started to do this. I had raised the muzzle possibly six inches when the tiger slid backwards as if drawn by a powerful spring. With rifle to shoulder and elbows on knees I now waited for the tiger to project his head a second time, and this I felt sure he would presently do.

Minutes passed, and then I heard the tiger. He had skirted round the bushes and, approaching from behind, started to claw my tree where the thick growth of small branches on the trunk made it impossible for me to see him. Purring with pleasure, the tiger once and again clawed the tree with vigour, while I sat on my branch and rocked with silent laughter.

I know that crows and monkeys have a sense of humour, but until that day I did not know that tigers also possessed this sense. Nor did I know that an animal could have the luck, and the impudence, that particular tiger had. In five days he had killed five cows, four of them in broad daylight. In those five days I had seen him eight times, and on four occasions I had pressed a trigger on him. And now, after staring at me for half an hour and eating while doing so, he was clawing the tree on which I was sitting, and purring to show his contempt of me.

The tiger was now, in his own way, confirming what the temple priest had said. Well, the tiger had made the last move in the exciting game we had played, without injury to either of us, but I was not going to give him the satisfaction of having the last laugh. Laying down the rifle and cupping my hands, I waited till he stopped clawing, and then sent a full-throated shout echoing over the hills, which sent him careering down the hill at full speed and brought my men down from the village at a run. 'We saw the tiger running away with his tail in the air,' the men said when they arrived, 'and just see what he has done to the tree.'

Next morning I bade farewell to all my friends at Dabidhura, and assured them I would return when the man-eating leopard got active again. I visited Dabidhura several times in subsequent years while hunting man-eaters, and I never heard of anyone having killed the temple tiger. So I hope that in the fullness of time this old warrior, like an old soldier, just faded away.

CHAPTER SEVEN

Going to War

When war broke out in Europe in 1914, Jim was eager to join the army. The railway authorities were reluctant to let him go, but consented when he guaranteed that he would return when hostilities ended. Having summoned his staff at Mokameh Ghat to a conference, he found it impossible to explain the implications of the distant war that was going on 5.000 miles away; yet every one of them declared themselves willing to carry on while he was absent. He therefore hastened to Calcutta, to volunteer for military service, only to be told that, at thirty-eight, he was too old. His response was to return home to Kumaon, and there carry out his own recruitment. Such was his status and renown in the area that by 1917 he had he raised a work-force of 500 men – the 70th Kumaon Labour Corps.

On 22 May he wrote home from Mokameh Ghat:

When you all get used to the idea of my going to France for one year, you will have the same feeling of pride and satisfaction as I have, that I was not found wanting when the call came. After all, it's little enough that I am going to do for my country, just a year's holiday in France, that and no more. Making roads or unloading goods at the docks – what could it be but a holiday after my twenty years in the sun and sand of Mokameh Ghat, with cholera, plague, snakes and a thousand other forms of sudden death to contend with?

While waiting for a summons to action, he bought an abandoned village called Choti Haldwani, some two miles from Kaladhungi. Dividing the land into forty plots, he set about repairing the least decrepit of the houses, and directed the construction of some simple new ones, which he let at very low rents. In all he created forty holdings. The fields had been over-run by weeds, but he had the whole area fenced-in, did much of the heavy clearing work himself, and built a six-foot wall around the perimeter to keep out the deer and wild pigs which would otherwise destroy the villagers' crops. Later he supervised the construction of a concrete water conduit which supplied all the houses. He also encouraged the people to plant fruit trees, and in due course the place became an attractive model village. To the locals he was a patriarch, known as 'Carbet Sahib' or 'Carpet Sahib' – the nearest they could get to an English pronunciation of his name. In the words of the biographer Martin Booth, 'The Indians loved and feared, respected and admired him. Of simple peasant stock, they saw him not only as a benefactor and surrogate tribal leader of sorts, but they prided themselves on being of his village.'

For himself and his sister Maggie, in due course he built a new house at Kaladhungi – a substantial, stone-built bungalow containing several rooms, with a separate, single-roomed hut next to it. This was supposed to be his bedroom, but although there was plenty of space in the house – Maggie had a room of her own – he was inclined to sleep in a tent in the garden.

In 1917, with his labour force, he made the long journey by rail and sea to Flanders, and there he looked after his men with exemplary efficiency and imagination. The men were never involved in fighting; they were mainly engaged in salvage work and the laying of railway lines; but one of his most difficult tasks must have been the maintenance of morale for Indians living in tents in a cold, wet, alien environment. With strange food, constant danger, and no knowledge of how long this unpleasant existence might last, the men of Kumaon needed endless encouragement. Jim looked after them like a father – and one manifestation of his energy was the bath-house he built for the detachment at Tincourt, a ruined village which the British had occupied earlier in the year as the Germans retreated towards the Hindenburg line. When a senior officer, Lord Ampthill (a former Governor of Madras) visited the detachment at the beginning of 1918, he was amazed to find the substantial brick building apparently undamaged.

> *On my enquiring how it came to escape the ravages of war [he wrote in his report] Captain Corbett told me that he had built it himself with salved materials and no labour except that of his own men. The building contains a bathroom and a drying room, both of which are to be heated by an incinerator. It has good, solid walls of red brick, and the mortar was made with nothing more than chalk and rice water.*

Jim's men, Ampthill continued, were 'greatly inconvenienced by the repeated theft of their ablution benches, and other things capable of being turned into fuel... by the men of neighbouring units.' Nevertheless, they remained in good spirits. The atmosphere was less cheerful at No. 73 Kumaon Company, where several officers had fallen ill.

When the war ended in November 1918, the Indian units headed for home via England. While the men were parked for a few days in a barracks in the Home Counties, Jim, now with the substantive rank of Major, realised his long-held ambition to see London, and booked into a hotel in Great Russell street, opposite the front of the British Museum. For years he had been fascinated by accounts and photographs of the capital's great buildings – the Tower, Buckingham Palace, St Paul's Cathedral – and now he walked at his usual energetic pace, taking in all he could see; but when the winter dusk began to close in, and he tried to turn for home, he found himself in trouble, because he could not remember the address or even the name of his hotel. In search of directions he approached a policeman; but the copper, baffled by this strange officer, could not help him – and so he was left to find his way back by the only method he knew, retracing his steps by noting the odd statue or bombed house or town poster which he had spotted on his way out, just as he would navigate by reference to a particular tree or stream or rock in the jungle round Kaladhungi.

The 70th Kumaon Labour Company re-embarked at Tilbury, on the Thames, and sailed home via the Mediterranean and the Suez Canal, docking at Bombay and travelling overland by train and road to Nainital, where the unit was paid off. Jim had taken 500 men to the war, and by an extraordinary feat of organisation he brought 499 back, the single casualty being a man who died of sea-sickness. He rewarded the survivors by having them paid in newly-minted silver rupees.

At Mokameh Ghat things had gone well in his absence. Ram Saran had performed admirably, but now the authorities wanted Jim to return to the railways, and offered him a post nearer home. He, however, at the age of forty-four, felt footloose – as he admitted to his mother and Maggie in a letter sent from Lucknow in February 1919:

I don't feel ancient enough yet to sit down and wait for old age. The only question is whether I could do anything better for us all than take the billet at Gorakhpur. I would have liked to go to British East Africa and British Columbia, but the question is whether we could have withstood the transplanting at our time of life. After my free and easy life I will not take very kindly to an office, but I could stand it if I thought it was for the best.

For the moment the need for decisions was taken from him by the fact that the Army promoted him to major and sent him to Waziristan, to support troops in the third Afghan war as Commandant of 144 Labour Battalion. From Kohat, on the North-West Frontier, he sent home a cheerful despatch:

A man who has put in a few years as a Labour Corps officer should be able to do almost anything in the world. Take myself, for instance. At 6am I am having wagons unloaded and bags and bales built into huge stacks. At 7am I am two miles away seeing that my unskilled labour is turning out good iron, wood, brick work, and at 8am I am three miles further on, sweating to get a five-mile, three-inch pipe laid in record time – and so throughout the whole day. I love the kind of work we are on, and the people we are working for love us and can't do enough for us.

Some day when the war is over you all must come to Kohat with me and have a look at the prettiest cantonment station in India. We must come in the fruit season, for here the flowers that border the roads and the fruit that hangs over them are the property of the public. If you wish to pluck a bunch of violets or roses as big as a haystack, or fill half a dozen baskets with grapes, mulberries etc., you are quite at liberty to do so. The mulberries fall in such quantities that the roads are stained black with their juice.

CHAPTER EIGHT

Into Business
1920s

After the war, freed from the shackles of the railway, he was able to live at home, at Kaladhungi in winter, and in summer at Nainital. He and Maggie would often eschew transport and walk the thirteen miles between the two, up or down. For the descent they sent their luggage by bullock cart a day ahead, so that their arrival in the village was heralded, and all the people would come out to welcome them.

In Nainital Jim had taken control of the leading firm in town – F.E.G. Matthews & Co., a hardware store with a profitable side-line in estate agency. It is not clear how he amassed the funds, first to buy a share in the company in 1906, and then to acquire the whole of it; but he soon proved himself an able and popular businessman, helped in no small measure by his mother, Mary Jane, who taught herself the basics of book-keeping, and by Maggie, who looked after his interests whenever he was away. Always a shrewd investor, he steadily bought more properties in the town and invested money in other commercial enterprises.

After leaving the railway in 1919, he returned to Nainital and was appointed a member of the town's Municipal Board, and soon rose through the civic hierarchy to become Vice-Chairman – an elevation no doubt accelerated by the fact that he gave a large amount of money for the completion of a bandstand beside the lake.

He did much to enhance Nainital's environment – for instance by limiting the felling of trees inside the town boundary, by enforcing the licensing of goats, which, uncontrolled, had done serious damage in the surrounding forest, and by putting restrictions on fishing in the lake.

With things going well at home, he had plenty of time for hunting, and made many forays in the company of Percy Wyndham, an Oxford graduate with a double first who had come out to India as a junior member of the Indian Civil Service in 1889, and in 1914 had been appointed District Commissioner in Nainital. A powerful character, short and sturdy, liable to be aggressive and offensively rude in dealings with subordinates, he was also a formidably keen hunter, and often joined Jim in organising tiger shoots, in which teams of beaters drove the quarry to guns mounted on elephants or *machans*.

In 1922 Wyndham suggested that Jim should go hunting with him in Africa, where he had bought a coffee plantation on an estate called Kikafu, in what was then Tanganyika, and a British Protectorate. The journey to it was a long one – by train (which Jim hated) to Bombay, across the Arabian sea to Mombasa, then by train again up country to Moi and on by road. At first the only house on the property was a mud-and-wattle hut with a thatched roof, and the amenities were minimal. But Jim was so enthused by the place and its surroundings that he agreed to become a partner in the enterprise, and helped in clearing some of the thorn bush to make way for coffee.

The setting was spectacular, but entirely different from the one to which he was accustomed: instead of the abrupt hills and dense forests of close-quarter Kumaon, here were vast sweeps of open country, much of it virgin grass-land, commanded to the north by the magnificent, permanently snow-capped hulk of the extinct volcano Mount Kilimanjaro

In contrast with the denizens of the Indian jungle, the animals were visible from miles away: no tigers or bears, but lions, leopards, cheetahs, elephants, rhinos, hippos, antelopes galore, and million-strong herds of wildebeest that stretched as far across the plains as eye could see. Riding out with Wyndham on horses or in sturdy trucks, and camping in the wilds, Jim hunted with enthusiasm, seeing that in this wonderful environment there was an unlimited abundance of big game. He also made numerous expeditions with his cameras, and worked on the plantation, especially on irrigation projects.

There is no evidence that he ever shot a lion, a leopard or an elephant, but he certainly shot antelopes, and took some of his trophies home; and once he had seen the possibilities around Kikafu, he went over for a few months almost every year. Yet the fact that he published hardly a word about hunting in Africa strongly suggests that he regarded it as a lesser form of sport, markedly inferior to the pursuit of tigers in the jungle.

For Jim and Maggie a sad moment came in May 1924, when their mother Mary died at the age of eighty-nine. Ever since the death of Jim's father Christopher in 1881, she had held the family together, and she was widely known in Nainital, for she had long acted as an estate agent, brokering Jim's lets and sales; yet her passing must also have been a relief to the family, for in old age she had become increasingly eccentric, and had taken to walking out of Gurney House stark naked on her way to the town, so that retainers had to rush after her and escort her back.

Until then, in summer Jim and Maggie had lived in a house called Mount Pleasant, on the south-west edge of the town, but after their mother's death they moved into Gurney House. By then Jim was a prominent figure in Nainital. As a leading member of the municipal board, he did much to improve Nainital's environment, for instance by enforcing limitations on tree-felling and promoting the control of goats, which did immense damage to the surrounding forest. Inevitably some people were jealous of his reputation as a hunter, and of his ability to associate equally with Indians and Europeans. He always described himself as 'white', rather as 'Anglo Indian', but, unlike many officials of the Raj, he treated members of either race with the same courtesy.

Perhaps it was his mother's departure from the scene that encouraged him to pursue an eighteen-year-old girl called Helen, sister-in-law of one of the forest officers, who came out from England for a long holiday with her parents. Entranced by her looks and intelligence, he mounted a serious campaign, and went so far as to ask her parents for permission to marry; they, however, declined to give it – deterred not least by the fact that Jim, at fifty, was more than double their daughter's age. So struck with her was he that, three years later, he followed her trail all the way to Edinburgh, via the Ibbotsons in Kenya, only to find that she was about to marry someone else.

CHAPTER NINE

The Man-Eating Leopard
of Rudraprayag
1925-26

To Jim, leopards were 'the most beautiful and the most graceful of all the animals in our jungles.' When cornered or wounded they were second-to-none in courage and ferocity; yet, less admirably, they were also scavengers, and would eat any dead creature they could find. Tigers become man-eaters when some disability like the loss of a canine tooth makes it impossible for them to catch and kill their normal prey. A few leopards, in contrast, simply get a taste for human flesh, especially if an epidemic provides them with a copious supply – as when influenza swept through India in 1918, and the inhabitants of mountain country performed the last rites for their dead by placing a live coal in the mouth and casting the body off a cliff-top into the valley below.

So it was in Garhwal, a district north-west of Nainital. Between 9 June 1918 and 14 April 1926 the leopard known as the man-eater of Rudraprayag was officially credited with 126 kills; its fame spread all over the world, and Jim called it 'the most publicised animal that has ever lived.' For eight years it ranged over an area of 500 square miles, and although most of its victims were local people, it also preyed heavily on the Hindu pilgrims trudging barefoot up and down the trail to the age-old shrines of Kedarnath and Badrinath.

Every attempt to kill it had been frustrated: the Government had offered substantial rewards; the best *shikaris* were liberally paid to go out after it; men of the Garhwal regiments were permitted to take their rifles with them when going home on leave; 300 special licences were issued (in addition to the 4,000 already in force); scores of drop-door traps were built and baited with goats; human corpses were laced with poison – all to no avail. People began to believe that the killer was not an animal, but an evil spirit proof against all normal methods of assassination. Suspicion often fell on the local *sadhu*, or holy man, who was thought to harbour the malign being, and at least one was burnt to death when villagers set his house on fire.

In the summer of 1926 Jim was galvanised into action by a letter from his friend and hunting companion William Ibbotson, the vigorous new Deputy Commissioner for Garhwal, who was said to administer his affairs by striking terror into the hearts of his subordinates, and was a formidable hunter of tigers in his own right. Jim described him in fulsome terms: 'Of all the men I have been on *shikar* with, Ibbotson is by far and away the best, for not only has he the heart of a lion, but he thinks of everything, and with it all is the most unselfish man that carries a gun.' He might have added that Ibby cut his own hair, using two mirrors, and wove ropes as a hobby.

Now he was eager to rid his district of its scourge. In spite of a clamour in the press for the destruction of the man-eater, he had had only one offer – from a sportsman who reckoned the easiest way to kill the leopard was to paint a goat over with arsenic, sew up its mouth to prevent it licking the poison off, and then tie it up in a place where the leopard would find it, eat it, and so destroy itself.

At the centre of the leopard's territory lay the village of Rudraprayag, on the confluence of two rivers, the

Alaknanda and the Mandakini, both flowing down from the north until they join and become the Ganges. At Ibbotson's summons Jim, now aged fifty-one, set off from Nainital on an eleven-day trek to the north-west, escorted by his servant, his cook and six local men carrying his kit. *'However little I merit it,'* he wrote later,

> *the people of our hills credit me with supernatural powers where man-eaters are concerned. News that I was on my way to try to rid Garhwal of the man-eater preceded me, and while I was still many days' march from Rudraprayag the men I met on the roads, and those who from their fields or village homes saw me passing, greeted me with a faith in the accomplishment of my mission that was as touching as it was embarrassing, and which increased in intensity the nearer I approached my destination.*

The terrain at the end of his trek was fierce:

> *The cultivated land in the distance shows up as a series of lines drawn across the face of the steep mountains. These lines are terraced fields, which vary in width from one yard to fifty or more yards. The village buildings are invariably set at the upper end of the cultivated land; this is done with the object of overlooking and protecting the cultivation from stray cattle and wild animals, for except in very rare cases there are no hedges or fences round the fields. The brown and the green patches that make up most of the landscape are, respectively, grassland and forests. Some of the villages are entirely surrounded by grasslands, while others are entirely surrounded by forests. The whole country is rugged and rough, and is cut up by innumerable deep ravines and rock cliffs.*

Jim found that leopards were relatively easy to track, locate and stalk. For one thing, they have tender pads, and keep to game tracks and footpaths as much as possible, leaving prints in sand, earth or mud; for another, every bird and animal in the jungle 'assists the hunter' by giving tongue when it spots a predator on the move.

His object in going to Rudraprayag (he wrote) was to prevent further loss of human life, and once he had reached his destination, he did not intend to wait for another person to be killed before taking action. He therefore quickly bought two goats and staked them out, one on the pilgrim road, the second on the far side of the Alaknanda, on a path which bore the pugmarks of a big male leopard. Next day he found that goat dead, clearly killed by a leopard, so for three hours that evening he sat up in a small tree about fifty yards from the body.

When night fell, and no predator had come, he walked back to the bungalow in which he was staying. Only in the morning did he realise how lucky he had been. Outside his building he picked up the tracks of a big male leopard which led all the way to the body of the goat. The kill had not been touched, but Jim realised that the tracks could only have been those of the man-eater, and that it had followed him back to his lodging in the dark.

For the rest of the day I walked as many miles as my legs would carry me, telling all the people in the villages I visited, and all whom I met on the roads, that the man-eater was on our side of the river, and warning them to be careful.

Very soon his warning was vindicated. One evening later a woman was snatched from the doorway of her house as she washed pots after a meal, and her body was carried away onto a tiny terraced field above a ravine. Pug marks on the path were identical with those of the animal which had followed Jim back to his bungalow – an outsized male leopard, long past his prime, with a slight defect on his left hind paw.

Rapidly constructing an ambush at the scene of the kill, Jim lashed his spare rifle and shotgun to two stout bamboos driven into the ground, and stretched fishing lines tied to their triggers across a path that approached the body. He also took a slab of white rock from the ravine, and set it a foot from the woman's naked corpse as a marker. He then withdrew to a comfortable roost in a stack of straw built against a stunted walnut tree, and prepared for an all-night vigil.

Night had hardly fallen when there was a flash of lightning, followed by distant thunder, and in a few minutes the sky was heavily overcast. Just as the first big drops of a deluge began to fall, I heard a stone roll into the ravine, and a moment later the loose straw on the ground below me was being scratched up. The leopard had arrived; and while I sat in torrential rain, with the icy-cold wind whistling through my wet clothes, he lay dry and snug in the straw below.

The rain was soon over – leaving me chilled to the bone – and the clouds were breaking up when the white stone was suddenly obscured, and a little later I heard the leopard eating. The night before, he had lain in the ravine and eaten from that side; so, expecting him to do the same this night, I had placed the stone on the near side of the kill. Obviously the rain had formed little pools in the ravine, and to avoid them the leopard had taken up a new position and in doing so had obscured my mark.

Ten minutes later the stone was visible, and almost immediately thereafter I heard a sound below me and saw the leopard as a light-yellowish object disappearing under the rick. His light colour could be accounted for by old age, but the sound he made when walking I could not then, nor can I now, account for; it was like the soft rustle of a woman's silk dress, and could not be explained by stubble in the field – for there was none – or by the loose straw lying about.

Waiting a suitable length of time, I raised the rifle and covered the stone, intending to fire the moment it was again obscured; but there is a limit to the time a heavy rifle can be held to the shoulder, and when the limit had been reached I lowered the rifle to ease my aching muscles. I had hardly done so when the stone for the second time disappeared from view. Three times within the next two hours the same thing happened, and in desperation, as I heard the leopard approaching the rick for the fourth time, I leant over and fired at the indistinct object below me.

Examining the spot next morning, Jim found the hole made by his bullet in the centre of the tiny terrace, only two feet wide, with a little hair cut from the leopard's neck. Chagrined to have missed, he reckoned that the 'fickle jade chance' had played both the region of Garhwal and himself a dirty trick. But his spirits rose with the arrival of 'an electric shooting light' – a lamp specially sent from Calcutta.

The Alaknanda, at that point, was a fast-flowing torrent, and Jim felt sure that no leopard would try to ford it. But the man-eater could cross the river on either of two bridges, one at Rudraprayag and the other at Chatwapipal, fourteen miles upstream. Jim reckoned that if he could deny the leopard access to these crossing-points, he could confine it to his side of the stream, and so reduce by half the area in which to hunt it. To close the bridges was simple. The plank walk-ways were suspended from steel cables fixed at either end in a stone tower, and in the middle of each tower was a four-foot-wide arch. By having the arches blocked with thorn bushes every evening, Jim could be sure that no man or animal crossed the river during the night.

His plan was to guard the Rudraprayag bridge by spending the night on top of the tower – but reaching that vantage point by means of a rickety ladder was no easy matter:

The ladder — two uneven lengths of bamboo connected with thin sticks loosely held in position with string — only reached to within four feet of the platform. Standing on the top rung of the ladder, and dependent for a hand-hold on the friction of the palms of my hands on the smooth masonry, the safe gaining of the platform was an acrobatic feat that had less appeal the oftener it was tried.

All the rivers in this part of the Himalayas flow from north to south, and through the valleys in which they flow blows a wind which changes direction with the rising and setting of the sun. During daylight hours the wind — locally called dadu — blows from the south, and during the night it blows from the north.

At the time when I used to take up my position on the platform, there was usually a lull in the wind, but shortly thereafter it started blowing as a light zephyr, gaining in strength as daylight faded, and amounting by midnight to a raging gale. There was no hand-hold on the platform, and even when lying flat on my stomach to increase friction and reduce wind-pressure, there was imminent risk of being blown off on to the rocks sixty feet below. Added to the discomfort of the wind, I suffered torment from a multitude of small ants, which entered my clothes and ate away patches of skin.

In spite of the hazards and the discomfort, Jim spent twenty nights on that high perch, with the arches left open, in the hope that the leopard would try to cross, and give him an easy downward shot. But during all that time the only animal that came over the bridge was a jackal.

One morning, as he descended from his vigil, he met a strange, white-robed figure standing on a rock by the river. When asked what had brought him there, the stranger replied that he had come from a far land to free the people of Garhwal from the evil spirit that was tormenting them. This he proposed to achieve by fashioning an effigy of a tiger: then, having induced the spirit to enter his creation, he would launch it into the river, which would carry it down to the sea.

Split bamboos, string, paper and cheap coloured cloth went into his construction, and on the final day the tiger – according to Jim 'about the size of a horse, and resembling no known animal'– was lashed to a long pole and carried down to a beach, escorted by more than a hundred men, many of them beating gongs and blowing long trumpets.

At the river's edge the effigy was unlashed from the pole. The white-robed man, with his silver crosses on headgear and breast, and his six-foot cross in his hands, knelt on the sand and with earnest prayer induced the evil spirit to enter his handiwork – whereupon the effigy, with a crash of gongs and a blare of trumpets, was consigned to the Ganges, and sped on its way to the sea by a liberal offering of sweets and flowers.

Jim did not say whether or not he told the old man that the animal he was hunting was a leopard, rather than a tiger. But his pursuit continued, soon reinforced by the arrival of Ibbotson and his wife Jean, who took over the bungalow in which Jim had been staying. Driven into the open, he and his men set up a little tented camp, protected by a circle of thorn bushes, and there they lived for several weeks.

One great advantage of having Ibby along was his perennial optimism: he always believed that if they did not get the man-eater that day, they would surely get it tomorrow. At school he had been captain of the rugger XV, and 'of all the men I have been on *shikar* with,' Jim wrote, 'he is far and away the best, for not only has he the heart of a lion, but he thinks of everything, and with it all is the most unselfish man who carries a gun.' Another advantage of having the Ibbotsons in camp was that Jean appealed strongly to Jim: attractive, intelligent and a good shot, she was at home in the jungle, and in every way a useful addition to the team.

Within days there came two reports of cows being killed by a leopard, one inside a house, the other in the open. Over one of the bodies Jim and his colleague set up an ambush, building a *machan* inside a hayrick, and reinforcing their armament with a huge gin trap, weighing 80 lbs. An hour after dark, angry roars betrayed the fact that the leopard was in the trap, and in the beam of the electric light Jim saw the raider rearing up with the, trap dangling from his forelegs. He took a hurried shot, but all his bullet did was to sever the chain which had secured the trap, and the leopard went off along a field in a series of great leaps, carrying the trap in front of him, hastened by a bullet from Jim's second barrel and by two slugs from Ibbotson's shotgun.

Hearing the roars of the leopard and our four shots, the people in Rudraprayag bazaar and in nearby villages swarmed out of their houses carrying lanterns and pine torches, and converged from all sides. Shouting to them to keep clear was of no avail, for they were making so much noise that they could not hear us. So while I climbed down the tree, Ibbotson lit and pumped up the petrol lamp we had taken into the machan.

Together we went in the direction the leopard had taken. Half way along the field there was a hump caused by an outcrop of rock; this hump we approached, with Ibbotson holding the lamp high above his head, while I walked by his side with rifle to shoulder. Beyond the hump was a little depression, and crouching down in this depression and facing us and growling, was the leopard.

Within a few minutes of my bullet crashing into his head, we were surrounded by an excited crowd, who literally danced with joy round their long-dreaded enemy. For the first night in many years, every house in the bazaar was open, with women and children standing in the doorways. Progress was slow, for every few yards the leopard was put down to let the children cluster round. At the father end of the long street our escort left us, and the leopard was carried in triumph to the bungalow by our men.

99

Ibbotson, and all the men who came to see it, were convinced that the man-eater was dead; Jim, in contrast, found it hard to believe that this was the leopard he had seen at such close range while sitting up over the body of the woman. But after a long debate, he and his colleague agreed that this was the killer, and that in the morning they would return to their civilian pursuits. Both were exhausted, and went to bed early.

Next morning, while it was still dark, and Jim was having his *chota hazri* (early breakfast), he heard men outside, and when he called to ask what they were doing, four of them climbed the path to his camp, sent by the *patwari* (village headman) to tell him that a woman had been killed by the man-eater on the far side of the river, about a mile from the Chatwapipal bridge.

With a swift change of plan, he and Ibbotson procured two good horses and set off for the north. At the bridge they were met by a waiting guide, who led them down into a densely-wooded ravine with a stream flowing through it. There they found the *patwari* and some twenty men, beating drums to guard the body.

The kill was a very robust and fair girl, some eighteen or twenty years of age, lying on her face with her hands by her sides. Every vestige of clothing had been stripped from her, and she had been licked by the leopard from the soles of her feet to the neck, in which were four great teeth-marks. Only a few pounds of flesh had been eaten from her body.

The house from which she had been snatched had only one room, and was made of stone. Early in the night she had handed her baby to her father-in-law and had gone outside (as Jim put it) 'to squat down'. Close inspection of the surroundings showed that the leopard had crouched behind a rock about thirty yards from the door, and that it had lain there for some time before creeping forwards, belly to the ground, to grab its victim from behind.

It had then picked her up, and holding her high, so that no mark of hand or foot showed in the soft, newly-ploughed ground, had carried her across one field, down a three-foot bank and across another field which ended in a twelve-foot drop onto a well-used path. Down this drop the leopard had sprung with the girl – who weighed about eleven stone – and some idea of his strength could be gained from the fact that when he landed on the footpath he did not let any portion of her body come in contact with the ground.

Again Jim and his colleague set up an ambush, climbing into a stunted oak some sixty yards from the kill. As Ibbotson had a telescopic sight on his rifle, it was agreed that he should shoot first; but it was only after dark that they heard the leopard stealthily approaching, and they could not get a shot. They then had a terrifying walk, through buffalo wallows and sunken rocks, back to the building allotted to them for accommodation, spurred on by fear that the leopard was almost certainly following them. 'There are events in one's life which, no matter how remote, never fade from memory,' wrote Jim. 'That climb up the hill was for me one of them.'

Next morning the kill had not been touched; so, besides setting the huge gin-trap again, Jim inserted capsules of cyanide into the body. He hated resorting to poison – he would far rather use his rifle 'as rifles were intended to be used, to put a bullet truly and accurately into the man-eater's body.' But as Government wanted him to try every means of killing the leopard, he felt that extreme measures were justified. He and Ibbotson then spent the night on a *machan* built in a big pine tree – but once more they were disappointed: in the morning the body lay exactly as they had left it.

The hunters had run out of time. After an early breakfast Ibbotson left for Rudraprayag, and Jim was preparing to set out for home on his fifteen-day trek to Nainital when a party of four men arrived with the news that a cow had been killed by a leopard in a village four miles away. They suspected that the villain was the man-eater, because in the early hours of the morning a leopard had made a determined effort to scratch its way through the door of the headman's house.

Postponing his departure, Jim accompanied the four men back to their village, taking the trap and a supply of poison. He was soon escorted to the kill – a young heifer, lying in a position ideal for setting the trap.

Having dug away the ground between the cow's legs and removed it to a distance, I set the trap where the leopard had placed his paws, and covered it over with big green leaves. Then, after sprinkling on a layer or earth, I replaced the dead leaves, bits of dry sticks and splinters of bone in the exact position in which I had found them. Not one of a hundred human beings going to the kill would have noticed that the ground had been in any way disturbed, and a deadly trap set.

For part of that night Jim sat up a tree. No predator came to the kill; but, as he walked back to the headman's house in the dark, he suddenly felt he was being followed. His reaction was not to accelerate, but to lie down behind a big rock and cover a stretch of open ground with his rifle. After ten minutes, and no action, he went on to the house, 'taking every precaution.' Daylight revealed that the man-eater had indeed followed him to the building and walked round it several times; it had also dragged the remains of the cow away, but had avoided springing the trap. 'Up to that time,' Jim wrote, 'I had not fully realised the degree of cunning that a man-eating leopard can acquire after eight years of close association with human beings.'

Trying yet again, he put 'a liberal dose of cyanide' into the remains of the cow, and when he visited the site next morning, he found that a leopard had eaten all the part

he had poisoned. Any other *shikari* might have rejoiced –
but he knew instinctively that this was not the work of his
great enemy: some other leopard had come on the carcass by
chance. He told the headman he would pay a hundred rupees
to anyone who found it and took its skin to the *patwari*. He
then set off for home.

*Shortly after midday we started on our long journey back to
Nainital. As we went down a narrow footpath to the Chatwapipal
bridge, a big rat-snake leisurely crossed the path, and as I stood
and watched it slip away, Madho Singh – a seasoned retainer
who had fought in the Garhwalis during the First World War
– said from behind me: 'There goes the evil spirit that has been
responsible for your failure.'*

*My action in leaving Garhwal to the tender mercies of the
man-eater may appear heartless to you – it did so to me – and was
adversely criticised in the press – for the leopard at that time was
daily mentioned in the Indian papers. In extenuation, I would
urge that an effort entailing great strain cannot be indefinitely
sustained. Time and again, after sitting up all night, I walked
endless miles next day, visiting distant villages from which
reports had come of unsuccessful attacks by the man-eater. On
many moonlit nights, when sitting in an uncomfortable position,
physical endurance had reached its limit, and when sitting where
it would have been easy for the leopard to have got at me, I had
no longer been able to keep my eyes open.*

*I had for hours walked the roads which were alone open to
me and to the leopard, trying every trick I knew of to outwit my
adversary, and the man-eater had, with luck beyond his deserts
or with devilish cunning, avoided the bullet that a press of my
finger would have sent into him – for in retracing my steps in the
morning after these night excursions I had found from the pug-
marks on the road that I was right in assuming I had been closely
followed. To know one is being followed at night – no matter*

how bright the moon may be — by a man-eater intent on securing a victim, gives one an inferiority complex that is very unnerving, and that is not mitigated by repetition.

Tired out in mind and in body, my longer stay at Rudraprayag would not have profited the people of Garhwal, and it might have cost me my own life. Knowing that the abandonment of my self-imposed task would be severely criticised by the press, but that what I was now doing was right, I plodded on towards my distant home, having assured the people of Garhwal that I would return to help them as soon as it was possible for me to do so.

In a letter to the *Pioneer,* Ibbotson declared that 'the man-eater should be left alone from now until March. He gets very few human kills in the cold weather, and constant pursuit will only increase his already phenomenal wariness. If he is left alone for three months, Captain Corbett will come again in March, and we will both then make a protracted and determined attempt to get him.'

Jim duly resumed the attack in the spring of 1926. During his brief absence the leopard had killed ten more people — the most recent a small boy, who had died two days before they reached Rudraprayag. As he had met his end on the near side of the Alaknanda, and had furnished the leopard with two good meals, it seemed reasonable to suppose that the killer had not gone away over the river — so Jim immediately took steps to close the far end of the first suspension bridge.

His aim was to man the near tower and, if the leopard tried to cross, to drive it into a net. 'The trouble is (he told Ibbotson in a letter) I cannot swarm down the iron guys with a rifle in my hand, so the job will have to be finished in the dark with a knife.'

Already he had had another tantalisingly close encounter with their quarry. One evening, hoping to lure the leopard to a kill, he perched on a stack of hay; the killer duly arrived on the scene, but out of sight, while Jim was being drenched by a heavy rain storm.

Some hay had drifted off the stack when I was climbing up, and in this he made himself comfortable. Then for an hour or more we sat within six feet of one another, with the advantage in his favour, for while he could move about and was quite dry and warm, I had to sit tight, was wet to the skin and was freeezing in the cold wind.

In the winter Ibbotson had organised an efficient local intelligence service, offering two rupees for information about any goat that had been killed, and up to twenty for news about a human death. The result was that dozens of rumours, of sightings and alleged attacks, were reported to the *shikaris*, and this led to them walking a great many miles on false trails – but, as Jim remarked, it was only to be expected, for in an area in which an established killer is operating, 'everyone suspects their own shadows, and every sound at night is attributed to the man-eater.'

The leopard was highly active, and soon killed a dog, four goats and two cows. Jim sat up over the cows for two nights, but although the man-eater came to one of them, he could not get a shot.

Then one day at the end of March he at last got a break from his dogged pursuit. He was walking down a road alongside the Mandakini river when he saw a group of men sitting at the head of a waterfall on the far bank. Below them was a long, deep pool of crystal-clear water, flanked by vertical walls of rock. The roar of the river made conversation impossible, but he could tell that they were after the big mahseer which were jumping up the fall.

Presently two of the men lowered a triangular net on a pole and by expert manipulation caught a ten-pounder as it was falling back from the lip. Within an hour they had landed three more fine fish, and Jim – himself a keen angler – decided to come back in the morning with his fourteen-foot salmon rod.

He found the local fishermen again in action, and they watched appreciatively from the far bank as he assembled his tackle. Casting was no easy matter, for he was high above the water, but at the first attempt he hooked a hefty mahseer, which took off for a hundred yards downstream. Using various stratagems, he played the fish for half an hour, but was reluctantly deciding that he would have to cut it loose when a man appeared beside him and said, 'Wait, *Sahib*. I will fetch my brother.' Away he went, and came back with 'a long and lanky stripling' who smelled so strongly of cow manure that Jim ordered him to go and wash. They then devised a plan whereby, with Jim holding the fish steady on his tight line, the boy would climb down a crack in the rock-face to a narrow ledge a few inches above the water, while his brother, above him in the crack, held his left hand, and Jim, face-down on the rock, grasped the brother's other hand.

The snag was that I could not hold the rod and at the same time make a link in the chain. However, some risk had to be taken, so I put the rod down and held the line in my hand, and when the brothers had taken up position I sprawled on the rock, and, reaching down, got hold of the elder brother's hand. Then very gently I drew the fish towards the rock, holding the line alternately with my left hand and with my teeth. There was no question that the stripling knew how to handle a fish, for before the mahseer had touched the rock he had inserted his thumb into one side of its gills and his fingers into the other, getting a firm grip on its throat. Up to this point the fish had been quite amenable, but on having its throat seized it lashed out, and for several seconds it appeared that the three of us would go tumbling into the river.

*Both brothers were bare-footed, and when I had been relieved of the necessity of holding **the line** and was able to help with both hands, they turned, and, facing the rock, worked their way up with their toes, while I pulled lustily from the top.*

The mahseer was in grand condition, and weighed just over 30lbs. When Jim asked the boys if they ate fish, they said they certainly did – so he promised to give it to them if they helped him catch another for his own men. This he proceeded to do, with a skilful cast and less of a struggle. The elder brother then set off for home with the first mahseer slung over his shoulder on a grass cable, and the younger boy accompanied Jim back to the inspection bungalow, carrying the second fish and the rod, and hanging back a little, 'so that all the people who see me on the road and in the bazaar will think that I have caught this great fish, the like of which they have never seen.'

With Ibbotson back in harness, the pair resumed their hunt by buying a white goat, staking it out and sitting up over it with their rifles. The animal proved one of the most admirably vociferous that Jim had ever known, and called persistently as night fell, but no leopard appeared. As the goat was such a good decoy, they decided to take it with them to the village; but on the way it broke loose and disappeared, and the two men ran after it in hot pursuit.

Keeping to the track, we went to the shoulder of the hill, where a considerable extent of the hill, clothed in short grass, was visible, and as the goat was nowhere in sight, we decided it had taken a short cut back to the village, and started to retrace our steps. I was leading, and as we got half-way along the hundred yards of track, I saw something white in front of me. The light had nearly gone, and on approaching the white object I found it was the goat, in the only position in which it could have been laid to prevent it rolling down the steep hillside. Blood was oozing from its throat, and when I put my hand on it the muscles were still twitching.

It was as if the man-eater − for no other leopard would have killed the goat and left it on the track − had said: 'Here, if you want your goat so badly, take it; and as it is now dark and you have a long way to go, we will see which of you lives to reach the village.'

I do not think either of us would have reached the village alive if I had not, very fortunately, had a full box of matches with me. Striking a match, and casting an anxious look all round, and then again striking another match, we stumbled down the rough track until we got within calling distance of the village. Then, at our urgent summons, men with lanterns and pine torches came up to meet us.

We had left the goat lying where the leopard had placed it, and when I returned at daybreak next morning I found the pug-marks of the man-eater where he had followed us down to the village, and I found the goat untouched and lying just as we had left it.

That same day Jim was again called into action. After failing to bag one of the *shikaris*, the leopard had killed a man who lived in a small forest-clearing, grabbing him outside his house and dragging him off to a little hollow surrounded by dense brushwood, where it ate the throat and jaw and part of one shoulder and thigh. The riflemen lay in wait for two hours, but when evening drew on and the killer had not returned, they put three doses of poison into the body and retired to their bungalow.

Next morning they were up early, but were disappointed to find that the leopard had not touched the places at which the poison was buried; instead, it had eaten the other shoulder and leg, and carried the body away and hidden it under some bushes. That night – one of brilliant moonlight – they again sat up, Ibbotson on a *machan* and Jim fifteen feet up on top of an old rhododendron. Both were guarding paths that led to the kill, and although neither saw the leopard, separate outbreaks of barking from a *kakar* told them he had come to the kill and spent two hours there – 'sufficient time,' as Jim remarked, 'for him to have had a good meal, and for him to have poisoned himself several times over.' They also heard the leopard lapping at a spring, which further raised their hopes that the cyanide was taking effect.

Once more they were disappointed. Morning showed that the leopard had eaten meat containing three doses of poison, but although 200 men turned out to search for his body, the only traces they found were some hairs left on a rock at the entrance to a large cave. Jim quickly had the opening blocked with stones, and then reinforced the closure with wire netting and stakes. For the next ten days he visited the site morning and evening; the netting remained undisturbed – and since no news of the man-eater's activities came in during that time, he began to hope that his enemy had died in the cave. Not so: on the tenth morning news arrived that during the night a woman had been killed in a village five miles away.

Quite evidently, cyanide was not the right poison for an animal that had the reputation of thriving on, and being stimulated by, arsenic and strychnine. That the leopard had eaten the cyanide there could be no doubt whatever, nor was there any doubt that he had entered he cave, for his hairs were adhering to the rock where his back had come in contact with it.

An overdose might account for the poison not having had the desired effect, and a second opening somewhere farther up the hill might account for his escape from the cave. Even so, it was no longer any matter of surprise to me – who had only been acquainted with the leopard for a few short months – that the people of Garhwal, who had lived in close and intimate association with him for eight long years, should credit him – animal or spirit – with supernatural powers, and that they should cling to the belief that nothing but fire would rid them of this evil spirit.

Setbacks served only to increase Jim's determination. A morning stalk on foot nearly paid off, when he flushed the leopard out of a shallow depression but slipped on wet rocks before he could bring his rifle to bear. Next he constructed an elaborate trap next to the remains of the latest victim, a woman, whose naked body was lying on a long, narrow strip of flat ground, only four yards wide.

First he poisoned the kill, of which the leopard had eaten only a small amount. Then he bent over the woman in an attitude the leopard was likely to adopt when eating, while Ibbotson lashed both their rifles to saplings about fifteen yards away and sighted them on him, with a length of fishing line looped through their triggers and tied round the body. Next they buried the gin trap and covered it with green leaves and a sprinkling of earth, so that it precisely resembled its surroundings. Finally they blocked any approach from an awkward direction by making foot-deep holes with a crowbar and ramming cut thorn bushes into them.

Both *shikaris* then retired to a substantial *machan* up a mango tree, made comfortable by a covering of straw, and took turns to keep watch and doze. The light gradually faded. Night came on, and with it rain.

Then suddenly:

A succession of savage and angry roars came from the direction of the kill. The leopard – the much-famed, man-eating leopard of Rudraprayag – was at last in the gin-trap. Ibbotson took a flying leap from the machan, while I swung down from a branch. In a very short time he had the petromax lamp lit, and we set off over the rough ground as hard as we could go, circling wide to avoid the fishing lines and a possible angry leopard, and approached the kill from above.

When we got to the high bank and looked down, we saw the hole in the ground, but no gin-trap. Just as our hopes were bounding up, the brilliant light of the petromax revealed the trap, with its jaws closed and roughly ten yards down the hillside. The kill was no longer lying with its head against the bank, and a glance revealed that a considerable portion of it had been eaten.

Our thoughts were too bitter to give expression to as we went back to the mango tree and climbed into the machan. There was no longer any need for us to keep awake, so, heaping some of the straw over ourselves, for we had no bedding and the night was cold, we went to sleep.

At the first streak of dawn a fire was built and water heated, and after we had drunk several cups of tea and warmed ourselves at the fire, we set off for the kill, accompanied by the patwari and several of Ibbotson's and my men, together with a number of men from the village.

Had I been alone, I would have hesitated to relate what I am now going to tell you. Fiend or animal, had the slayer of the old woman been present and watched our overnight preparations, it would even then have been difficult to understand how it had, on a dark and rainy night, avoided capture or death in one form or another. But the rain, though light, had been enough to soften the ground, and we were able to reconstruct and follow his every movement of the previous night.

The leopard had come from the direction we expected, and on arrival at the flat strip of ground, had skirted round and below it, and had approached the kill from the side where we had firmly planted the thorn bushes. Three of these bushes he had pulled up, making a sufficiently wide gap to go through, and then, getting hold of the kill, he had drawn it a foot or so towards the rifles, thus slackening off the fishing lines. Having done this, he had started to eat, avoiding contact with the line that was tied round the woman's body.

We had not thought it necessary to poison either the head or the neck. These he had eaten first, and then – very carefully – he had eaten all that portion of the body between the many doses of poison we had inserted in different places.

After satisfying his hunger, the leopard left the kill with the intention of seeking shelter from the rain, and while he was doing so, what I feared would happen actually happened. The weight of rainwater on the very finely-set trap had depressed the plate that constituted the trigger, and released the springs just as the leopard was stepping over the trap, and the great jaws had met on either side of the stifle, or knee-joint, of his hind leg.

And here was the greatest tragedy of all, for when bringing the trap up from Rudraprayag the men carrying it had let it fall, and one of the three-inch long teeth had broken off, and the stifle of the leopard's left hind leg had been caught by the jaws exactly where the missing tooth formed a gap in the otherwise perfectly fitting set of teeth. But for this missing tooth, the leopard would have been fixed to the trap without any possibility of getting free, for the grip on his leg had been sufficiently good for him to lift the eighty-pound trap out of the hole in which we had buried it, and carry it ten yards down the hillside. And now, instead of the leopard, the jaws of the trap held only a tuft of hair and a small piece of skin.

However unbelievable the actions of the leopard may appear to have been, they were in fact just what one would have expected from an animal that had been a man-eater for eight years. Avoiding the open ground, and approaching the kill under cover; removing *the thorn obstruction we had erected across the blood trail he had left that morning, and rejecting those portions of the kill that we had poisoned – cyanide, of which he now had experience, has a very strong smell – were all quite normal and natural actions.*

I need not tell those of you who have carried a sporting rifle in any part of the world that all these many repeated failures and disappointments, so far from discouraging me, only strengthened my determination to carry on until that great day or night came when, having discarded poison and traps, I would get an opportunity of using my rifle as rifles should be used, to put a bullet truly and accurately into the man-eater's body.

The leopard continued its depredations, killing the prize goat of an old packman who was taking salt and gur from the bazaar at Hardwar to distant villages. One afternoon, in the hope of catching it napping, Jim lay on a projecting rock, high above the valley of the Alaknanda, with the 'river showing as a gleaming silver ribbon winding in and out,' and in the distance the eternal snows, standing out 'against the intense blue sky as clear as if cut out of white cardboard.' The view was magical; and yet, he knew, when the sun set, terror would grip the rows of slate-roofed houses on the opposite hill, 'as it had done for eight long years.'

He spent that night at the top of a single pine tree, with a goat at its foot as bait, and called up a leopard to within sixty yards, only for it to be lured away by the siren summons of a female from further off.

For the next few days he lost touch with the man-eater, but he kept hearing of instances in which the animal had broken down the door of a house or dug through the mud wall, in attempts to secure a victim. Its next kill, however, was a cow, which one of the villagers found dead in a deep ravine. As there was no tree nearby, Jim decided to sit the night out in a little rock hollow, only thirty yards from the body. He hoped the leopard would return to the kill while there was still some light, but it did not appear. When a bank of cloud came over, intensifying the darkness, heavy drops of rain began to fall, and he was afraid that the leopard might suddenly land on him before he could bring his rifle to bear.

Where there had been absolute and complete silence, there was now sound and movement all round – the opportunity the leopard had been waiting for had come. Hastily taking off my coat, I wound it round my neck, fastening it securely in place with the sleeves, I unsheathed my Afridi stabbing knife, which I knew had figured in three murders, and clutched it tight while the rain lashed down.

Should I go or should I remain? If the leopard up to then had not seen me, it would be foolish to give my position away and possibly fall across him on the difficult ground I should have to negotiate on my way up to the pilgrim road. On the other hand, to remain where I was for another six hours – momentarily expecting to have to fight for my life with an unfamiliar weapon – would put a strain on my nerves which they were not capable of standing. So, getting to my feet and shouldering the rifle, I set off.

I had not far to go, only about five hundred yards, half of which was over wet clay and the other half over rocks worn smooth by bare feet and the hooves of cattle. Afraid to use the torch for fear of attracting the man-eater, and with one hand occupied with the rifle and the other with the knife, my body made as many contacts with the ground as my rubber-shod feet. When I eventually reached the road, I sent a full-throated cooee into the night, and a moment later I saw a door in the village far up the hillside open, and Madho Singh and his companion emerge, carrying a lantern.

Both men were willing to accompany me back to Rudraprayag, so we set out on our seven-mile walk, Bachi Singh leading, Madho Singh carrying the lantern, and I bringing up the rear. When I returned next day, I found the kill had not been touched, and on the road I found the tracks of the man-eater.

When I look back on that night, I look back on it as my night of terror. I have been frightened times without number, but never have I been as frightened as I was that night when the unexpected rain came down and robbed me of all my defences, and left me for protection a murderer's knife.

By then the annual pilgrim season had begun, and because in previous years the leopard had killed one or two travellers on the road, Jim spent two comfortable but fruitless nights on a hay-rick overlooking the track. On the third morning he walked six miles down the road and six back, checking other villages, and he was having a late breakfast at midday when two men arrived with the news that a boy had been killed at Bhainswara, a hamlet eighteen miles to the south-east. When he handed each of the men a ten-rupee note, one of them volunteered to act as guide, and they set off together. In the first three miles they climbed 4,000 feet, and Jim had difficulty keeping up; thereafter he led the way, and in every village he found the population waiting for him, some to give him their blessings, others to beg him not to leave the district until he had killed their enemy. Those eighteen miles, he remembered, were the longest and hardest miles he had ever walked.

At Bhainswara, immediately surrounded by a crowd a hundred strong, he learnt that a leopard had snatched a twelve-year-old boy from the centre of the village and carried him off downhill, dropping him on a cattle track. When the raid was discovered, men ran to their houses for drums or guns, which they played or fired all night. In the morning searchers following the blood trail found the body and brought it home.

Refreshed by a dish of tea, Jim also followed the trail, down over three high walls to the place where the leopard had earlier abandoned his kill. But because there was no tree in which he could sit, he decided to return to the village and try to lure the killer there. He therefore sunk a stout wooden peg into the floor of the courtyard, chained the boy's body to it and took up station on the verandah of the nearest house, lying on his side in some straw.

Straining into the black darkness, I first heard the sound when it was level with my feet. Something was creeping, very stealthily creeping, over the straw. I was wearing the article of clothing called shorts, which left my legs bare in the region of my knees. Presently against this bare skin I felt the hairy coat of an animal brushing. It could only be the man-eater, creeping up until he could lean over and get a grip of my throat. A little pressure now on my left shoulder – to get a foothold – and then, just as I was about to press the trigger of the rifle to cause a diversion, a small animal jumped down between my arms and my chest. It was a little kitten, soaking wet, that had been caught out in the storm and, finding every door shut, had come to me for warmth and protection.

The kitten had hardly made itself comfortable inside my coat, and I was just beginning to recover from the fright it had given me, when, from beyond the terraced fields, there came some low growling, which gradually grew louder, and then merged into the most savage fight I have ever heard. Quite evidently, the man-eater had returned to the spot where the previous night he had left his kill, and while he was searching for it, in none too good a temper, another male leopard who looked upon this particular area as his hunting ground, had accidentally come across him and set on him.

The man-eater, though old, was a big and very powerful male, and in the 500 square miles he ranged over there was possibly no other male capable of disputing his rule; but here at Bhainswara he was a stranger and a trespasser, and to get out of the trouble he had brought on himself he would have to fight for his life. And this he was undoubtedly doing.

My chance of getting a shot had now gone. The first round, lasting about five minutes, was fought with unabating savagery, and was inconclusive, for at the end of it I could still hear both animals. After an interval of ten or fifteen minutes the fight was resumed, but at a distance of two to three hundred yards from where it had started. Quite evidently, the local champion was getting the better of the fight and was gradually driving the intruder out of the ring. The third round was shorter than the two that had preceded it, but was no less savage; the scene had receded to the shoulder of the hill, where after a few minutes it died of hearing.

Jim's experience told him that, after such a battle, the man-eater would never return to the village; so at first light he carried the dead boy into a shed and covered him with a blanket. Then he knocked up the headman, and got him to promise that he would immediately arrange for the body to be taken to the burning-*ghat*. With that, he set off on the long walk back to Rudraprayag, deeply depressed by his succession of failures, and by the fact that he had let down so many village folk.

Only after he had stopped and drunk a cup of tea in the last village before his destination did his spirits lift. Suddenly he noticed, in the rain-softened red clay of the path, the fresh pug-marks of the man-eater. He could tell that for a while the leopard had been moving at a steady pace; then he had begun placing his hind feet in front of his fore feet, which showed that he had accelerated as he neared home territory.

Here he had a better reason [than hunting] for the long walk he had undertaken, for he was anxious to put as great a distance as possible between himself and the leopard who had given him a lesson in the law of trespass.

By then the annual pilgrim season was under way, and in the village of Golabrai Jim warned the pundit to take extra precautions, both for his own safety, and for that of any strangers who might be staying in his shelter. Years earlier, the pundit himself had had a miraculous escape when the leopard seized him and tried to drag him off his own verandah; though severely wounded, the priest had recovered, and now regarded the man-eater as 'the evil spirit',

Together with Ibbotson, who had returned to the fray, Jim built a *machan* in a mango tree that overlooked the pilgrim road, and tethered a goat in the middle of the track. That night, and for the nine nights that followed, he sat up on the platform wrapped in a rug, but saw nothing; yet he knew that the man-eater was still in the neighbourhood, for during that time it broke into two houses and carried off a goat and a sheep.

For both *shikaris*, time was running out. Ibbotson had urgent work awaiting him in his office in Pauri, and Jim had booked a passage to Africa. Should they both cancel their arrangements? They decided to postpone a decision until next day, and in the evening, while Ibbotson retired to the Inspection Bungalow, Jim went up his mango tree for his eleventh consecutive night aloft. The moon was a few days past the full, and the valley was in darkness when, just after nine, some dogs guarding sheep and goats in an enclosure in the valley began barking furiously.

The dogs were unmistakably barking at a leopard, which was now coming down the road on its way to the pilgrim shelter. At

first they barked in the direction of the road, but after a while they turned and barked in my direction. The leopard had now quite evidently caught sight of my sleeping goat and lain down out of sight of the dogs – which had stopped barking – to consider his next move.

I knew that the leopard had arrived, and I also knew that he was using my tree to stalk the goat – and the question that was tormenting me as the long minutes dragged by was whether he would skirt round the goat and kill one of the pilgrims, or whether he would kill the goat and give me a shot.

The distance between the goat and my machan was about twenty feet, but the night was so dark under the dense foliage of the tree that my straining eyes could not penetrate even this short distance, so I closed them and concentrated on my hearing.

My rifle, to which I had a small electric torch attached, was pointing in the direction of the goat, and I was just beginning to think that the leopard – assuming it was the man-eater – had reached the shelter and was selecting a human victim, when there was a rush from the foot of the tree, and the goat's bell tinkled sharply. Pressing the button of the torch, I saw that the sights of the rifle were aligned on the shoulder of the leopard, and without having to move the rifle an inch I pressed the trigger, and as I did so the torch went out.

The echo of my shot was dying away in the valley when the pundit opened his door and called out to ask if I needed any help. I was at the time listening with all my ears for any sounds that might come from the leopard, so I did not answer him, and he hurriedly shut his door.

The leopard had been lying across the road with his head away from me when I fired, and I was vaguely aware of his having sprung over the goat and gone down the hillside, and just before the pundit had called I thought I heard what may have been a gurgling sound, but of this I could not be sure. The pilgrims had been aroused by my shot, but after murmuring for a few minutes, they resumed their sleep. The goat appeared to be unhurt, for from the sound of his bell I could tell that he was moving about and apparently eating the grass, of which he was given a liberal supply each night.

I had fired my shot at 10pm. As the moon was not due to rise for several hours, and as there was nothing I could do in the meantime, I made myself comfortable, and listened and smoked. Hours later the moon lit up the crest of the hills on the far side of the Ganges and slowly crept down into the valley, and a little later I saw it rise over the top of the hill behind me. As soon as it was overhead, I climbed to the top of the tree, but found that the spreading branches impeded my view. Descending again to the machan, I climbed out on the branches spreading over the road, but from here also I found it was not possible to see down the hillside in the direction in which I thought the leopard had gone.

It was then 3am, and two hours later the moon began to pale. When nearby objects became visible in the light of the day that was being born in the east, I descended from the tree, and was greeted by a friendly bleat from the goat. Beyond the goat, and at the very edge of the road, there was a long, low rock, and on this rock there was an inch-wide streak of blood. The leopard from which that blood had come could only have lived a minute or two; so, dispensing with the precautions usually taken when following up the blood trail of carnivores, I scrambled down off the road and, taking up the trail on the far side of the rock, followed it for fifty yards to where the leopard was lying dead.

He had slid backwards into a hole in the ground, in which he was now lying crouched up, with his chin resting on the edge of the hole. No marks by which I could identify the dead animal were visible; even so, I never for one moment doubted that the leopard in the hole was the man-eater. But here was no fiend, who, while watching me through the long night hours, had rocked and rolled with silent fiendish laughter at my vain attempts to *outwit him, and licked his lips in anticipation of the time when, finding me off my guard for one brief moment, he would get the opportunity he was waiting for of burying his teeth in my throat.*

Here was only an old leopard, who differed from others of his kind in that his muzzle was grey and his lips lacked whiskers – the best-hated and the most-feared animal in all India, whose only crime – not against the laws of nature but against the laws of man – was that he had shed human blood, with no object of terrorising man, but only in order that he might live, and who now, with his chin resting on the rim of the hole and his eyes half-closed, was sleeping peacefully his long last sleep.

While I stood unloading my rifle, I heard a cough, and on looking up saw the pundit peering down at me from the edge of the road. I beckoned to him, and he came gingerly down the hill. On catching sight of the leopard's head he stopped, and asked in a whisper whether it was dead, and what it was. When I told him it was dead, and that it was the evil spirit that had torn open his throat five years ago, he put his hands together and attempted to put his head on my feet.

Next minute there was a call from the road above of 'Sahib, where are you?' It was one of my men calling in great agitation, and when I sent an answering call echoing over the Ganges, four heads appeared, and, snatching sight of us, four men came helter-skelter down the hill, one of them swinging a lighted lantern which he had forgotten to extinguish.

The leopard had got stiff in the hole, and was extracted with some little difficulty. While it was being tied to the stout bamboo pole the men had brought with them, they told me they had been unable to sleep that night, and as soon as Ibbotson's jemadar's watch showed them it was 4.30am, they lit the lantern, and, arming themselves with a pole and a length of rope, had come to look for me, for they felt that I was in urgent need of them. Not finding me in the machan, and seeing the goat unhurt, and the streak of blood on the rock, they concluded the man-eater had killed me, and not knowing what to do they had in desperation called to me.

The four men and I, with the goat trotting alongside, set off for the Inspection Bungalow. The goat, who had escaped with very little injury owing to my having fired the moment the leopard caught him, little knew that his night's adventure was to make him a hero for the rest of his life, and that he was to wear a brass collar and be a source of income to the man from whom I had purchased him, and to whom I gave him back.

Ibbotson was still asleep when I knocked on the glazed door, and the moment he caught sight of me he jumped out of bed, and dashing to the door flung it open, embraced me and next minute was dancing round the leopard, which the men had deposited on the veranda. Shouting for tea, and a hot bath for me, he called for his stenographer and dictated telegrams to the government, the Press and my sister, and a cable to Jean.

Ibbotson had carried a heavy responsibility, for his position had for a long time been like that of the head of a police force who, knowing the identity of a noted criminal, was unable to prevent his committing further crimes, and for this was being badgered on all sides. Little wonder that on the 2nd of May 1926 he was the happiest man I had ever seen, for not only was he now able to inform all concerned that the criminal had been executed, but he was also able to tell the people from the bazaars, and from the surrounding villages, and the pilgrims, all of whom were swarming into the compound of the Inspection Bungalow, that the evil spirit that had tormented them for eight long years was now dead.

The two *shikaris* measured the old warrior, and found him to be 7' 6" between pegs, 7' 10" over curves. They recorded his coat as 'Light Straw', and found that his teeth were worn and discoloured, with one canine broken. Jim was puzzled by the fact that his tongue and mouth were black, but thought this might have been from contact with cyanide. The leopard's body bore evidence of several partially-healed wounds, but the one which clinched his identity was on the stifle of his left hind leg, which perfectly fitted the piece of skin which he had left in the gin trap weeks before.

Jim was much moved by the scenes that followed, and wrote:

When the people of our hills visit an individual to show their gratitude or to express their thanks, it is customary for them not to go on their mission empty-handed. A rose, a marigold or a few petals of either flower suffice, and the gift is proffered in hands cupped together. When the recipient has touched the gift with the tips of the fingers of his right hand, the person proffering the gift goes through the motion of pouring it onto the recipient's feet, as if his cupped hands contained water.

I have on other occasions witnessed gratitude, but never as I witnessed it that day at Rudraprayag, first at the Inspection Bungalow, and later at a reception in the bazaar.

'He killed our only son, Sahib, and we being old, our house is now desolate.'

'He ate the mother of my five children, and the youngest is but a few months old, and there is no one in the home now to care for the children, or to cook the food.'

'My son was taken ill at night, and no one dared to go to the hospital for medicine, and so he died.'

Tragedy upon pitiful tragedy... and while I listened, the ground around my feet was strewn with flowers.

Effusive thanks came from the Maharajah of Dhar, whose private secretary wrote on 19 May:

'I have been directed by Colonel His Highness the Maharajah Sahib Bahadur to convey to you His Highness's very best congratulations on your keen sportsmanship in putting an end to

the Notorious Man-Eating Leopard. His Highness also wishes me to express his great delight at your being able to get rid of that terrible enemy and pest of the public of Garhwal.

CHAPTER TEN

The Talla Des Man-eater
April 1929

When Jim set out to hunt the Talla Des tiger in the spring of 1929, he was by no means in the best of health. A few weeks earlier, as he conducted a bird-shoot from elephant-back, another man, sitting behind him on the *howdah*, had inadvertently let off a high-velocity rifle so close to his head that the blast scorched the inner lining of his left ear and burst the ear-drum. 'For me,' he recorded, 'the rest of that February day was torture. After a sleepless night I excused myself on the plea that I had urgent work to attend to, and at dawn, while the camp was asleep, I set out on a twenty-five mile walk to my home at Kaladhungi.'

The young doctor there confirmed that the eardrum had been destroyed. A month later, in the hospital at Nainital, Colonel Barber, the Civil Surgeon, agreed with the diagnosis, and found that abscesses were forming inside the patient's head. 'My condition was distressing my two sisters as much as it was distressing me,' Jim wrote, 'and as the hospital was unable to do anything to relieve me, I decided – much against the wishes of my sisters and the advice of Colonel Barber, to go away.'

Two Deputy Commissioners – Bill Baynes of Almora and Ham Vivian of Nainital – had been imploring him to

125

deal with man-eaters in their areas, and he decided to try to help Baynes first by going after the Talla Des killer. 'The pursuit of this tiger would, I hoped, tide me over my bad time and enable me to adjust to my new condition.'

He left Nainital on 4 April, accompanied by six Garhwalis, a cook named Elahai and a Brahmin, Ganga Ram, Having walked the fourteen miles down to Kathgodam, they caught the evening train and, travelling through Bareilley and Pilibhit, reached Tanakpur at noon next day. There they learned that a boy had been killed at Kaladhunga (not to be confused with Jim's home village Kaladhungi), some twenty-four miles further on, and they set out to walk to their destination that day. After only sixteen miles, however, darkness caught them in the Sarda river gorge, where they camped on a narrow rock shelf for the night.

As Jim rested on his bed after supper, he was startled to see lights appear in the vertical cliff face across the river. At first there were three, each about two feet in diameter. Then two more shone out, and the left-hand one moved slowly down the hill until it merged into the centre of the first trio. Presently more appeared, until all faded away. The night was very quiet; the Sarda flowed silently past below them, and no alien sound reached the travellers. Jim was fascinated. In the morning he scanned every foot of the opposite rock face through binoculars for a clue as to the lights' origin – and only later did he learn that at Purnagiri, high on the mountain, there were two shrines dedicated to the goddess Bhagbatti.

The more sacred shrine could be reached only by going along a narrow crack, or fault, running across the face of a more or less perpendicular rock cliff. Nervous people, children and the aged are carried across the cliff in a basket slung on the back of a hillman. Only those whom the goddess favours are able to reach

*the upper shrine; the others are struck blind, and have to make
their offerings at the lower shrine.*

*Puja (prayer) at the upper shrine starts at sunrise and ends
at midday. After this hour, no one is permitted to pass the lower
shrine. Near the upper and more sacred shrine is a pinnacle of
rock a hundred feet high, the climbing if which is forbidden by the
Goddess. In the days of long ago a sadhu, more ambitious than
his fellows, climbed the pinnacle with the object of putting himself
on an equality with the Goddess. Incensed at his disregard of
her orders, the Goddess hurled the sadhu from the pinnacle to
the hill on the far-side of the snow-fed river. It is this sadhu
who, banished for ever from Purnagiri, worships the Goddess
2,000 feet above him by lighting lamps to her. These votive
lights appear only at certain times (we saw them on 5 April) and
are only visible to favoured people. The favour was accorded to
me and to the men with me because I was on a mission to the
hillfolk over whom the Goddess watches.*

By morning Jim and his party were advancing through
man-eater territory, evident from the many scratch-marks
along the track. In spite of the danger, he rejoiced in the
beauty of the forest, whose white butterfly orchids hung down
in showers, veiling the trees in which they were rooted. When
he came out on a grassy ledge overlooking a village, the whole
population turned out to greet him. 'I was possibly the first
white man who had ever approached that village alone and on
foot,' he wrote, 'and yet, by the time I reached the assembled
people, a square of carpet had been produced, a *mohra* (rush
seat) placed on it, and I had hardly sat down before a brass
vessel containing milk was placed in my hands.'

The village had been terrorised by the man-eater for
nearly ten years. Outlying fields were no longer cultivated,
and no one was prepared to walk to Tanakpur to get
much-needed food. The people begged Jim to stay and release

them from fear; but he insisted on pressing on to the place where the most recent kill had been reported, and promised to return as soon as possible.

In the next village he fell in with Dungar Singh, a fearless young man whose mother had just become the man-eater's latest victim. Together they walked down through dense scrub until they came out in a clearing, and on the way Jim warned his companion that he was deaf in his left ear: if Dungar Singh wanted to communicate anything, he was to point or whisper in Jim's right ear.

By then a posse of men had appeared higher up the hill, and by listening intently with a hand cupped to his ear, Dungar Singh picked up a message from one of the group: 'My brother says to tell you that in the *wyran* field below you there is something red lying in the sun.' A *wyran* field was one that had gone out of cultivation. The red object could have been some dry bracken, but to Jim it seemed a heaven-sent chance, and, taking Dungar Singh with him, he immediately began a stalk along narrow terraces.

Bending down and keeping to the inner edge of the field, we crept along until we came to the far end. Here we lay down, and, crawling on hands and knees to the edge of the field, parted the grass and looked down. Below us was a small valley with, on the far side, a steep, grassy slope fringed on the far side by a dense growth of oak saplings. Beyond the saplings was the deep ravine in which the man-eater had eaten Dungar Singh's mother. The grassy slope was about thirty yards wide, and on its near side was a terraced field, a hundred yards long and some ten yards wide. At our end the field had a small patch of short, emerald green grass. Lying on it, in brilliant sunlight, about ten feet apart, were two tigers.

The nearer tiger had its back to us, with its head towards the hill, and the farther one had its stomach to us, with its tail towards the hill. Both were fast asleep. The nearer offered the better shot, but I was afraid that on hearing the smack of the bullet the farther one would go straight down the hill into dense cover, in the direction in which its head was pointing. Whereas if I fired at the farther one first, the smack of the bullet — not to be confused with the crack of the rifle — would either drive the nearer one up the hill where there was less cover, or else drive it towards me. So I decided to take the farther one first.

The distance was approximately 120 yards, and the angle of fire was not so steep that any allowance had to be made for the lift of the bullet — a point which has to be kept in mind when shooting downhill in the Himalayas. Resting the back of my hand on the edge of the field to form a cushion, and holding the rifle steady, I took careful aim at where I thought the animal's heart would be, and gently pressed the trigger.

The tiger never moved a muscle, but the other one was up like a flash and in one bound landed on a five-foot-high bank of earth that divided the field from a rainwater channel. Here it stood, broadside on to me, looking back over its right shoulder at its companion. At my shot it reared up and fell over backwards into the rainwater channel, and out of sight.

After my second shot I saw a movement in the aromatic weeds, which started close to where the tigers had been lying. A big animal was going at full gallop straight along the field. Having started from so close, this third animal could only be another tiger. I could not see the animal, but I could follow its movements by the parting of the weeds which were white on the underside. Flicking up the 200-yard sight, I waited for the animal to break cover.

Presently out onto the grassy slope dashed a tiger. I have seen animals fall over at a shot, and I have seen them crumple up, but I have never seen an animal fall as convincingly dead as that tiger fell at my shot. For a few moments it lay motionless, then it started to slide down, feet foremost, gaining momentum as it went. *Directly below it, and within a few feet of the brink of the rock cliff, was an oak sapling eight to ten inches thick. The tiger struck this sapling with its stomach and came to rest with its head and forelegs hanging down on one side, and its tail and hindlegs hanging down on the other.*

With rifle to shoulder and finger on trigger, I waited, but there was not so much as a quiver in the tiger. When I saw the two lying asleep I concluded that the man-eater had found a mate, but later, when my third shot flushed a third tiger, I knew I was dealing with a tigress and her two cubs. Which of the three was the mother and which the cubs it was not possible to say, for all three looked about the same size when I had viewed them over the sights of my rifle. That one was the man-eater of Talla Des there could be no question, for tigers are scarce in those hills, and the three had been shot close to where a human being had recently been killed and eaten. The cubs had died for the sins of their mother. They had undoubtedly eaten the human flesh their mother had provided for them from the time they were weaned; this, however, did not mean that when they left the protection of their mother they would have become man-eaters themselves.

Sitting on the edge of the field with my legs dangling down and the rifle resting on my knees, I handed cigarettes to my companions and told them I would go and have a look at the tiger that had fallen into the rainwater channel, after we had finished our smoke. That I would find the tiger dead I had no doubt whatsoever; even so, nothing would be lost by waiting a few minutes, if for no other reason than to give myself a little time to rejoice over the marvellous luck I had met with.

Within an hour of my arrival at Talla Des I had, quite by accident, got in touch with a man-eater that had terrorised an area of many hundreds of square miles for eight years, and in a matter of a few seconds had shot dead the man-eater and her two cubs. To the intense pleasure that all sportsmen feel at having held a rifle steady when every drop of blood in one's body is pounding with excitement, was added the pleasure and relief of knowing that there would be no necessity to follow up a wounded animal – a contingency that has to be faced when hunting tigers on foot.

The four of us sitting on the edge of the field had nearly finished our cigarettes when I noticed that the tiger resting against the oak sapling was beginning to move. The blood from the body had evidently drained into the forward end of the animal, making that end heavier than the tail end, and it was now gently slipping down head-foremost. Once it was clear of the sapling the tiger glissaded down the grassy slope and over the brink of the rock cliff. As it fell through space I threw up the rifle and fired. I fired that shot on the spur of the moment to give expression to my joy at the success of my mission to Talla Des, and also, I am ashamed to admit, to demonstrate that there was nothing – not even a tiger falling through space – that I could not hit on a day like this.

The exuberant discharge of that last bullet proved a dangerous mistake, for it left Jim with only one live round, and after he had missed the wounded animal with a further shot as she painfully climbed the hill, he had no ammunition left. One of his men, Madho Singh, soon came running with a fresh supply, but by then the light was failing, and he decided to postpone a follow-up until the next day.

The two tigers he had killed turned out to be nearly full-grown cubs – and this convinced him not only that the third animal was their mother, but that she was the man-eater. He followed her trail for the whole of the next day – no easy task, as her wound had stopped bleeding, and he had to rely on finding tracks and bits of crushed vegetation. His men came along behind him at a distance, but in the evening a heavy rain-storm blotted out all traces, and he abandoned the pursuit for the day.

131

Next morning he treated the cubs' skins, rubbing wood ashes and powdered alum on the damp parts. Then in the afternoon he again took up the pursuit of the tigress, with four of his men acting as scouts. He was in constant danger, as he himself emphasised.

Under normal conditions man-eating tigers limit the range of their attack to the distance they can spring, and for this reason they are more difficult to cope with than wounded tigers, who invariably launch an attack from a little distance, maybe only ten or twenty yards, but possibly as much as a hundred yards. This means that whereas the former have to be dealt with in a matter of split seconds, the latter give one time to raise a rifle and align the sights. In either case it means rapid shooting and a fervent prayer that an ounce or two of lead will stop a few hundred pounds of muscle.

Four days had passed since he had wounded the tigress: he knew that by now she must be hungry, and in spite of her wound liable to attack any human she came near. For him, the danger was increased by the fact that he had become extremely ill. His head, face and neck had swollen to such a degree that he could no long move his head up and down or from side to side. Although he could still see out of his right eye, his left eye was closed, and he could still hear a little.

In this diminished and dangerous state he followed the tigress all day along water channels, game tracks and cattle paths, avoiding thick cover wherever possible. His difficulties were exacerbated by the fact that he did not know the ground, and so could not ambush the tigress by anticipating her movements. Back in camp, he was forced to admit that a crisis had come.

I realised that the 'bad time' I had foreseen and dreaded was approaching. Electric shocks were stabbing through the enormous abscess, and the hammer blows were increasing in intensity. Sleepless nights and a diet of tea had made a coward of me, and I could not face the prospect of sitting on my bed through another long night, racked with pain and waiting for something, I knew not what, to happen.

I had come to Talla Des to try and rid the hill people of the terror that menaced them, and to tide over my bad time – and all that I had accomplished so far was to make their condition worse. Deprived of the ability to secure her natural prey, the tigress, who in eight years had only killed 150 people, would now, unless she recovered from her wound, look to her easiest prey – human beings – to provide her with most of the food she needed. There was therefore an account to be settled between the tigress and myself – and that night was as suitable a time as any to settle it.

Calling for a cup of tea – made hill-fashion with milk – which served me as dinner, I drank it while standing in the moonlight. Then, calling my eight men together, I instructed them to wait for me in the village until the following evening, and if I did not return by then, to pack up my things and start early the next morning for Nainital. Having done this, I picked up my rifle and headed down the valley. My men, all of whom had been with me for years, said not a word, either to ask where I was going or to try to dissuade me from going. They just stood silent in a group and watched me walk away. Maybe the glint I saw on their cheeks was only imagination, or maybe it was only the reflection of the moon. Anyway, when I looked back not a man had moved. They were just standing in a group as I had left them.

Driven by pain and guilt, he picked up the trail where he had left it earlier, and walked through the moonlit night until he came to a large oak in which a troop of langurs were sleeping. Knowing that the monkeys would give warning of danger, he sat down and rested with his back against the trunk. For half an hour all was quiet. Then an old langur gave an alarm call, and presently Jim saw the tigress walk out into the open. Had he been fully fit, he could have shot her where she lay down, a hundred yards away, but with his left eye closed by the swelling he could not take a risk at that range, and he waited until she got up and started to walk slowly away. For half an hour he crept after her, gradually closing the distance between them until she disappeared over the edge of a ravine.

I bent down and ran forward on silent feet. Bending down and running was a very stupid mistake for me to have made, and I had only run a few yards when I was overcome by vertigo. Near me were two oak saplings, a few feet apart and with interlaced branches. Laying down my rifle, I climbed up the saplings to a height of ten or twelve feet. Here I found a branch to sit on, another for my feet, and yet other small branches for me to rest against. Crossing my arms on the branches in front of me, I laid my head on them, and at that moment the abscess burst, not into my brain, as I feared it would, but out through my nose and left ear.

'No greater happiness can man know, than the sudden cessation of pain,' was said by someone who had suffered and suffered greatly, and who knew the happiness of sudden relief. It was round about midnight when relief came to me, and the grey light was just beginning to show in the east when I raised my head from my crossed arms. Cramp in my legs, resulting from my having sat on a thin branch for four hours, had roused me, and for a little while I did not know where I was or what had happened to me. Realisation was not long in coming. The great swelling on my head, face and neck had gone, and with it had gone the pain. I could now move my head as I liked, my left eye was open and I could swallow without discomfort. I had lost an opportunity of shooting the tigress, but what did that matter now, for I was over my bad time, and no matter how far she went, I would follow her, and sooner or later I would surely get another chance.

Having washed in a stream, he found his way back to his camp in the village of Talla Kote. His men, ignoring his instructions to sleep in the safety of a hut, had sat round a fire all night, nursing a kettle of water kept hot in case he should want tea. When they saw him, they sprang up with cries of *'Sahib! Sahib!* You have come back, and you are well!' 'Yes,' he answered. 'I have come back, and I am now well.' Afterwards, all he remembered was someone easing off his shoes as he drifted into a peaceful sleep.

His respite did not last long. In the morning he was woken by an excited throng of young men and boys, all telling him that the man-eater had just killed six goats on the far side of the village. Grabbing his .275, he set off with Dungar Singh along a track into the valley to the place where the tiger had suddenly appeared and struck down six of a large flock. Three of the dead animals had already been taken back to the village, but three, with broken backs, lay dying in a hollow.

The only trees round the site were enormous pines, which had no branches for the first thirty or forty feet and were therefore unclimbable. Jim had no choice of an ambush-point but a small rock, on which he could shelter behind a bigger one, with only his head protruding on the side from which he expected the tigress to come. When a kalege pheasant began giving its chattering alarm call from round a corner of the hill, he told Dungar Singh to run back to the village as fast and he could, and covered him with his rifle for as long as he was in sight.

Half an hour later a pair of blue Himalayan magpies came up the valley, and after several false alarms they landed on the goat with a ripped back and began to feed. Next on the scene was a king vulture, with white shirt-front, black coat and red head and legs, which quartered the sky for a while, then came sailing down and landed light as a feather

135

on a dead pine branch. Jim welcomed the bird's presence, for as long as it remained aloft, it had a wide view of its surroundings, and if it stayed there, it would mean that the tigress was lying up somewhere close by. If it came down to feed, it would mean that the tigress had gone.

For the next half hour the scene remained unchanged – the magpies continued to feed, and the vulture sat on the dead branch. Then the *kalege* pheasant started chattering again, and the magpies flew screaming down the valley.

The tigress was coming, and sooner than I expected. A few light bushes obstructed my view in the direction of the ravine, and presently through these bushes I saw her. She was coming, very slowly, along a flat bit of ground above a twenty-foot-high bank, and was looking straight towards me. With only head exposed and my soft hat pulled down to my eyes, I knew she would not notice me if I made no movement. So, with the rifle resting on the flat rock, I sat perfectly still. When she had come opposite to me, she sat down, with the bole of a big pine tree directly between us. I could see her head on one side of the tree and her tail and part of her hindquarters on the other. Here she sat for minutes, snapping at the flies that, attracted by her wound, were tormenting her.

To put her out of her misery I several times aligned the sights of my rifle on her head, but the light, owing to the heavy clouds, was not good enough for me to make sure of hitting a fairly small object at sixty yards. Eventually she stood up and then stood broadside-on to me, looking down at the goats. With my elbows resting on the flat rock I took careful aim at the spot where I thought her heart would be, pressed the trigger and saw a spurt of dust go up on the hill on the far side of her. The thought flashed through my mind that not only had I missed the tigress's heart, but that I had missed the whole animal. And yet, after my careful aim, that could not be. What undoubtedly had happened was that my bullet had gone clean through her without meeting any resistance.

Blood splashes along a path made the trail easy to follow; but on a spur of the hill the track bent back at an acute angle, and Jim, moving fast, over-ran the corner and dropped, feet first, down a sheer face, with his heels cutting furrows in the soft earth. Had he not managed to grab hold of a rhododendron sapling which arrested his fall, he would have plunged into 'a dark and evil-looking ravine.'

A tiger that has made up its mind to avenge an injury is the most terrifying animal to be met with in an Indian jungle. The tigress had a very recent injury to avenge, and she had demonstrated – by striking down six goats and by springing and dashing away when I fired at her – that the leg wound she had received five days before was no handicap to rapid movement. I felt sure, therefore, that as soon as she became aware I was following her and she considered that I was within her reach, she would launch an all-out attack on me, which I would possibly have to meet with a single bullet. Drawing back the bolt of the rifle, I examined the cartridge very carefully, and, satisfied that it was one of a fresh lot I had recently got from Manton in Calcutta, I replaced it in the chamber, put back the bolt and threw off the safety-catch.

The path ran through bracken, which was waist-high, and which met over it. The blood trail lay along the path into the bracken, and the tigress might be lying on the path or on the right- or left-hand side of it. So I approached the bracken foot by foot and looking straight ahead – for, on these occasions it is unwise to keep turning the head. When I was within three yards of the bracken I saw a movement a yard from the path on the right. It was the tigress, gathering herself together for a spring. Wounded and starving though she was, she was game to fight it out. Her spring, however, was never launched, for, as she rose, my first bullet raked her from end to end, and the second bullet broke her neck.

Days of pain and strain on an empty stomach left me now trembling in every limb, and I had great difficulty in reaching the spot where the path bent back at an acute angle and where, but for the chance dropping of a rhododendron seed, I would have ended my life on the rocks below.

The entire population of the village, plus my own men, were gathered on the saddle of the hill and on either side of it, and I had hardly raised my hat to wave when, shouting at the top of their voices, the men and boys came swarming down. My six Garhwalis were the first to arrive. Congratulations over, the tigress was lashed to a pole, and six of the proudest Garhwalis in Kumaon carried the Talla Des man-eater in triumph to Talla Kote village. Here the tigress was laid down on a bed of straw for the women and children to see, while I went back to my tent for my first solid meal in many weeks.

An hour later, with a crowd of people around me, I skinned the tigress. The cause of her man-eating was quickly revealed. In the muscle of her right foreleg and shoulder were embedded twenty porcupine quills from two to six inches long. This injury, acquired some eight years earlier, had reduced her ability to secure normal prey and made her rely on humans, of whom she had killed about 150, inflicting widespread terror on the people of Talla Des.

Jim's first bullet, fired on 7 April, had bushed (flattened) and lodged in the ball-and-socket joint of her right shoulder. The second and third bullets, fired as she was falling through the air and climbing the hill, had missed. The fourth, fired on April 12, had gone through her without striking any bones, and the fifth and sixth had killed her.

He recorded:

I spent the following day in partly drying the skin, and three days later I was back in my home with my bad time behind me. Baynes very kindly sent for Dungar Singh and his brother, and at a public function in Almora thanked them for the help they had given me, and presented them with a token of my gratitude. A week after my return to Nainital Sir Malcom Hailey gave me an introduction to Colonel Dick, an ear specialist, who treated me for three months in his hospital in Lahore and restored my hearing sufficiently for me to associate with my fellow men without embarrassment, and gave me back the joy of hearing music and the song of birds.

CHAPTER ELEVEN

The Chowgarh Tigers
1930

Between 15 December 1925 and 21 March 1930 a tiger killed at least sixty-four people in the Chowgarh district, to the south-east of Nainital. Having committed himself at a District Conference to have a try for it, Jim set off on foot one morning in April 1929, with his usual retinue augmented by four young buffaloes which he planned to use as bait. After a four-day march, culminating in a stiff climb of 4,000 feet, he arrived at the Kala Agar forest bungalow; but after a night there, and a discussion with the headmen, he decided to press on to the next settlement, Dalkania, round which there had been many casualties.

At about 2pm he met a number of men from the village who had come up to tell him that the tiger had that morning attacked a party of women cutting their crops. Sending his own men on to Dalkania, he decided to visit the scene himself, and after what he described as 'a substantial meal' prepared by his servant, he walked on alone. The track along the face of a hill proved so difficult that dark began to fall before he reached his destination, and he opted to spend the night in the branches of an oak tree. As he wrote, 'to have spent the night on the ground would have been to court death in a very unpleasant form.'

In the morning he walked on to the next tiny village, which consisted of two huts and a cattle-shed in a clearing.

The inhabitants, overjoyed to see him, and hearing he had spent the night in the jungle, offered to make him a meal; but, seeing their extreme poverty, he settled for a bowl of fresh milk 'sweetened to excess with jaggery', and then mounted guard over the women while they cut the rest of their wheat.

Once again he set off on his own, walking up a long valley until dusk without seeing any sign of tigers, and then choosing what turned out to be a very comfortable tree for a second night aloft. Next morning, on the way to rejoin his team at Dalkania, he fell in with a man who told him that, the day before, tigers had stampeded his cattle out of a ravine and killed one of them, a white cow. Thanking him for his information, Jim quickly set off to investigate, and after making a wide detour, approached the spot where he expected the kill to be.

This side of the ravine was deep in young bracken — ideal for stalking over. Step by step, silently as a shadow, I made my way through the bracken, which reached above my waist, and when I was some thirty yards from the bed of the ravine a movement in front of me caught my eye. A white leg was suddenly thrust up into the air and violently agitated, and the next moment there was a deep-throated growl. The tigers were on the kill and were having a difference of opinion over some toothful morsel.

For several minutes I stood perfectly still; the leg continued to be agitated, but the growl was not repeated. A nearer approach was not advisable, for even if I succeeded in covering the thirty yards without being seen, and managed to kill one of the tigers, the other, as likely as not, would blunder into me, and the ground I was on would give me no chance of defending myself.

Twenty yards to my left front, and about the same distance from the tigers, there was an outcrop of rock some ten to fifteen feet high. If I could reach this rock without being seen, I should in all probability get an easy shot. Dropping on hands and knees, and pushing the rifle before me, I crawled through the bracken to the shelter of the rocks, paused a minute to regain my breath and make quite sure the rifle was loaded, and then climbed the rock. With my eyes level with the top, I looked over, and saw two tigers.

One was eating at the hindquarters of the cow, while the other was lying nearby licking its paws. Both tigers appeared to be about the same size, but the one that was licking its paws was several shades lighter than the other; and concluding that her light colouring was due to age, and that she was the man-eater, I aligned the sights very carefully on her, and fired. At my shot she reared up and fell backwards, while the other bounded down the ravine and was out of sight before I could press the second trigger. The tiger I had shot did not move again, and after pelting it with stones to make sure it was dead, I approached and met with great disappointment; for a glance at close quarters showed me that I had made a mistake and shot the cub – a mistake that during the ensuing twelve months cost the district fifteen lives and incidentally nearly cost me my own life.

Pug-marks showed that the tigress which had got away was old, and almost certainly the man-eater; but Jim's disappointment was mitigated by the fact that the animal he had shot had been living partly on human flesh, and therefore almost certainly had developed man-eating proclivities. Having skinned the body with a pen-knife – no easy task – he again sought refuge in a tree, where he spent twelve miserable hours, drenched by rain. Then in the morning, after sixty hours without food, he set off on the fifteen-mile trek to Dalkania, carrying the skin, head and paws, which between them weighed 40lbs but felt – by the time he reached his destination – like 200.

In a courtyard, flagged with great slabs of blue slate, and common to a dozen houses, I found my men in conference with a hundred or more villagers. My approach, along a yard-wide lane between two houses, had not been observed, but the welcome I received when, bedraggled and covered with blood, I staggered into the circle of squatting men, will live in my memory as long as memory lasts. Refusing to believe that that the man-eater had claimed me as a victim, my men had kept a kettle on the boil day and night in anticipation of my return.

A hot bath, taken of necessity in the open and in full view of the village – I was too dirty and too tired to care who saw me – was followed by an ample dinner, and with a loaded rifle for company, I settled down to a sleep which lasted for twelve hours.

Jim spent the next ten days scouring the forests for signs of the tigress and staking-out his buffaloes in the evenings; but it was only on the eleventh morning that the man-eater made her next strike, seizing a girl by the head and starting to drag her away before being scared off. Summoned for help by the village women, Jim washed the victim's wounds and poured into them the contents of a small bottle of yellow fluid given him by a doctor years before. The worst injury was a claw-cut that ran from between the eyes, over the top of the head and down to the nape of the neck, leaving the scalp hanging in two halves. With strips torn from his shirt Jim bandaged the flaps together and carried the girl to her home – where, ten days later, he found to his amazement that her wounds were almost all healed. Less fortunate was another woman – also caught in the open – who saw the tigress about to spring on her and jumped down an almost perpendicular slope, only to be seized in mid-air. By the time Jim reached her, her wounds had turned septic, and she died during the night.

After nearly a month in Dalkania, he was eager to return home; but before he left he agreed to shoot some game for the villagers. Among legitimate targets were bears, which local people valued highly for their skins and fat, and he went out with a party of six men, one armed with an axe. As usual he took only five rounds of ammunition with him – and very soon he had used three of them, killing two ghoorals, the second of which tumbled down a steep face.

The ghooral had hardly come to rest when a big Himalayan bear came lumbering out of a ravine on the side of the grassy slope, and, with never a pause or backward look, came at a fast trot along the cattle track. On reaching the dead goat he sat down and took it into his lap, and as he started nosing the goat, I fired. Maybe I hurried over my shot, or allowed too much for refraction; anyway, the bullet went low and struck the bear in the stomach instead of in the chest.

To the six of us who were intently watching, it appeared that the bear took the smack of the bullet as an assault from the ghooral, for, rearing up, he flung the animal from him and came galloping down the track, emitting angry grunts. As he passed a hundred yards below us, I fired my fifth and last cartridge, the bullet, as I found later, going through the fleshy part of his hindquarters.

As it was now 2pm, it would not be possible to fetch more ammunition, track down and kill the bear, and get home by dark; so it was unanimously decided that we should follow up the wounded animal and try to finish it off with stones and the axe.

After a fast chase along the side of a hill, the pursuers flushed their quarry into open farm land, where it went to ground in a rainwater channel. The first attempt to finish it off was made by the axe-carrier, who brought the square head of his weapon down on the bear's head, only to see it bounce off – whereupon Jim took over, and after a great deal of manoeuvring 'buried the entire blade in the bear's skull.' The owner of the axe was delighted to be told that he could have not only the victim's skin, but also a double ration of ghooral meat.

Early next morning Jim left Dalkania for home. Having told his men to prepare for an early start, he set off alone before sunrise, leaving the team to pack up. There had been no news of the tigress for a week, but the absence of information made him all the more careful, and he reached a commanding ridge without mishap, coming out into a glade near the top of the hill.

The glade was pear-shaped, roughly a hundred yards long and fifty wide, with a stagnant pool of water in the centre. Sambar and other game used this pool as a drinking place and to wallow, and, curious to see the tracks round it, I left the path. As I approached the pool I saw the pug-marks of the tigress in the soft earth at the edge of the water. She had approached the pool from the same direction as I had, and, evidently disturbed by me, had crossed the water and gone into the dense tree and scrub jungle on the right-hand side of the glade. A great chance lost — for had I kept as careful a lookout in front as I had behind, I should have seen her before she saw me. However, though I had missed a chance, the advantages were now all on my side and distinctly in my favour.

The tigress had seen me, or she would not have crossed the pool and hurried for shelter, as her tracks showed she had done. Having seen me, she had also seen that I was alone, and, watching me from cover as she undoubtedly was, she would assume I was going to drink at the pool, as she had done. My movements up to this point had been quite natural, and if I could continue to make her think I was unaware of her presence, she would possibly give me a chance.

Stooping down, and keeping a very sharp look-out from under my hat, I coughed several times, splashed the water about, and then, moving very slowly and gathering dry sticks on the way, I went to the foot of a steep rock. Here I lit a small fire, and, resting my back against the rock, lit a cigarette. By the time the cigarette had been smoked, the fire had burnt out. I then lay down, and, pillowing my head on my left arm, placed the rifle on the ground with my finger on the trigger

The rock above me was too steep for any animal to find foothold on. I had therefore only my front to guard, and as the heavy cover nowhere approached to within less than twenty yards of my position, I was quite safe. I had all this time neither seen nor heard anything — nevertheless, I was convinced that the tigress was watching me. The rim of my hat, while effectually shading my eyes, did not obstruct my vision, and inch by inch I scanned every bit of the jungle within my range of view. There was not a breath of wind blowing, and not a leaf or a blade of grass stirred. My men, whom I had instructed to keep close together and sing from the time they left camp until they joined me on the forest road, were not due for an hour and a half, and during this time it was more than likely that the tigress would break cover and try to stalk, or rush, me.

There are occasions on which time drags, and others when it flies. My left arm, on which my head was pillowed, had long since ceased to prick and gone dead, but even so the singing of the men in the valley below reached me all too soon. The voices grew louder, and presently I caught sight of the men as they rounded a sharp bend. Another failure, and the last chance on this trip gone.

As his men came along the forest road, heading home, Jim joined them, and presently the group met a man herding buffaloes. Jim warned him that the man-eater was somewhere very close, and told him to keep his animals together. Not until months later did Jim hear what happened next. As the man had leant forward to light a cigarette, he was seized by the right shoulder from behind and pulled backwards. His shout, combined with a growl from the tigress, brought the buffaloes charging to him, and although both his arms and one shoulder were broken, he managed to ride one of them home. Villagers carried him thirty miles non-stop to the hospital at Haldwani, but there he died, causing Jim to reflect:

When Atropos, who snips the threads of life, misses one thread, she cuts another, and we who do not know why one thread is missed and another cut, call it Fate, Kismet, or what we will. For a month I had lived in an open tent, a hundred yards from the nearest human being, and from dawn to dusk had wandered through the jungles, and on several occasions had disguised myself as a woman and cut grass in places where no local inhabitant dared to go. During this period the man-eater had quite possibly missed many opportunities of adding me to her bag, and now, when making a final effort, she had quite by chance encountered this unfortunate man and claimed him as a victim.

By the time Jim returned to Dalkania in February 1930, several more human beings had been killed, and many wounded. He had hardly arrived in the village when he learnt that a cow had been killed the day before Vultures, visible from the village, were circling over the body and sitting on a tree above it, so he quickly set off to investigate. After a difficult approach, he found the remains of the cow lying in the open in a narrow abandoned field, and positioned himself about twenty yards away on a branch of the tree occupied by the vultures. From the circumstances, he already had a strong suspicion that the killer was a leopard, rather than a tiger – and sure enough, after only ten minutes, out of the bushes and into the open stepped a fine male leopard.

Those who have never seen a leopard under favourable conditions in his natural surroundings can have no conception of the grace of movement, and beauty of colouring, of this the most graceful and the most beautiful of all animals in our Indian jungles. Nor are his attractions limited to outward appearances, for, pound for pound, his strength is second to none, and in courage he lacks nothing. To class such an animal as VERMIN, as is done in some parts of India, is a crime which only those could perpetrate whose knowledge of the leopard is limited to the miserable, underfed and mangy specimens seen in captivity.

But, beautiful as the specimen was that stood before me, his life was forfeit, for he had taken to cattle-killing, and I had promised the people of Dalkania and other villages on my last visit that I would rid them of this their minor enemy, if opportunity offered. The opportunity had now come, and I do not think the leopard heard the shot that killed him.

Next morning, in response to another appeal for help, Jim walked four miles down the valley, and he had completed a reconnaissance of the deep ravines around the village of Nandhour when two men came running after him with the news that a tiger had killed a bullock in a spot that he had visited earlier. By the time he returned to the site, vultures had cleaned out the carcass, leaving nothing but skin and bones; so he got the Headman of a nearby village to provide him with a young buffalo, which he had tied to the stump of a fallen pine. Then – as there were no trees to climb – he scrambled up to a ledge in the rocky face and prepared for an uncomfortable vigil.

The sun had set when the buffalo, who had been lying down, scrambled to his feet and faced up the ravine. A moment later a stone came rolling down. After some time the buffalo gradually turned to his left until he was facing in my direction. This showed that whatever he was frightened of was in the recess below me. Presently the head of a tiger appeared directly under me. A head shot at a tiger is only justified in an emergency, and any movement on my part would have betrayed my presence. For a long minute or two the head remained perfectly still, and then, with a quick dash forward and one great bound, the tiger was on the buffalo.

To avoid a frontal attack, with the possibility of injury from the buffalo's horns, the tiger's dash carried him to the left of his target, and he made his attack at right angles. There was no fumbling for tooth-hold, no struggle, and no sound beyond the impact of two heavy bodies, after which the buffalo lay quite still with the tiger lying partly over it and holding it by the throat. It is generally believed that tigers kill by delivering a smashing blow on the neck. This is incorrect. Tigers kill with their teeth,

The tiger's right side was towards me, and, taking careful aim with the .275, I fired. Relinquishing its hold on the buffalo, the tiger, without making a sound, turned and bounded off up the ravine and out of sight. Clearly a miss, for which I was unable to assign any reason.

If the tiger had not seen me or the flash of the rifle, there was a possibility that it would return; so, recharging the rifle, I sat on. The buffalo lay without movement, and the conviction grew on me that I had shot him rather than the tiger. Ten, fifteen minutes dragged by, when the tiger's head for a second time appeared from the recess below me. Again there was a long pause, and then, very slowly, the tiger emerged, walked up to the buffalo and stood looking down at it. With the whole length of the back as a target, I was going to make no mistake the second time. Very carefully the sights were aligned and the trigger slowly pressed; but instead of the tiger falling dead, as I expected it to, it sprang to the left and went tearing up a little ravine, dislodging stones as it went up the steep hillside.

Two shots fired in comparatively good light at a range of thirty yards, and heard by anxious villagers for miles around – and all I should have to show for them would be certainly one, and quite possibly two, bullet holes in a dead buffalo. Clearly my eyesight was failing, or in climbing the rock I had knocked the foresight out of alignment. But in focusing my eyes on small objects, I found there was nothing wrong with my eyesight, and a glance along the barrel showed that the sights were all right, so *the only reason I could assign for having missed the tiger twice was bad shooting.*

Jim felt certain that the tiger would not return a third time. He was cold and stiff, and his thin khaki shorts gave little protection from the hard, cold rock. The idea of a dish of hot tea beckoned strongly. Yet prudence told him to stay on his ledge: the path to the village wound through dense undergrowth, and the man-eater might be watching him from close quarters. He therefore remained where he was until dawn broke and the light was strong enough to shoot by; he then climbed down, but stiff and chilled, slipped on the wet-rock and landed with his feet in the air, luckily on a bed of sand.

Early as it was, I found the village astir, and I was quickly in the middle of a small crowd. In reply to the eager questions from all sides, I was only able to say that I had been firing at an imaginary tiger with blank ammunition. A pot of tea, drunk while sitting next to a roaring fire, did much to restore warmth to my inner and outer man, and then, accompanied by most of the men and all the boys of the village, I went to where a rock jutted out over the ravine directly above my overnight exploit.

To the assembled throng I explained how the tiger had appeared from the recess under me and had bounded on the buffalo, and how after I had fired it bounded off in that direction. As I pointed up the ravine there was an excited shout of 'Look, Sahib! There's the tiger lying dead!' My eyes were strained with an all-night vigil, but even after looking away and back again, there was no denying the fact that the tiger was lying there dead.

To the very natural question of why I had fired a second shot after a period of twenty or thirty minutes, I said that the tiger had appeared a second time from exactly the same place, and that I had fired at it while it was standing near the buffalo, and that it had gone up that side ravine. There were renewed shouts, in which the women and girls, who had come up, now joined, of 'Look, Sahib – there is another tiger lying dead! Both tigers appeared to be about the same size, and both were lying about sixty yards from where I had fired.

Followed by the entire population of the village, Jim went down to inspect the bodies. For a moment his hopes were high, for he saw at once that the first was an old tigress; but they were soon dashed, for close inspection of her feet showed that they by no means matched the distinctive pug-marks of the man-eater which he had seen on the edge of the field where women were cutting corn. His second victim turned out, as he expected, to be a male. The villagers were dreadfully disappointed by his verdict, that neither of these animals was the killer they had been dreading. Had he not already told them that the man-eater was an ancient tigress? The first animal he had now shot was only a few yards from the spot on which four of their number had been killed a few days ago. How could this not be the man-eater? What did the shape of a tiger's feet count against such evidence?

Next morning Jim had to leave for home. He assured the Headmen who had come in from nearby villages that the tigress which had been troubling them was not dead. On the contrary: she was very much alive, and he warned them to maintain all possible precautions, to deny her the opportunities for which she was waiting. As he remarked later, had they heeded his words, the man-eater would have claimed far fewer victims.

A few weeks later, at the end of March 1930, he was on her trail again, this time around Kala Agar, ten miles north-west of Dalkania. Attempts to kill the tigress had been made by Vivian, the District Commissioner, and his colleagues, but it was left to Jim to take over the pursuit. For fourteen days he ranged over the mountain terrain on foot – and once he came uncomfortably close to his quarry. He had been to look at a village abandoned by its inhabitants because of the threat from the killer, and was on his way back to camp along a cattle track, when, approaching a pile of rocks, he suddenly felt danger ahead.

I had been along this track many times, and this was the first occasion on which I hesitated to pass the rocks. To avoid them I should either have had to go several hundred yards through dense undergrowth, or make a wide detour round and above them; the former would have subjected me to very great danger, and there was no time for the latter, for the sun was near setting, and I still had two miles to go. So, whether I liked it or not, there was nothing for it but to face the rocks.

A hundred feet would see me clear of the danger zone, and this distance I covered foot by foot, walking always with my face to the rocks and the rifle to my shoulder; a strange mode of progression, had there been anyone to see it. Thirty yards beyond the rocks was an open glade, starting from the right-hand side of the track and extending up the hill for fifty or sixty yards, and screened from the rocks by a fringe of bushes. In this glade a kakar was grazing. I saw her before she saw me, and watched her out of the corner of my eye. On catching sight of me she threw up her head, and as I was not looking in her direction, and was moving slowly on, she stood stock still, as these animals have a habit of doing when they are under the impression that they have not been seen.

On arrival at the hairpin bend I looked over my shoulder and saw that the kakar had lowered her head and was once more cropping the grass. I had walked a short distance along the track when the kakar went dashing up the hill, barking hysterically. In a few quick strides I was back at the bend, and was just in time to see a movement in the bushes on the lower side of the track. That the kakar had seen the tigress was quite evident, and the only place where she could have seen her was on the track.

A trickle of water seeping out from under the rocks had damped the red clay of which the track was composed, making an ideal surface for the impression of tracks. In this damp clay I had left footprints, and over these footprints I now found the splayed-out pugmarks of the tigress, where she had jumped down from the rocks and followed me, until the kakar had seen her and given its alarm-call. She was undoubtedly familiar with every foot of the ground, and not having had an opportunity of killing me at the rocks – and her chance of bagging me at the first hairpin bend having been spoilt by the kakar – she was now probably making her way through the dense undergrowth to try to intercept me at the second bend. Further progress along the track was now not advisable, so I followed the kakar up the glade, and turning to the left worked my way down over open ground, to the forest road below.

The sense that warns us of impending danger is a very real one. I do not know, and therefore cannot explain, what brings it into operation. On this occasion I had neither heard nor seen the tigress; nor had I received indication from bird or beast of her presence; and yet I know, without any shadow of doubt, that she was lying up for me among the rocks. I had been out for many hours that day and had covered many miles of jungle with unflagging caution, but without one moment's unease, and then, on cresting the ridge and coming in sight of the rocks, I knew they held danger for me – and this knowledge was confirmed a few minutes later by the kakar's warning to the jungle folk, and by my finding the man-eater's pugmarks superimposed on my own footprints.

Jim's first and final meeting with the Chowgarh tigress took place in the early afternoon of 11 April 1930. After nineteen days patrolling around Kala Agar, he went out at 2pm to tie up his three buffaloes as baits at selected places along the forest road. A mile from base, he came on a party of men collecting firewood, among them an old fellow who told him that, a month ago, a tiger had killed and eaten his eighteen-year-old son in a thicket of young oaks some 500 yards down the hill. More to placate the old man than in the hope of doing any good, Jim agreed to stake out one of his buffaloes on the spot where the lad had died.

In a patch of open ground alongside the thicket he tethered the buffalo, set one man to cut a supply of grass for it, and sent Madho Singh up an oak tree with instructions to strike a dead branch with the head of his axe and to call at the top of his voice, as hill people did when cutting leaves for their cattle. Jim then took up position on a big rock on the lower edge of the open ground.

The grass-cutter made several trips with fresh fodder, and Madho Singh, up the tree, shouted and sang lustily, while Jim stood on the rock smoking, with the rifle in the angle of his left arm. Then, all at once, he became aware that the man-eater had arrived. How he sensed this, he did not say, but suddenly he knew he was in danger.

Waiting in a state of maximum alert, he surmised that the tigress had come as far as the base of the rock behind him, preparing to attack him from there, but then had changed her mind. A few minutes later he heard a dry twig snap lower down the hill. His nervous tension eased, and he decided on new tactics. He would cross the valley and go up the other side, taking his two men with him – for to leave them with the buffalo would, as he put it, be nothing short of murder. If the tigress came to the bait, he would get a long-range shot at her. The three set out along a path, but when Jim saw that, about 100 yards ahead, the track went into heavy undergrowth, he branched off it into a ravine. The gully was about ten yards wide and four or five feet deep, and as he stepped down into it, a nightjar fluttered off a rock on which he had laid a hand.

On looking at the spot from which the bird had risen, I saw two eggs, strawberry-coloured with rich brown markings, and of a most unusual shape, one being long and very pointed, while the other was as round as a marble. As my collection lacked nightjar eggs, I decided to add this odd clutch to it. I had no receptacle of any kind in which to carry the eggs — so, cupping my left hand, I placed them in it and packed them round with a little moss.

As I went down the ravine, the banks became higher, and sixty yards from where I had entered it I came on a deep drop of some twelve to fourteen feet. The water that rushes down all these hill ravines in the rains had worn the rock as smooth as glass, and as it was too steep to offer a foothold, I handed the rifle to the men, and, sitting on the edge, proceeded to slide down. My feet had hardly touched the sandy bottom when the two men, with a flying leap, landed one on either side of me, and, thrusting the rifle into my hand asked in a very agitated manner if I had heard the tiger. As a matter of fact I had heard nothing, possibly due to the scraping of my clothes on the rocks; and when questioned, the men said what they had heard was a deep-throated growl from somewhere close at hand.

Tigers do not betray their presence by growling when looking for their dinner, and the only and very unsatisfactory explanation I can offer is that the tigress had followed us after we left the open ground, and on seeing that we were going down the ravine, had gone ahead and taken up a position where the ravine narrowed to half its width, and that when she was on the point of springing out on me, I had disappeared out of sight down the slide, and she had involuntarily given vent to her disappointment with a low growl.

Where the three of us now stood in a bunch, we had the smooth, steep rock behind us, to our right a wall of rock leaning slightly over the ravine and fifteen feet high, and to our left a tumbled bank of big rocks thirty or forty feet high. The sandy bed of the ravine, on which we were standing, was roughly forty feet long and ten feet wide. At the lower end of this sandy bed a great pine tree had fallen across, damming the ravine, and the collection of the sand was due to this dam. The wall of overhanging rock came to an end twelve or fifteen feet from the fallen tree, and as I approached the end of the rock, my feet making no sound on the sand, I very fortunately noticed that the sandy bed continued round to the back of the rock.

The rock about which I have said so much I can best describe as a giant school slate, two feet thick at its lower end, and standing up, not quite perpendicularly, on one of its long sides. As I stepped clear of it, I looked behind me over my right shoulder, and – looked straight into the tigress's face. The sandy bed behind the rock was quite flat, enclosed by three natural walls, and about twenty feet long and half as wide. Lying on it, with her fore-paws stretched out and her hind legs well tucked under her, was the tigress. Her head, which was raised a few inches off her paws, was eight feet (measured later) from me, and on her face was a smile, similar to that one sees on the face of a dog welcoming his master home after a long absence.

Two thoughts flashed through my mind, one that it was up to me to make the first move, and the other, that the move would have to be made in such a manner as not to alarm the tigress or make her nervous. The rifle was in my right hand, held diagonally across my chest, with the safety-catch off, and in order to get it to bear on the tigress the muzzle would have to be swung round three-quarters of a circle.

The movement of swinging round the rifle, with one hand, was begun very slowly, and hardly perceptibly, and when a quarter of a circle had been made, the stock came in contact with my right side. It was now necessary to extend my arm, and as the stock cleared my side, the swing was very slowly continued. My arm was now at full stretch, and the weight of the rifle was beginning to tell. Only a little further now for the muzzle to go, and the tigress — who had not once taken her eyes off mine — was still looking up at me with the pleased expression still on her face.

How long it took the rifle to make the three-quarter circle, I am not in a position to say. To me, looking into the tigress's eyes and unable therefore to follow the movement of the barrel, it appeared that my arm was paralysed, and that the swing would never be completed. However, the movement was completed at last, and as soon as the rifle was pointing at the tigress's body, I pressed the trigger.

I heard the report, exaggerated in that restricted space, and felt the jar of the recoil, and but for these tangible proofs that the rifle had gone off, I might, for all the immediate result the shot produced, have been in the grip of one of those awful nightmares in which triggers are vainly pulled of rifles that refuse to be discharged at the critical moment.

For a perceptible fraction of time, the tigress remained perfectly still, and then, very slowly, her head sank on to her outstretched paws, while at the same time a jet of blood issued from the bullet-hole. The bullet had injured her spine and shattered the upper portion of her heart.

The two men who were following a few yards behind me, and who were separated from the tigress by the thickness of the rock, had come to a halt when they saw me stop and turn my head. They knew instinctively that I had seen the tigress, and judged from my behaviour that she was close at hand. Madho Singh said afterwards that he wanted to call out and tell me to drop the eggs and get both hands on the rifle.

When I had fired my shot and lowered the point of the rifle on to my toes, Madho Singh, at a sign, came forward to relieve me of it, for very suddenly my legs appeared to be unable to support me, so I made for the fallen tree and sat down. Even before looking at the pads of her feet I knew it was the Chowgarh tigress I had sent to the happy hunting grounds, and that the shears that had assisted her to cut the threads of sixty-four human lives — the people of the district put the number at twice that figure — had, while the game was in her hands, turned, and cut the threads of her own life.

Three things, each of which would appear to you to have been to my disadvantage, were actually in my favour. These were (a) the eggs in my left hand, (b) the light rifle I was carrying and (c) the tiger being a man-eater. If I had not had the eggs in my hand, I should have had both hands on the rifle, and when I looked back and saw the tigress at such close quarters, should instinctively have tried to swing round to face her, and the spring that was arrested by my lack of movement would inevitably have been launched.

Again, if the rifle had not been a light one, it would not have been possible for me to have moved it in the way it was imperative I should move it, and then discharge it at the full extent of my arm. And lastly, if the tiger had been just an ordinary tiger, and not a man-eater, it would, on finding itself cornered, have made for the opening and wiped me out of the way — and to be wiped out of the way by a tiger usually has fatal results.

While the men made a detour and went up the hill to free the buffalo and secure the rope, which was needed for another and more pleasant purpose, I climbed over the rocks and went up the ravine to restore the eggs to their rightful owner. I plead guilty of being as superstitious as my brother sportsmen. For three long periods, extending over a whole year, I had tried — and tried hard — to get a shot at the tigress, and had failed; and within a few minutes of my having picked up the eggs, my luck had changed.

The eggs, which all this time had remained safely in the hollow of my left hand, were still warm when I replaced them in the little depression in the rock that did duty as a nest. When

I again passed that way half an hour later, they had vanished under the brooding mother whose colouring so exactly matched the mottled rock that it was difficult for me, who knew the exact spot where the nest was situated, to distinguish her from her surroundings.

The buffalo, who after months of care was now so tame that he followed like a dog, came scrambling down the hill in the wake of the men, nosed the tigress and lay down on the sand to chew the cud of contentment while we lashed the tigress to the stout pole the men had cut.

I tried to get Madho Singh to return to the bungalow for help, but this he would not hear of doing. With no one would he and his companion share the honour of carrying-in the man-eater – and if I would lend a hand, the task, he said, with frequent halts for rest, would not be too difficult. We were three hefty men – two accustomed since childhood to carry heavy loads – and all three hardened by a life of exposure; but, even so, the task we set ourselves was a herculean one.

The sun was still shining on the surrounding hills when three dishevelled and very happy men, followed by a buffalo, carried the tigress to the Kala Agar forest bungalow; and from that evening to this day no human being has been killed – or wounded – over the hundreds of square miles of mountain and vale over which the Chowgarh tigress, for a period of five years, held sway.

The tigress's claws were broken, and bushed out, and one of her canine teeth was broken, and her front teeth were worn down to the bone. It was these defects that had made her a man-eater and were the cause of her not being able to kill outright – and by her own efforts – a large proportion of the human beings she had attacked since the day she had been deprived of the assistance of the cub I had, on my first visit, shot by mistake.

Some critics have raised doubts about the veracity of this astonishing account, partly because the first version of it – sent by Jim in a letter to Maggie – differed slightly from the published text. One or two experts have claimed that it would hardly be possible for anyone, however strong, to bring a .275 Mauser to bear using only one arm, and fire the weapon like a pistol. Others, who have owned rifles of that make and calibre (including the author of this book) say that the feat would be perfectly possible, especially if a rush of adrenalin was boosting normal strength. Apart from such purely physical considerations, it seems unlikely that Jim, who always played down his own heroics, would have invented the story or even embroidered it with fictitious details.

Whatever his precise movements, his triumph resounded throughout the area. On 17 May 1930 the Deputy Inspector of Schools sent out a notice:

> *The teachers are informed that the schools of Patti Chaugarh will remain closed for five days from 4th to 8th June, in honour of Major Corbett's success in shooting the man-eater which was causing havoc and reducing general attendance. We should show our gratitude for the enterprising and beneficent act, and pray for his long life and happiness.*

CHAPTER TWELVE

The Bachelor of Powalgarh
1930

All thoughts of conservation seem to have deserted Jim when he went after the tiger known throughout the United Provinces as the Bachelor of Powalgarh. This huge animal was no man-eater, and no Government rewards had been offered for his destruction. Jim was already well aware of the need for conservation. Why, then, did he pursue the creature so eagerly at the age of fifty-five? One can only suppose that the sheer size of the tiger overcame his normal scruples.

The Bachelor had become the most sought-after big game trophy in the Province, and numerous efforts had been made to bag him with the help of buffalo baits, but his luck seemed phenomenal, and he had never been fired at. Once during a beat he had been saved when a guy-rope suspending a *machan* from a tree-branch had obstructed the weapon of the rifleman about to pull the trigger, and during another drive he had arrived so far ahead of the beaters that he caught the *shikari* filling his pipe. Both men had seen him within a few feet; one described him as 'big as a Shetland pony', the other as 'big as a donkey.'

Jim first set eyes on the monster just after sunrise on a winter morning, when he came out into a forest glade three miles from home, to the east of Kaladhungi. Red jungle fowl were scratching among dead leaves, and fifty or more chital

161

were feeding on the dew-laden grass when the Bachelor stepped out of the bushes.

In his rich winter coat, which the newly-risen sun was lighting up, he was a magnificent sight as, with head turning now to the right and now to the left, he walked down the wide lane the deer had made for him. At the stream he lay down and quenched his thirst, then sprang across, and, as he entered the dense tree jungle beyond, called three times in acknowledgement of the homage the jungle folk had paid him – for from the time he had entered the glade every chital had called, every jungle fowl had cackled, and every one of a troupe of monkeys on the trees had chattered.

The Bachelor was far afield that morning, for his home was in a ravine six miles away. Living in an area in which the majority of tigers are bagged with the aid of elephants, he had chosen his home wisely. The ravine, running into the foot-hills, was half a mile long, with steep hills rising on either side to a height of a thousand feet. At the upper end of the ravine there was a waterfall some twenty feet high, and at the lower end, where the water had cut through the red clay, it narrowed to four feet. Any sportsman, therefore, who wished to try conclusions with the Bachelor, while he was at home, would of a necessity have to do so on foot. It was this secure retreat, and Government rules prohibiting night shooting, that had enabled the Bachelor to retain his much sought-after skin.

Things changed in the winter of 1930 when the Forest Department began extensive felling around the ravine, and the big tiger shifted his ground. Jim first heard about his move from two shooting parties who had tried but failed to bag him – and then one evening the old *dak* runner who came past Kaladhungi every day dropped in to tell him that he had seen the biggest tiger tracks he had known in thirty years of service.

Early next morning Jim was on the trail, with his spaniel Robin at his heels. When they reached the spot where the runner had seen the pugmarks, they changed positions and the little dog took the lead. Jim could tell from his behaviour that he was on the scent of a tiger, and that the scent was hot. Sure enough, prints in a patch of soft ground confirmed that they were on the heels of the Bachelor, and only a minute or two behind him.

We had gone another fifty yards when Robin stopped and, after running his nose up and down on the left of the track, turned and entered the grass, which here was about two feet high. On the far side of the grass there was a patch of clerodendron, about forty yards wide. This plant grows in dense patches to a height of five feet, and has widely spread leaves and a big spread of flowers not unlike horse-chestnut. It is greatly fancied by tiger, sambar and pig because of the shade it gives.

When Robin reached the clerodendron he stopped and backed towards me, thus telling me that he could not see into the bushes ahead and wished to be carried. Lifting him up, I put his hind legs into my left-hand pocket, and when he had hooked his forefeet over my left arm, he was safe and secure, and I had both hands free for the rifle.

Proceeding very slowly, we had gone half-way through the clerodendron when I saw the bushes directly in front of us swaying. Waiting until the tiger had cleared the bushes, I went forward expecting to see him in the more-or-less open jungle, but he was nowhere in sight, and when I put Robin down he turned to the left and indicated that the tiger had gone into a deep and narrow ravine nearby. This ran to the foot of an isolated hill on which there were caves frequented by tigers, and as I was not armed to deal with a tiger at close quarters, and further, as it was time for breakfast, Robin and I turned and made for home.

After breakfast Jim returned alone, armed with a heavy .450 rifle, and on top of the hill he found a man up a tree, shouting and striking a dead branch with the head of his axe, in an attempt to keep the tiger away from his herd of buffalos. The man – an old friend and a veteran poacher – begged Jim to help him drive the cattle safely out of the jungle, and exhorted him to kill the tiger, which he said was big enough to kill and eat a buffalo a day.

By then the Bachelor was calling from a grass-covered hill some three-quarters of a mile away. Rather than go after him, Jim decided that 'he should come and look for me', so he sprinted forward, climbed to the top of a high tree and called three times. Getting an immediate answer from a distance, he climbed down and ran to find a spot with a good field of fire.

Something would have to be done, and done in a hurry, for the tiger was rapidly coming nearer; so, after rejecting a little hollow which I found to be full of black, stinking water, I lay down flat in the open, twenty yards from where the track entered the scrub. From this point I had a clear view up the track for fifty yards, to where a bush, leaning over it, impeded my further view. If the tiger came down the track, as I expected him to, I decided to fire at him as soon as he cleared the obstruction.

After opening the rifle to make quite sure it was loaded, I threw off the safety catch, and with elbows comfortably resting on the soft ground, waited for the tiger to appear. To give him directions, I now gave a low call, which he immediately answered from a distance of a hundred yards. If he came on at his usual pace, I judged he would be clear of the obstruction in thirty seconds. I counted the number very slowly, and went on counting up to eighty, when out of the corner of my eye I saw a movement to my right front, where the bushes approached to within ten yards of me.

Turning my eyes in that direction, I saw a great head projecting from the bushes, which here were four feet high. The tiger was only a foot or two inside the bushes, but all I could see of him was his head. As I very slowly swung the point of the rifle round and ran my eye along the sights, I noticed that his head was not quite square on to me, and as I was firing up, and he was looking down, I aimed an inch below his right eye, pressed the trigger – and for the next half-hour nearly died of fright.

Instead of dropping dead, as I expected him to, the tiger went straight up into the air above the bushes to his full length, falling backwards on to a tree a foot thick which had been blown down in a storm and was still green. With unbelievable fury he attacked this tree and tore it to bits, emitting as he did so roar upon roar, and, what was even worse, a dreadful blood-curdling sound as though he was savaging his worst enemy. The branches of the tree tossed about as though struck by a tornado, while the bushes on my side shook and bulged out, and every moment I expected to have him on top of me, for he had been looking at me when I fired and knew where I was.

Too frightened even to recharge the rifle, for fear the slight movement and sound should attract his attention, I lay and sweated for half an hour with my finger on the left trigger. At last the branches of the tree and the bushes ceased waving, and the roaring became less frequent, and eventually, to my great relief, ceased. For another half-hour I lay perfectly still, with arms cramped by the weight of the heavy rifle, and then started to pull myself backwards with my toes. After progressing for thirty yards in this manner I got to my feet, and, crouching low, made for the welcome shelter of the nearest tree. Here I remained for some minutes, and as all was now silent, I turned and made for home.

Next morning I returned, accompanied by one of my men, an expert tree-climber. I had noticed the previous evening that there was a tree growing on the edge of the open ground, about forty yards from where the tiger had fallen. We approached this tree very cautiously, and I stood behind it while the man climbed to the top. After a long and careful scrutiny he looked down and shook his head, and when he rejoined me on the ground he told me that the bushes over a big area had been flattened down, but that the tiger was not in sight.

I sent him back to his perch on the tree with instructions to keep a sharp lookout and warn me if he saw any movement in the bushes, and went forward to have a look at the spot where the tiger had raged. He had raged to some purpose, for, in addition to tearing branches and great strips of wood off the tree, he had torn up several bushes by the roots and bitten down others. Blood in profusion was sprinkled everywhere, and on the ground were two congealed pools, near one of which was lying a bit of bone two inches square, which I found on examination to be part of the tiger's skull.

No blood trail led away from this spot, and this, combined with the two pools of blood, was proof that the tiger was still here when I left on the previous evening and that the precautions I had taken had been very necessary, for when I started on my 'getaway' I was only ten yards away from the most dangerous animal in the world − a freshly-wounded tiger.

Jim was well aware that a tiger shot in the head could live for days, so he proceeded with the utmost caution and climbed another tree, hoisting his rifle, a shotgun and a bag of a hundred cartridges on a cord. He then bombarded the bushes with shot, yard by yard, hoping to flush out the wounded beast. But when the hail of small pellets produced no result, he came down and again went back to base.

Returning to the scene next morning, he found the old poacher there with his buffaloes, greatly mystified by the multiple reports he had heard the day before. He, too, had seen the patches of blood and the piece of bone from the tiger's skull. With a wound like that, he said, no animal could live for more than a few hours, and he offered to take his cattle into the jungle to find the body. Having heard about the ability of buffaloes to find a casualty, Jim agreed to a search.

We made for the semul tree, followed by the buffaloes. Our progress was slow, for not only had we to move the chin-high bushes with our hands to see where to put our feet, but we also had frequently to check a very natural tendency on the part of the buffaloes to stray. As we approached the semul tree, where the bushes were lighter, I saw a little hollow filled with dead leaves that had been pressed flat, and on which were several patches of blood, some dry, others in the process of congealing, and one quite fresh; and when I put my hand to the ground, I found it was warm.

Incredible as it may appear, the tiger had lain in this hollow the previous day while I had expended a hundred cartridges, and had only moved off when he saw us and the buffaloes approaching. The buffaloes had now found the blood and were pawing up the ground and snorting, and as the prospect of being caught between a charging tiger and angry buffaloes did not appeal to me, I took hold of my friend's arm, turned him round and made for the open plain, followed by the buffaloes. When we were back on safe ground, I told the man to go home, and said I would return next day and deal with the tiger alone.

The path through the jungles that I had taken each day when coming from and going home ran for some distance over soft ground, and on this soft ground, on this fourth day, I saw the pugmarks of a big male tiger. By following these pugmarks I found the tiger had entered the dense brushwood a hundred yards to the right of the semul tree. Here was an unexpected complication, for if I now saw a tiger in this jungle, I should not know — unless I got a very close look at it — whether it was the wounded or an un-wounded one. However, this contingency would have to be dealt with when met, and in the meantime worrying would not help, so I entered the bushes and made for the hollow at the foot of the semul tree.

There was no blood trail to follow, so I zig-zagged through the bushes, into which it was impossible to see more than a few inches, for an hour or more, until I came to a ten-foot-wide dry watercourse. Before stepping down into it I looked up and saw the left hind leg and tail of a tiger, standing perfectly still, with its body and head hidden by a tree, and only this one leg visible. I raised the rifle to my shoulder and then lowered it. To have broken the leg would have been easy, for the tiger was only ten yards away, and it would have been the right thing to do if its owner was the wounded animal; but there were two tigers in this area, and to have broken the leg of the wrong one would have doubled my difficulties, which were already considerable.

Presently the leg was withdrawn and I heard the tiger moving away. Going to the spot where he had been standing, I found a few drops of blood – too late now to regret not having broken that leg. A quarter of a mile further on there was a little stream, and it was possible that the tiger, now recovering from his wound, was making for this stream.

With the object of intercepting him, or, failing that, waiting for him at the water, I took a game path which I knew went to the stream, and had proceeded along it for some distance when a sambar belled to my left and went dashing off through the jungle.

It was now evident that I was abreast of the tiger, and I had only taken a few more steps when I heard the loud crack of a dry stick breaking, as though some heavy animal had fallen on it. The sound had come from a distance of fifty yards, and from the exact spot where the sambar had belled. The sambar had, in unmistakable tones, warned the jungle folk of the presence of a tiger, and the stick therefore could only have been broken by the same animal; so, getting down on my hands and knees, I started to crawl in the direction from which the sound had come.

The bushes here were from six to eight feet high, with dense foliage on the upper branches and very few leaves on the stems, so that I could see through them for a distance of ten to fifteen feet. I had covered thirty yards, hoping fervently that if the tiger charged he would come from my front (for in no other direction could I have fired), when I caught sight of something red on which the sun, drifting through the upper leaves, was shining. It might only be a bunch of dead leaves; on the other hand, it might be the tiger.

I could get a better view of this object from two yards to the right; so, lowering my head until my chin touched the ground, I crawled this distance with belly to ground, and on raising my head saw the tiger in front of me. He was crouching down looking at me, with the sun shining on his left shoulder, and on receiving my two bullets he rolled over on his side without making a sound.

As I stood over him and ran my eyes over his magnificent proportions, it was not necessary to examine the pads of his feet to know that before me lay the Bachelor of Powalgarh. The entry of the bullet fired four days previously was hidden by a wrinkle of skin, and at the back of the head was a big hole, which, surprisingly, was perfectly clean and healthy.

The report of my rifle was, I knew, being listened for; so I hurried home to relieve anxiety, and while I related the last chapter of the hunt and drank a pot of tea, my men were collecting. Accompanied by my sister and Robin and a carrying party of twenty men, I returned to where the tiger was lying, and before he was roped to a pole my sister and I measured him from nose to tip of tail, and from tip of tail to nose. At home we again measured him to make quite sure we had made no mistake the first time.

These measurements were valueless, for there were no witnesses present to certify them. They are, however, interesting as showing the accuracy with which experienced woodsmen can

169

judge the length of a tiger from his pugmarks. [Percy] Wyndham had said the tiger was ten feet between pegs, which would give roughly 10' 6" over curves. The other had said he was 10' 6" or a little more. Seven years after these estimates were made, my sister and I measured the tiger as being 10' 7" over curves.

CHAPTER THIRTEEN

The Mohan Man-eater
1931

At a conference in Almora Jim had promised that, once he had dealt with the Bachelor of Powalgarh, he would go after the tiger which was terrorising people around the village of Kartkanoula, to the west of Nainital. For once he did not make the whole journey on foot. Instead, on a blistering hot day in May 1931, with two servants and six Garhwalis, he took the train as far as Ramnagar – and still was faced with a twenty-four mile walk to the village of Kartkanoula. There he found that the man-eater had killed three people during the past week.

For accommodation, he had been offered the Foresters' Hut, but when he found that the wooden building had a mouldy, disused smell, and that the roof was swarming with bats, he announced that he would sleep in his tent. This alarmed the villagers greatly. Did he not realise that the man-eater came along the road every night? If he doubted local reports, let him come and see the claw-marks on the doors of houses. If the tiger did not eat him in the tent, it would certainly eat his men in the hut, were he not there to protect them. He therefore agreed to sleep in the main room of the hut, with his servants and bearers in the two small rooms at either end.

The most interesting piece of information given by the villagers was that they knew when the tiger was present from the moaning sound it made as it passed between the houses: sometimes the noise was continuous, and sometimes intermittent. From this information Jim concluded (a) that the tiger was suffering from a wound, (b) that the wound was of such a nature that the tiger felt it only when in motion, and that therefore (c) the wound was in one of its legs. The men were curious to know why he was so interested in the sound, but when he told them that it indicated the animal had a wound in one of its legs, and that the wound had been caused either by a bullet or by porcupine quills, they disagreed with his reasoning and said that on the occasions they had seen the tiger, it appeared to be going sound, and further, that the ease with which it killed and carried off its victims was proof that it was not crippled in any way. Nevertheless, what Jim told them was later remembered and earned him the reputation of being gifted with second sight.

One night in the damp hut left him and his men with sore throats – but, rummaging in his gun case, he found a paper packet of permanganate, given him some time earlier by his sister Maggie. The paper was soaked through with gun oil, but the crystals were still soluble, and by mixing them with iodine in hot water he made a potent gargle, which turned his and the men's teeth black but eased the soreness in their throats. Even so, he decided not to sit up for the tiger, as he would not be able to suppress his cough; rather, he would stalk it on foot, using two buffalos tethered as baits in the jungle.

Reconnoitring a disused road overgrown with grass, he found scratch marks left by a tiger, and then the pug-marks of a big, old male. At one point an over-hanging rock towered ten feet above the track, with a small, flat piece of ground on top – an ideal place from which a tiger might launch an attack. As Jim approached it one evening, he marked it as quite the most dangerous spot in all the ground he had gone over so far – 'for a tiger lying on the grass-covered bit of ground above the rock would only have to wait until anyone going either up or down the road was under it, or had passed it, to have them at his mercy – a very dangerous spot indeed, and one that needed remembering.'

On the fourth evening, when I was returning at sunset, after I came round a bend in the road thirty yards from the overhanging rock, I suddenly felt I was in danger, and that the danger that threatened me was on the rock in front of me. For five minutes I stood perfectly still with my eyes fixed on the upper edge of the rock, watching for movement. At that short range the flicker of an eyelid would have caught my eyes, but there was not even this small movement; and after going forward ten paces I again stood watching for several minutes. The fact that I had seen no movement did not in any way reassure me. The man-eater was on the rock, of that I was sure; and the question was: what was I going to do about it?

The hill was very steep, had great rocks jutting out of it, and was overgrown with grass and trees and scrub jungle. Bad as the going was, had it been earlier in the day I would have gone back and worked round and above the tiger to try to get a shot at him, but with only half an hour of daylight left, and the best part of a mile still to go, it would have been madness to have left the road.. So, slipping up the safety catch and putting the rifle to my shoulder, I started to pass the rock.

The road here was about eight feet wide, and going to the outer edge I started walking crab-fashion, feeling each step with my feet before putting my weight down, to keep from stepping off into space. Progress was slow and difficult, but as I drew level with the overhanging rock and then began to pass it, hope rose high that the tiger would remain where he was until I reached

173

Hero of Kumaon

that part of the road from which the flat bit of ground on which he was lying was visible. The tiger, however, having failed to catch me off my guard, was taking no chances, and I had just got clear of the rock when I heard a low, muttered growl above me, and a little later first a kakar went off barking to the right, and then two sambar started belling near the crest of the triangular hill. The tiger had got away with a sound skin, but, for that matter, so had I, so there was no occasion for regrets.

Next morning Jim found that one of the buffalos, which he had tethered with four ropes twisted together, had been killed and hauled off downhill. Rain during the night had softened the ground, so that he found the line of the drag easy to follow, until he came out on a huge rock which commanded a view of the ground below. There he sat down, and as he did so, he caught sight of a red-and-white object in a patch of short undergrowth forty or fifty yards below.

When one is looking for a tiger in a dense jungle, everything red that catches the eye is immediately taken for the tiger, and here, not only could I see the red of the tiger but I could also see his stripes. For a long minute I watched the object intently, and then, as the face you are told to look for in a freak picture suddenly resolves itself, I saw that the object I was looking at was the kill, and not the tiger. The red was blood where he had recently been eating, and the stripes were the ribs from which he had torn away the skin.

Knowing from experience that the tiger was almost certainly lying-up somewhere close, Jim sat still on his rock and waited; but then he felt an irritation building in his throat, and knew he was going to have to relieve it. In desperation he converted the cough into the alarm call of a *langur – khok, khok, khok,* ending with *khokorror –* a sound which the tiger probably heard every day of its life, and to which it would

174

pay no attention. Some thirty minutes later, having seen no movement, he went cautiously down to the kill, to find that the tiger had eaten about half the buffalo and then moved off, leaving a faint track.

As silently and as slowly as a shadow I took up the track, knowing that the tiger would be somewhere close at hand. When I had gone a hundred yards I came on a flat bit of ground, twenty feet square and carpeted with that variety of short, soft grass that has highly-scented roots; on this grass the tiger had lain, the imprint of his body being clearly visible. As I was looking at the imprint and guessing at the size of the animal that had made it, I saw some of the blades of grass that had been crushed down spring erect. This indicated that the tiger had been gone only a minute or so. My first thought was that he had seen me and moved off, but this I soon found was not likely, for neither the rock nor the kill was visible from the grass plot. Why then had he left his comfortable bed and gone away? The sun shining on the back of my neck provided the answer. It was now nine o'clock of an unpleasantly hot May morning, and a glance at the sun and the tree-tops over which it had come showed that it had been shining on the grass for ten minutes. The tiger had evidently found it too hot, and had gone away to look for a shady spot.

On the far side of the twenty-foot grass plot there was a fallen tree, lying north and south. This tree was about four feet in diameter, and as it was lying along the edge of the grass, in the middle of which I was standing, it was ten feet away from me. The root end of the tree was resting on the hillside, which here went up steeply and was overgrown with brushwood, and the branch end (which had been snapped off when the tree had fallen) was projecting out over the hillside. Beyond the tree the hill appeared to be more or less perpendicular, and running across the face of it was a narrow ledge of rock, which disappeared into the dense jungle thirty yards further on.

If my surmise – that the sun had been the cause of the tiger changing his position – was correct, there was no more suitable place than the lee of the tree for him to have taken shelter in, and the only way of satisfying myself on this point was to walk up to the tree and look over.

Here a picture seen long years ago in Punch flashed into memory. The picture was of a lone sportsman who had gone out to hunt lions, and who, on glancing up onto the rock he was passing, looked straight into the grinning face of the biggest lion in Africa. Underneath the picture was written, 'When you go out looking for a lion, be quite sure that you want to see him.' True, there would be this small difference, that whereas my friend looked up, into the lion's face, I would look down, into the tiger's. Otherwise the two cases – assuming that the tiger was on the far side of the tree – would be very similar.

Slipping my feet forward an inch at a time on the soft grass, I now started to approach the tree, and had covered about half the distance - that separated me from it when I caught sight of a black-and-yellow object about three and a half inches long on the rocky ledge, which I now saw was a well-used game path. For a long minute I stared at this motionless object, until I was convinced that it was the tip of the tiger's tail. If the tail was pointing away from me, the head must obviously be towards me, and as the ledge was only two feet wide, the tiger could only be crouching down and waiting to spring the moment my head appeared over the bole of the tree.

The tip of the tail was twenty feet from me, and allowing eight feet for the tiger's length while crouching, his head would be twelve feet away. But I should have to approach much nearer before I should be able to see enough of his body to get in a crippling shot – and a crippling shot it would have to be, if I wanted to leave on my feet. And now, for the first time in my life, I regretted my habit of carrying an uncocked rifle. The safety catch of my 450/400 makes a very distinct click when thrown off, and to make any sound now would either bring the tiger right on top of me, or send him straight down the steep hillside without any possibility of my getting in a shot.

Inch by inch I again started to creep forward, until the whole of the tail, and after it the hindquarters, came into view. When I saw the hindquarters I could have shouted with delight, for they showed that the tiger was not crouching and ready to spring, but was lying down. As there was only room for his body on the two-foot-wide ledge, he had stretched his hind legs out and was resting them on the upper branches of an oak sapling growing up the face of the almost perpendicular hillside.

Another foot forward, and his belly came into view, and from the regular way in which it was heaving up and down, I knew that he was asleep. Less slowly now I moved forward, until his shoulder, and then his whole length, was exposed to my view. The back of his head was resting on the grass plot, which extended for three or four feet beyond the fallen tree; his eyes were fast shut, and his nose was pointing to heaven.

Aligning the sights of the rifle on his forehead, I pressed the trigger, and, while maintaining a steady pressure on it, pushed up the safety catch. I had no idea how this reversal of the normal method of discharging a rifle would work; but it did work, and when the heavy bullet at that short range crashed into his forehead, not so much as a quiver went through his body. His tail remained straight out; his hind legs continued to rest on the upper branches of the sapling, and his nose still pointed to heaven. Nor did his position change in the slightest when I sent a second, and quite unnecessary, bullet to follow the first. The only change noticeable was that his stomach had stopped heaving up and down, and that blood was trickling down his forehead from two surprisingly small holes.

I do not know how the close proximity of a tiger reacts on others, but me it always leaves with a breathless feeling — due possibly as much to fear as to excitement — and a desire for a little rest. I sat down on the fallen tree and lit the cigarette I had denied myself from the day my throat got bad, and allowed my thoughts to wander. Any task well accomplished gives satisfaction, and the one just completed was no exception. The reason for my presence at that spot was the destruction of the man-eater, and from the time I had left the road two hours previously, right up to the moment I pushed up the safety-catch, everything – including the langur call – had worked smoothly and without a single fault. In this there was great satisfaction – the kind of satisfaction I imagine an author must feel when he writes FINIS to the plot that, stage by stage, has unfolded just as he desired it to. In my case, however, the finish had not been satisfactory, for I had killed the animal that was lying five feet from me, in his sleep.

My personal feelings are, I know, of little interest to others, but it occurs to me that you also might think it was not cricket; and in that case I should like to put the arguments before you that I used on myself, in the hope that you will find them more satisfactory than I did.

These arguments were (a) the tiger was a man-eater, better dead than alive, (b) therefore it made no difference whether he was awake or asleep when killed, and (c) that had I walked away when I saw his belly heaving up and down, I should have been morally responsible for the deaths of all the human beings he killed thereafter.

All good and sound arguments, you will admit, for my having acted as I did; but the regret remains that through fear of the consequences to myself, or fear of losing the only chance I might ever get, or possibly a combination of the two, I did not awaken the sleeping animal and give him a sporting chance.

Leaning the rifle, for which I had no further use, against the fallen tree, I climbed up to the road and, once round the corner near the cultivated land, I cupped my hands and sent a cooee echoing over the hills and valleys. I had no occasion to repeat the call, for my men had heard my two shots and had run back to the

178

hut to collect as many villagers as were within calling distance. Now, on hearing my cooee, the whole crowd came helter-skelter down the road to meet me.

While a couple of saplings to assist in carrying the tiger back to the hut were being felled, I saw some of the men passing their hands over the tiger's limbs, and knew they were satisfying themselves that their assertion that the tiger had not been suffering from any old or crippling wounds was correct. At the hut the tiger was placed in the shade of a wide-spreading tree, and the villagers informed that it was at their disposal up to two o'clock. Longer I could not give them, for it was a very hot day and there was fear of the hair slipping and the skin being ruined.

I myself had not looked closely at the tiger, but at 2pm, when I laid him on his back to start skinning, I noticed that most of the hair from the inner side of his left foreleg was missing, and that there were a number of small punctures in the skin from which yellow fluid was exuding. I did not draw attention to these punctures, and left the skinning of the leg, which was considerably thinner than the right leg, to the last.

When the skin had been removed from the rest of the animal, I made a long cut from the chest to the pad of the festering left leg, and as I removed the skin, drew out of the flesh, one after another, porcupine quills, which the men standing round eagerly seized as souvenirs; the longest of these quills was about five inches, and their total number was between twenty-five and thirty. The flesh under the skin, from the tiger's chest to the pad of his foot, was soapy, and of a dark yellow colour; cause enough to have made the poor beast moan when he walked, and quite sufficient reason for his having become, and remained, a man-eater, for porcupine quills do not dissolve, no matter how long they are embedded in flesh.

I have extracted, possibly, a couple of hundred porcupine quills from the man-eating tigers I have shot. Many of these quills have been over nine inches in length and as thick as pencils.

Many were embedded in hard muscles, a few were wedged firmly between bones, and all were broken off short under the skin.

Unquestionably the tigers acquired the quills when killing porcupines for food, but the question arises − to which I regret I am unable to give any satisfactory answer − why animals with the intelligence, and the agility, of tigers should have been so careless as to drive quills deep into themselves, or so slow in their movements as to permit porcupines − whose only method of defending themselves is walking backwards − to do so; and further, why the quills should have broken off short, for porcupine quills are not brittle.

Leopards are just as partial to porcupines as our hill tigers, but they do not get quills stuck in them, for they kill porcupines − as I have seen − by catching them by the head, and why tigers do not employ the same safe and obvious method, and so avoid injury to themselves, is a mystery to me.

CHAPTER FOURTEEN

The Kanda Man-Eater
1933

PETITION FROM THE PEOPLE OF GARHWAL

Jirat, Negi   18th February 1933

From: The Public of Patty Painaum, Bungi and Bickla
Badalpur, District Garhwal

To: Captain J.E.Carbitt, Esq., I.A.R.O.
Kaladhungi Dist. Nainital.

Respected Sir,
    We, all the public (of the above three Patties), most
humbly and respectfully beg to lay the following few lines for
your kind consideration and doing needful,
    That in this vicinity a tiger has turned out man-eater
since December last. Up to this date he has killed 5 men and
wounded 2. So we the public are in a great distress. By the
fear of this tiger we cannot watch our wheat crop at night so
the deers have nearly ruined it. We cannot go in the forest for
fodder grass nor can we enter our cattles in the forest to graze
so many of our cattle are to die. Under the circumstances we
are nearly to be ruined.

The Forest Officials are doing every possible arrangement to kill this tiger but there is no hope of any success. 2 shikari gentlemen also tried to shoot it but unfortunately they could not get it. Our kind District Magistrate has notified Rs 150 reward for killing this tiger, so every one is trying to kill it but no success. We have heard that your kind self have killed many man-eater tigers and leopards, for this you have earned a good name specially in Kumaon revenue Division. The famous man-eater leopard of Nagpur has been shoot by you. This is the voice of all the public here that this tiger also will be killed only by you.

So we the public venture to request that you very kindly take trouble to come to this place and shoot this tiger (our enemy) and save the public from this calamity. For this act of kindness we the public will be highly obliged and will pray for your long life and prosperity.

Hope you will surely consider on our condition and take trouble to come here for saving us from this calamity. The route to this place is as follows Ramnagar to Sultan, Sultan to Lahachaur, Lahachaur to Kanda. If your honour kindly informs us the date of your arrival at Ramnagar we will send our men and cart to Ramnagar to meet you and accompany you.

We beg to remain, Sir, your most sincerely

Govind Singh, Headman Village Jharat

Followed by 40 signatures and 4 thumb impressions of inhabitants of Painaum, Bungi and Bickla Badalpur Patties.

In response to this appeal, in the summer of 1933, Jim travelled some forty miles west to Kanda, where a tiger had recently killed and eaten a young man. The lad had just been accepted as a recruit by the Royal Garhwal Rifles, and Jim was much moved by the courage of his father, who was devastated by the boy's death.

As always in such cases, the villagers were living in a state of terror. From dawn to dusk on fifteen of the hottest days in May, Jim climbed up and down what even he called 'the incredibly steep hills' around the settlement, searching for traces of the man-eater. On the fifteenth evening he returned to the Forest Bungalow in which he was staying, and heard the welcome news that the tiger had been seen that day on the outskirts of the village. Yet it was an encounter next morning that seemed to change his luck.

He had long held a superstitious belief that his chances of killing a man-eater were greatly improved if he could first despatch a snake – and on the sixteenth morning, as he circled the village, advancing awkwardly across a slope of scree, he came on large hamadryad, or king cobra, thirteen or fourteen feet long. 'It was the most beautiful snake I had ever seen,' he wrote:

> The throat, as it faced me, was deep orange-red, shading to yellow where the body met the ground. The back, olive green, was banded by ivory-coloured chevrons, and some four feet of its length from the tip of its tail upwards was shiny black, with white chevrons. If, as it seemed about to do, the snake attacked up or down hill, I should be at a disadvantage, but across the shale scree I felt I could hold my own. A shot at the expanded hood, the size of a small plate, would have ended the tension, but the rifle in my hands was a heavy one, and I had no intention of disturbing the tiger that had showed up after so many days of weary waiting and toil.

After an interminably long minute, during which time the only movement was the flicking in and out of a long and quivering forked tongue, the snake closed his hood, lowered his head to the ground and, turning, made off up the opposite slope. Without taking my eyes off him, I groped with my hand on the hillside and picked up a stone that filled my hand as comfortably as a cricket ball. The snake had just reached a sharp ridge of hard clay when the stone, launched with the utmost energy I was capable of, struck it on the back of the head. The blow would have killed any other snake outright, but the only, and very alarming, effect it had on the hamadryad was to make it whip round and come straight towards me. A second and larger stone fortunately caught it on the neck when it had covered half the distance between us, and after that the rest was easy.

Fortified by that stroke of luck, Jim set out yet again on the next morning, walking the four miles from the bungalow to the village; and as he approached the houses he was greeted with the 'gratifying news' that during the night the tiger had killed a buffalo and dragged it down into a heavily-wooded valley. A careful reconnaissance suggested that it would be unwise to follow the line of the drag downhill, so he made a lengthy detour and came up from below to the spot where he hoped the remains of the buffalo would be. He had just spotted it tucked away under a bank of ferns when a premonition of impending danger came over him.

For three or four minutes I had stood perfectly still, with no thought of danger, and then all at once I became aware that the tiger was looking at me at a very short range. The same sense had evidently operated in the same way on the tiger and awakened him from his sleep. To my left front were some dense bushes, growing on a bit of flat ground. On these bushes, distant fifteen to twenty feet from me, and about the same distance from the kill, my interest centred. Presently the bushes were gently stirred, and the next second I caught sight of the tiger going at full speed up the steep hillside.

Before I could get the rifle to bear on him, he disappeared behind a creeper-covered tree, and it was not until he had covered about sixty yards that I again saw him as he was springing up the face of a rock. At my shot he fell backwards and came roaring down the hill, bringing an avalanche of stones with him. A broken back, I concluded, and just as I was wondering how best to deal with him when he should arrive all-of-a-heap at my feet, the roaring ceased, and the next minute, as much to my relief as to my disappointment, I saw him going full-out and apparently unwounded, across the side of the hill. The momentary glimpses I caught of him offered no shot worth taking, and with a crash through some dry bamboos he disappeared round the shoulder of the hill into the next valley.

I subsequently found that my bullet, fired at an angle of seventy-five degrees, had hit the tiger on the left elbow and chipped out a section from that bone which some cynical humourist has named the 'funny bone'. Carrying on, the bullet had struck the rock, and, splashing back, had delivered a smashing blow on the point of the jaw. Neither wound, however painful it may have been, was fatal, and the only result of my following up the very light blood trail into the next valley was to be growled at from a dense thorn thicket, to enter which would have been suicidal.

On visiting the kill the following morning, I was very pleased and not a little surprised to find that the tiger had returned to it during the night and taken a light meal. The only way now of getting a second shot was to sit up over the kill; and here a difficulty presented itself. There were no suitable trees within convenient distance, and the very unpleasant experience I had on a former occasion had effectively cured me of sitting on the ground at night for a man-eater.

The tree I finally selected was growing on the very edge of a perpendicular bank and had a convenient branch about eight feet from the ground. When sitting on this branch I should be thirty feet from, and directly above, the boulder-strewn ravine up which I expected the tiger to come. The question of the tree settled, I returned to the ridge where I had instructed my men to meet me with breakfast and to cooee to me at sunrise next morning. If I answered with the call of a leopard, they were to sit tight; but if they received no answer, they were to form two parties with as many villagers as they could collect and come down on either side of the valley, shouting and throwing stones.

By four o'clock in the evening I was comfortably seated on the branch and prepared for a long and hard sit-up. I have acquired the habit of sleeping in any position on a tree, and as I was tired, the evening did not pass unpleasantly. As the setting sun was gilding the hilltops above me, I was roused to full consciousness by the alarm call of a langur. I soon located the monkey, sitting in a tree-top on the far side of the valley, and as it was looking in my direction, I concluded it had mistaken me for a leopard. The alarm call was repeated at short intervals, and finally ceased as darkness came on.

Hour after hour I strained my eyes and ears, and was suddenly startled by a stone rolling down the hillside and striking my tree. The stone was followed by the stealthy padding of a heavy, soft-footed animal, unmistakably the tiger. At first I comforted myself with the thought that his coming in this direction, instead of up the valley, was accidental, but this thought was soon dispelled when he started to emit low, deep growls from immediately behind me. Quite evidently he had come into the valley while I was having breakfast, and, taking up a position on the hill, where the monkey had later seen him, had watched me climbing into the tree.

Here was a situation I had not counted on, and one that needed careful handling. The branch that had provided a comfortable seat while daylight lasted, admitted of little change of position in the dark. I could, of course, have fired off my rifle into the air, but the terrible results I have seen following an attempt to drive away a tiger at very close quarters by discharging a gun dissuaded me from taking this action. Further, even if the tiger had not attacked, the discharge of the rifle (a 450/400) so near him would probably have made him leave the locality, and all my toil would have gone for nothing.

I knew the tiger would not spring, for that would have carried him straight down a drop of thirty feet onto the rocks below. But there was no need for him to spring, for by standing on his hind legs he could easily reach me. Lifting the rifle off my lap and reversing it, I pushed the barrel between left arm and side, depressing the muzzle and slipping up the safety-catch as I did so. This movement was greeted with a deeper growl than any that had preceded it.

If the tiger now reached up for me, he would in all probability come in contact with the rifle, round the triggers of which my fingers were crooked, and even if I failed to kill him, the confusion following on my shot would give me a sporting chance of climbing higher into the tree. Time dragged by on leaden feet, and, eventually tiring of prowling about the hillside and growling, the tiger sprang across a little ravine on my left, and a few minutes later I heard the welcome sound of a bone being cracked at the kill. At last I was able to relax in my uncomfortable position, and the only sounds I heard for the rest of the night came from the direction of the kill.

The sun had been up but a few minutes and the valley was still in deep shadow when my men cooeed from the ridge, and almost immediately afterwards I caught sight of the tiger making off at a fast canter, up and across the hill on my left. In the uncertain light, and with my nightlong-strained eyes, the shot was a very difficult one, but I took it, and had the great satisfaction of seeing the bullet going home. Turning with a great roar, he came straight for my tree, and as he was in the act of springing, the second bullet, with great good fortune, crashed into his chest. Diverted in his spring by the impact of the heavy bullet, the tiger struck the tree just short of me, and ricocheting off it went headlong into the valley below, where his fall was broken by a small pool. He floundered out of the water, leaving it dyed red with his blood, and went lumbering down the valley and out of sight.

Fifteen hours on the hard branch had cramped every muscle in my body, and it was not until I had swarmed down the tree, staining my clothes in the great gouts of blood the tiger had left on it, and had massaged my stiff limbs, that I was able to follow him. He had gone but a short distance, and I found him lying dead at the foot of a rock in another pool of water.

Contrary to my orders, the men collected on the ridge, hearing my shot and the tiger's roar, followed by a second shot, came in a body down the hill. Arriving at the blood-stained tree, at the foot of which my soft hat was lying, they not unnaturally concluded that I had been carried off by the tiger. Hearing their shouts of alarm, I called out to them, and again when, with a gasp of dismay, they saw my blood-stained clothes. Reassured that I was not injured, and that the blood on my clothes was not mine, a moment later they were crowding round the tiger. A stout sapling was soon cut and lashed to him with creepers, and the tiger, with no little difficulty and a great deal of shouting, was carried up the steep hill to the village.

Jim ended his account with a moving tribute to the boy's father, who had fearlessly searched for him all night, only to discover his remains at sunrise.

The people of our hills are very superstitious, and every hilltop, valley and gorge is credited with possessing a spirit in one form or another, all of the evil and malignant kind most to be feared during the hours of darkness. A man brought up in these surroundings, and menaced for over a year by a man-eater, who, unarmed and alone, from sunset to sunrise, could walk through dense forests which his imagination peopled with evil spirits, and in which he had every reason to believe a man-eater was lurking, was in my opinion possessed of a quality and a degree of courage that is given to few.

CHAPTER FIFTEEN

Hosting the Viceroy

1937

Increasingly keen as he had become on the need for conservation, Jim was startled when, one afternoon in March 1937, Ram Singh, whose duty it was to fetch the mail from the post office two miles away, ran up to the Corbetts' cottage at Kaladhungi with an urgent telegram. It came from Hugh Stable, Military Secretary to Lord Linlithgow, and said that the new Viceroy had changed his plans. Instead of touring the southern provinces – as was the custom of an incoming ruler – he was hoping to set up a ten-day shooting trip before moving to Simla for the summer, and asked if Jim could organise something on his behalf.

For a former railway manager, who described himself as 'a mere man in the street without any connexion with Government,' this was a startling idea. Seven years earlier, at Christmas 1929, he had organised a successful tiger shoot for Sir Malcolm Hailey – but this was on another plane. 'The Viceroy coming to Kaladhungi!' Jim wrote. 'Why, such a thing had never before been heard of.' The telegram called for a swift reply, so he sent Ram Singh off to the nearest telegraph station at Haldwani, fourteen miles distant, with a message asking Hugh Stable to be available on the telephone at 11 next morning. Jim, meanwhile, went off upriver to catch a fish for dinner, in a pool which, he knew, was inhabited by a three-pound mahseer. As a boy he had spent countless hours angling with a bamboo rod and a bent pin in the lake at Nainital; and, as he later remarked, 'one can do a lot of thinking while fishing.' By the time he had caught his fish and brought it home, he had made up his mind to meet the Viceroy's request.

Before dawn next morning Jim himself set out on foot for Haldwani. As so often, he soon had a big cat for company. For the first seven miles the road ran through jungle, and as the light came up he spotted the fresh pug-marks of a male leopard in the dust. Going round a bend, he saw the animal 200 yards ahead. It seemed to sense his presence, for it turned its head to look back; but it kept to the road until he had closed to within fifty yards. Then it moved off into a patch of grass and crouched down a few feet off the track. Jim walked steadily past, staring straight ahead and watching it out of the corner of one eye. When he looked back, a hundred yards further on, the leopard had come back onto the road, and was following him. As he remarked, 'to him I was just a wayfarer for whom he had made way.'

At Haldwani, an hour on the telephone with Stable revealed that the Viceroy was hoping for a major *bandobast*, or festivity. With him would come his wife Doreen, their daughters Anne, Joan and Doreen (known as 'Bunty'), his personal staff, a swarm of Government officials and a whole company of soldiers. In the end it turned out that there were 300 people in the camp.

In his memoir Jim passed over the details of the first four beats of the shoot, each of which yielded a single tiger. But the fifth and last beat caused him acute anxiety. He had armed the three girls with a rifle apiece, and positioned them and their father on separate *machans*, all of which were rather low and frail. Anne, Joan and the Viceroy were on their own, but he had given Bunty (who was only sixteen) a reinforcement in the form of Peter Borwick, one of the ADCs. Their platform was barely six feet off the ground.

With the ambush set, Jim went back to command the line of sixteen driving elephants. When, from the middle of the line, he took off his hat and waved it, his men gave a lusty shout and started clapping their hands, to push forward any tiger that might be lurking in the 500-yard patch of thick cover. Because there were numerous deer and peafowl in the area, Jim hoped to hear alarm calls from one species or another. When none came, he began to grow worried, and signalled another burst of noise.

This time, after a minute or two, a single shot rang out in the distance ahead. From the sound he could tell that the rifle had been fired in his direction. Holding his breath, he waited. After a few moments, two more shots rang out in quick succession, both (he could tell) fired facing away from him. Then came a fourth shot, again towards him. This, he feared, could only mean trouble. Both *machans* had been in action − but had one of the girls wounded a tiger? With his heart racing, he told Ajamat, his elephant's *mahout*, to go forward as fast as he could.

Straight through thorn bushes, over big rocks and broken ground and under over-hanging branches we went... and then as we crashed into a patch of twelve-foot high nal grass, the elephant hesitated... Ajmat leant back and whispered, 'She can smell the tiger. So hold tight, Sahib, for you are unarmed.'

Only another hundred yards to go, and then through the trees I caught sight of Joan, and could have shouted with joy and relief, for she was unconcernedly sitting on her machan with her rifle across her knees. On seeing me, she spread her arms wide − which I rightly interpreted as meaning a big tiger − and then pointed down to the front of Bunty's machan.

It turned out that the beaters' first shout and clapping of hands had shifted the tiger, which broke cover about sixty yards in front of *machan* No. 3 and came slowly along a game-track. At the second shout it stopped and looked over its shoulder. Satisfied that there was no need to hurry, it stood listening for a minute, then started up a bank. When it paused at a spot which Jim had marked with a dead stick, Bunty fired and hit it in the chest – at which the tiger sprang forward with a roar and attacked her *machan*. As she and Peter desperately pushed the muzzles of their rifles through the platform's floor, trying to get in another shot, Joan knocked the tiger down with a bullet from her perch thirty yards away, and gave it another as it fell to the ground. Finally, as it struggled to regain thick cover, Bunty put a bullet through the back of its head.

'That was our Viceroy's first visit to Kaladhungi,' Jim recalled years later, 'but it was not his last, and during the many subsequent occasions on which he honoured our small foothill village with his presence... I never again took risks such as I took on the last day of that memorable shoot.' Linlithgow reciprocated Jim's hospitality by inviting him and Maggie to stay in Simla, in Delhi and (much later) at Leadhills, his moor in Scotland, where Jim discovered that driven grouse were exceedingly elusive targets.

If it seems uncharacteristic that Jim was prepared to sacrifice a precious tiger simply to gratify three teenage girls and their father, on the other hand it was a measure of the Viceroy's admiration of Jim – of his absolute reliability and skill as a *shikari* – that he put his daughters at risk. The one member of the family who missed the excitement was Linlithgow's son John (later Lord Glendevon), who became a close friend of Jim and often went hunting with him.

In his memoir *The Viceroy at Bay* John recorded an unnerving experience suffered by his mother in 1941 when the family was again in camp at Kalahundi. Late one night she was woken by her *jemadar* standing by her bed and saying 'Light! Light!'

She shone a torch and saw by his eyes that he was out of his mind. She jumped out of bed but he caught hold of her ankles, prostrating himself on the ground. She had the presence of mind to stoop down and remove the dagger from his belt — to which he responded by imploring her to kill him. Kicking herself free, she fled from the tent. The poor jemadar also fled, and was found next morning sitting in the roadway covered in dust. It was a tragic as well as a frightening episode, for he had been a devoted personal guard to the Vicereine, and all the family were very fond of him.

CHAPTER SIXTEEN

Conservation with a Camera

Jim owed much to his friendship with F.W.Champion, an officer of the Indian Forestry Service who had come out to India in 1903, and first served in the Police Department in East Bengal, and then, during the First World War, joined the Army. After service on the North West Frontier, he joined the Imperial Forestry Service and became an ardent conservationist, passionately devoted to the jungle and its denizens. In his heavily-illustrated book *The Jungle in Sunlight and Shadow* he wrote lyrically of the mountains, the forests and their inhabitants, and in the 1920s and 1930s he became a pioneer of big game photography.

His particular skill was to develop the use of cameras set off by tripwires, with which he obtained wonderful black-and-white flashlight images of tigers, leopards, bears and lesser creatures such as snakes, porcupines, ratels (honey badgers) and pangolins (scaly ant-eaters). Such was the precision of his photographs taken at night that he became able to recognise individual tigers from the pattern of their stripes.

At first sight it seems strange that he and Jim came together in an informal partnership, for their characters were very different. Whereas Jim, especially in youth, had been a mercilessly keen hunter, and killed countless animals and birds, most of them for sport, Champion greatly disliked *shikar*, and stood up for the creatures of the forest, arguing that every one had its place in the Indian scheme of things. He exonerated the tiger from charges of cruelty, and headed one of his chapters with the question 'What is the use of leopards?', arguing that, far from being evil and a menace, they were an essential element in the preservation of a balance of nature: without their killing and eating power, the population of wild pigs and deer would rapidly run out of control.

What united the two men was their love of the great Indian forests, and their alarm at the speed with which they were being reduced by commercial exploitation. In a lyrical description of a perfect winter morning, Champion sounded a note of warning;

> *Every now and then comes a terrific heart-rending crash as some splendid tree which has stood for hundreds of years through storm and fire, frost and flood, is hacked mercilessly down to meet the ever-increasing demand for timber to supply the needs of India's millions. Timber is a vital necessity to mankind, and we must all bow to the inevitable, but no forester who loves his jungle can view with any feeling but deep regret the ultimate sacrifice of the trees which he has watched over with such care, and which to him are friends and companions in his beloved forests.*

Champion pointed out that commercial plantations of trees such as pine, teak and eucalyptus, which were taking the place of the original jungle, were positively hostile to wildlife. A natural forest contains shrubs, herbs, tubers, fruits, flowers, undergrowth, creepers and any amount of decaying vegetation, largely the decomposing leaves of deciduous trees, which shed their canopy at different times of the year. Worms in oak-leaf mulch sustain pheasants, jungle fowl, peacocks and other ground-feeders. The leaves of young oaks provide food for deer. Acorns sustain deer, pigs, porcupines, bears and any number of birds. The 'standardization of forests', as Jim called the establishment of plantations, provided neither shelter nor food, and the former jungle became a desert for wildlife.

It was the photographs in Champion's book that first gave Jim the idea of trying to catch tigers on camera – and his gradual change of focus may have been accelerated by a conversation with the Rev. A.G. Atkins, pastor of the Union Church in Nainital. One day, as the two men walked down the hill towards Gurney House, the priest asked Jim what it was that had turned him from hunter to photographer. The answer was a single, phenomenal duck-shoot on a lake, to which he had taken out three army officers. The party of guns blazed away until their barrels were too hot to hold, and killed over 300 water-fowl – far more than they could possibly retrieve or carry away – and Jim was sickened by the senseless slaughter of so many birds.

It was this incident (he told Atkins) that encouraged him to shoot more with a camera than with a rifle, and he came to realise that a good photograph, which he could show to friends anywhere in the world, was a far better souvenir than a tiger skin slowly decomposing on the wall or floor of his home. Spurred on by Champion's success with a still camera and flashlight, he decided to 'go one better' and film with a cine-camera in daylight; and when, in 1928, he was given a 16-millimetre Bell & Howell cine-camera by his friend Lord Strathcona, he began to experiment with moving film.

At first his results were only moderately successful, and his methods were amateurish: all he did was stalk about the jungle lugging his 11-lb burden, armed with a khaki cushion 'for any emergency', proposing to throw it in the face of any carnivore that threatened him. As he himself recorded, for ten years he walked through hundreds of miles of tiger country, sometimes seen off by tigers guarding their kills or by tigresses defending their cubs. Altogether he reckoned he saw tigers 200 times, but never got a single satisfactory picture.

In August 1932, in a long article for the journal *Indian Wildlife,* he deplored the way in which villagers had taken to shooting deer with their primitive weapons from *machans* built in trees beside ponds and water courses. He told them that God had given water free for all, and that to sit up over it waiting for creatures when they came to drink was 'to lower themselves below the level of a corpse-eating hyena, for even he, the lowest of all creation, did not lie in wait to kill defenceless animals while they were drinking.' His point was that the slaughter of *chital* and *sambar* was depriving tigers of their natural food, and that tiger numbers were dwindling. Exhorting people to show greater respect for wildlife, he wrote: 'If we do not bestir ourselves now, it will be to our discredit that the fauna of our province was exterminated in our generation, and under our very eyes, while we looked on and never raised a finger to protect it.'

A year later he urged Sir Malcolm Hailey, who had just become Governor of the United Provinces for the second time, to set about creating a wildlife sanctuary in Kumaon. Hailey was already a sympathetic ally, and recorded how, when he and Jim were out and about in the wilds, deputations of hill folk would come to them seeking help.

Now, putting his weight behind the Association for the Preservation of the Fauna in the U.P., he asked Jim to propose a suitable site for a park, and Jim suggested an area of jungle around the broad valley of the Ramganga, in the hills some fifty miles west of Nainital. He knew the country there well, not least because he had killed a man-eater the year before at Kanda, just to the north, and he had often fished the river for its celebrated golden and black mahseer.

Thanks largely to Hailey, the U.P. Government drafted a National Parks Bill and a new Wildlife Protection Act. A 160-square-mile sanctuary was demarcated by Evelyn Smithies (later Chief Conservator of Forests), and in 1935 it became India's first National Park. 'Few protected areas in India can match the Corbett Tiger Reserve for its astounding beauty and splendid wildlife,' wrote the distinguished naturalist A.J.T. Johnsingh. 'The outer Himalaya, which can be seen as a distant, blue-tinged range, the meandering Ramganga, the expansive sal forests with their stately trees, and the sombre-coloured Shivalik Hills add variety to the habitat.' Wildlife abounded: elephants, tigers, leopards, jackals, *chital,* hog deer, *muntjac,* exceptionally large wild pigs, *nilgai* antelopes, *ghoral,* sloth and black bears, rhesus macaques and *langurs,* marsh crocodiles and *gharials* (fish-eating crocodiles), pythons and fifteen-foot cobras, to say nothing of 500 species of birds.

By then Jim was giving lectures on wildlife to schools in Nainital and Lucknow. His favourite subject was 'A Tiger is Coming,' and he would herald the predator's approach with bird and animal calls, the performance culminating in growls and a roar that made members of the audience clutch their seats.

One boy who never forgot him was Billy Arjan Singh, scion of a noble clan, the Kapurthalas, who ruled the state of Balrampur, not far south-east of Kumaon. Like Jim, in youth he was a bloodthirsty hunter, with a leopard to his rifle at ten and a tiger at fourteen. His family had a summer home in Nainital, and for some reason Jim took a special interest in him, inviting him to call at Gurney House every Sunday morning, and holding him enthralled by his man-eater stories. Little could Jim know that after a mid-life epiphany the lad would dedicate the last fifty years of his life to the conservation of big cats, bringing up three leopards and a tiger at his home in nearby Dudhwa; that he would play a leading role in the creation of the Dudhwa National Park, and win an international award for conservation.

For years Jim persevered with his attempts to photograph tigers; but his ceaseless perambulations yielded poor results, and in 1938 he resorted to a new idea – of setting up a jungle studio close to home at Kaladhungi and luring tigers to it by dropping baits at ever-nearer points in the forest – as he put it, 'a few yards at a time.' His studio was built over a stream which he dammed to create several little falls, so that the splashing of water blotted out the whirr of his camera – and by this means he managed to assemble six tigers and film them in a single gathering, on which he exposed a thousand feet of film. 'The whole proceeding, from start to finish, took four and a half months,' he recorded, 'and during the countless hours I lay near the tiny stream and my miniature waterfalls, not one of the tigers ever saw me.' Another memorable film was of a leopard – which he called to him – attacking a goat. Four times the predator charged what looked like an easy victim, and four times the goat met it head-on, to repel it with its horns, until the leopard retired in disgust. The films, which Jim showed in schools and hospitals, became a valuable asset in his campaign to spread the need for conservation.

His endless wandering in the jungle inevitably brought some setbacks – as when he fell out of a tree and injured himself severely. Maggie thought he had broken his back – but if he really had, he might never have walked again: more likely he cracked some ribs, which the doctor bound up with strapping. Hailey remembered another set-back, and described Jim as emerging 'in some apparent disorder' from a tangled thicket in the jungle near Kaladhungi. 'He explained that he had been trying to get a picture of a tigress, but she was in a bad temper, and as often as he went into the thicket, she drove him out again. He added however, as one who was ready to make allowances, that she had her cubs with her. This seemed to be typical of the terms on which he now stood with the animals of Kumaon.'

Elsewhere Hailey recalled how, along with a diminution in the desire to kill, Jim's observation of jungle life 'became of increasing interest for its own sake.'

There could be nothing more enjoyable than to spend in his company long days on the hillside or in the jungle where every twisted twig, every call of bird or animal, seemed to carry its own meaning to him; or, if the interpretation was not at once clear, would provide him with matter for most engaging speculation.

CHAPTER SEVENTEEN

The Chuka Man-eater

1937

Chuka was a small village on the right bank of the Sarda river, east of Nainital, and there in the winter of 1936 a tiger attacked a man driving two bullocks along a fire-track. Providentially, he was carrying a wooden plough and a large bundle across his shoulders, and the tiger, hitting these burdens, bounced off — although its claws ripped the man's right arm from shoulder to wrist. Some weeks later, another potential victim had even greater luck: he too was carrying a heavy load — a sack of *gur* (unrefined sugar) — and when the tiger leapt on him, its teeth stuck in the sack, which it carried off down the hill without inflicting any injury.

Next summer — in June 1937 — seven men and two fourteen-year-old boys were herding cattle near Thak, a prosperous village of stone-built houses and slated roofs, some 3,000 feet higher than Chuka. When their beasts strayed off into the jungle, one of the boys was sent to drive them back, but the men lay down to sleep off the heat of the day. Only when, towards evening, a *kakar* began giving alarm calls did they stir themselves — and all they did then was to send the second boy to drive the cows back into the open. Soon after he had disappeared, the cattle stampeded, and a tiger sprang onto one of them and killed it, in full view of the men.

The bellowing of the cows brought people out of the village, among them the parents of the first boy and the mother of the second. She, distraught with anxiety and fear, went into the jungle in search of her son, and found him lying dead. The parents soon had the same awful experience, finding their son not only dead but partly eaten.

As Jim remarked, the Chuka man-eater was disorganising life for everyone in the area; and although he had almost always pursued dangerous tigers on his own, this time he joined forces with William Ibbotson. Together with him and his wife Jean, Jim made a leisurely two-day march to Chuka, fishing successfully in the Sarda river on the way, then setting up camp.

At their destination things moved slowly. Six young buffalos had been staked out for three nights as bait for the tiger, but none had been attacked. For another four days Jim visited the site in the early morning; but it was only on the fifth morning that a buffalo was killed on the edge of the jungle where the boys had lost their lives. Instead of dragging the carcass into thick forest – as Jim expected – the tiger had taken it up onto a rocky knoll, apparently to keep clear of a *machan* from which he had twice been fired at. Tracks in a nearby buffalo wallow showed that the killer was not – as local people thought – a tigress, but a big male.

Twenty yards from the kill stood a large jamun tree, with one branch which would offer a seat and give a commanding view of the dead buffalo. After a picnic lunch Jim climbed silently to the vantage-point while Ibby and his 'big-hearted man' Sham Singh carried out a diversionary manoeuvre by going into the jungle, then walking away and returning to camp. Soon after they had left, pheasants started chattering alarm calls, and a *kakar* began barking. The tiger was evidently on the move, and Jim was poised to deal with it.

*The red glow from the setting sun had faded from the Nepal hills
on the far side of the Sarda river, and the village sounds had
died down, when a kakar barked in the direction of the buffalo
wallow; the tiger was returning to his kill along the line he had
taken when leaving it. A convenient branch in front of me gave
me a perfect rest for my rifle, and the only movement it would
be necessary for me to make when the tiger arrived would be to
lower my head onto the rifle butt. Minute succeeded minute until
a hundred had been added to my age, and then, two hundred
yards up the hillside, a kakar barked in alarm, and my hope of
getting a shot, which I had put at ten to one, dropped to one in
a thousand.*

*At midnight these alarm calls ceased altogether, and the
jungle settled down to that nightly period of rest ordained by
Nature, when strife ceases and the jungle folk can sleep in peace.
Others who have spent nights in an Indian jungle will have
noticed this period of rest, which varies a little according to the
season of the year and the phases of the moon, and which as a
rule extends from midnight to 4am. Between those hours killers
sleep. And those who go in fear of them are at peace.*

All that night Jim sat in his tree, in vain. Next day he staked
out a buffalo, and again sat up over it all night, without result.
Next morning one buffalo had gone missing from a group of
five, and Jim, casting around, picked up a well-defined blood
trail which led him for several miles over difficult ground
and back to a narrow ravine, at a point where it closed into
a bottleneck only ten feet wide. Why the tiger had dragged
its kill all that way, Jim could not make out – but he was
sure that it would come back that night, and went off for a
morning's fishing.

Returning in the evening with Sham Singh and a
posse of three men, and (for safety's sake) walking well ahead
of the rest, he approached the bottleneck for the second time.

As I did so the tiger started growling. The ravine here was steep and full of boulders, and the tiger was growling from behind a dense screen of bushes, about twenty yards straight in front of me. An unseen tiger's growl at close range is the most terrifying sound in the jungle, and is a very definite warning to intruders not to approach any nearer. In that restricted space, and with the tiger holding a commanding position, it would have been foolish to have gone any farther. So, signalling to the men to retire, and giving them a few minutes to do so, I started to walk backwards very slowly – the only safe method of getting away from any animal with which one is anxious not to make contact.

I now knew exactly where the tiger was, and felt confident I would be able to deal with him; so, on rejoining the men, I told them to leave me and return to the fishing party. This, however, they were very naturally frightened to do. They believed, as I did, that the tiger they had just heard growling was a man-eater, and they wanted to have the protection of my rifle. To have taken them back myself would have lost me two hours, and as we were in a sal forest, and there was not a climbable tree in sight, I had of necessity to keep them with me.

Climbing the steep left bank, we went straight away from the ravine for 200 yards. Here we turned to the left, and after I had paced out 200 yards, we again turned to the left and came back to the ravine 100 yards above where we had heard the tiger growling. The tables were now turned, and we held the advantage of position. For ten minutes we sat on the edge of the ravine, scanning every foot of ground in front of us. Then, moving back a few paces, we went thirty yards to the left, and again sat down on the edge, and as we did so, the man sitting next to me whispered 'Sher!' and pointed across the ravine.

From the breathing of the men behind me it was evident that excitement was rising to a high pitch. Presently one of them stood up to get a better view, and the tiger, who had been lying down facing us, got up and started to go up the hill, and as his head appeared from behind a bush, I fired. My bullet, I subsequently found, went through the ruff on his neck and striking a rock splintered back, making him spring straight up into the air, and on landing he got involved with a big creeper from which he had some difficulty freeing himself. When we saw him struggling on the ground, we thought he was down for good, but when he regained his feet and galloped off, Sham Singh expressed the opinion, which I shared, that he was unwounded. Leaving the men, I crossed the ravine and on examining the ground found the long hairs the bullet had clipped, the splintered rock, and the torn and bitten creeper, but I found no blood.

For the next two days Jim's pursuit of the man-eater was interrupted by the appearance of another tiger, and another kill – that of a cow. Sitting up over it in a quickly-built *machan*, with the thermometer registering 110°F, he was fascinated by the sight of a tigress bringing her two cubs down to the site: the behaviour of the juveniles seemed to confirm his long-held belief that tigers have no sense of smell. The carcass of the cow was a day old, and stinking powerfully under the leaves with which the tigress had covered it; but although the cubs quested back and forth within a few feet of their target, they had difficulty finding it. As soon as they did discover it and started to feed, their mother rolled onto her back with her feet in the air and went to sleep.

Four nights later another captive buffalo was killed at Thak, about 200 yards from the first kill-site. Together with a son and two men to carry their lunch, Jim set off to follow the line of the drag for two miles, through dense undergrowth, down steep banks, through beds of nettles and raspberry bushes, over and under fallen trees, and over great masses of rock, until at last they found the kill lying in a hollow under a box tree shaped like an umbrella. Their hopes rose when they saw from teeth marks on the buffalo's neck that the killer had one broken incisor – and so was almost certainly the man-eater.

Our hot walk up to Thak and subsequent descent down the densely-wooded hillside, over difficult ground, had left us in a bath of sweat, and while we rested in the hollow having lunch and drinking quantities of tea, I cast my eyes round for a convenient place on which to sit and, if necessary, in which to pass the night. Growing on the outer edge of the hollow, and leaning away from the hill at an angle of forty-five degrees, was a ficus tree. This, having started life in some decayed part of a giant of the forest, had killed the parent tree by weaving a trellis round it, and this trellis was now in the course of coalescing to form a trunk for the parasite. Ten feet from the ground, and above where the trellis had stopped, and the parent tree had rotted and fallen away, there appeared to be a comfortable seat, on which I decided to sit.

Lunch eaten, and a cigarette smoked, Ibby took our two men sixty yards to the right and sent them up a tree to shake the branches and pretend they were putting up a machan, to distract the tiger's attention in case he was lying up close-by and watching us, while I as silently as possible climbed into the ficus tree.

The seat I had selected sloped forward and was cushioned with dead wood and rotten leaves. Fearing that if I brushed them off, the sound and movement might be detected by the tiger, I left them as they were and sat down on them, hoping devoutly that there were no snakes in the hollow trunk below me or scorpions in the dead leaves. Placing my feet in an opening in the trellis, to keep from slipping forward, I made myself as comfortable as conditions permitted, and when I had done so, Ibby called the men off the tree and went away talking to them in a loud voice.

Immediately below me there was a flat bit of ground about ten feet wide and twenty feet long. From this flat piece of ground the hill fell steeply away and was overgrown with tall grass and dense patches of brushwood, beyond which I could hear a stream running; an ideal place for a tiger to lie up in. Ibby and the two men had been gone about fifteen minutes when a red monkey on the far side of the valley started barking to warn the jungle folk of the presence of a tiger. From the fact that this monkey had not called when we were coming down the hill, following the drag, it was evident that the tiger had not moved off at our approach, and that he was now coming to investigate – as tigers do – the sounds he had heard in the vicinity of his kill.

I was sitting facing the hill, with the kill to my left front, and the monkey had only called eight times when I heard a dry stick snap down the steep hillside behind me. Turning my head to the right, and looking through the trellis, I saw the tiger standing and looking in the direction of my tree, from a distance of about forty yards, and then in the direction of the tree the men had climbed, until eventually, deciding to come in my direction, he started up the steep hillside. It would not have been possible for a human being to have got over that steep and difficult ground without using his hands, and without making considerable noise, but the tiger accomplished the feat without making a sound.

The nearer he came to the flat ground, the more cautious he became and the closer he kept his belly to the ground. When he was near the top of the bank, he very slowly raised his head, took a long look at the tree the men had climbed, and, satisfied that it was not tenanted, sprang up on to the flat ground and passed out of sight under me. I expected him to reappear on my left and go towards the kill, and while I was waiting for him to do so, I heard the dry leaves under the tree being crushed as he lay down on them.

For the next quarter of an hour I sat perfectly still, and as no further sounds came to me from the tiger, I turned my head to my right, and craning my neck looked through an opening in the trellis, and saw the tiger's head. If I had been able to squeeze a tear out of my eye and direct it through the opening, it would, I believe, have landed plumb on his nose. His chin was resting on the ground, and his eyes were closed. Presently he opened them, blinked a few times to drive away the flies, then closed them again and went to sleep.

The situation needed consideration. The bole of the tree against which I had my back was roughly three feet thick and afforded ideal cover, so there was no possibility of the tiger seeing me. That he would go to the kill if not disturbed was certain; the question was, when would he go? It was a hot afternoon, but the spot he had selected to lie on was in deep shade from my tree, and, further, there was a cool breeze blowing up the valley. In these pleasant conditions he might sleep for hours, and not approach the kill until daylight had gone, taking with it my chance of getting a shot. The risk of waiting on the tiger's pleasure could not be taken.

Physically and mentally, Jim was in an exceedingly awkward position. This might be his last chance of killing the tiger, 'and on that chance might depend the lives of many people.' Waiting for a shot was clearly inadvisable: a better alternative might be to deal with the tiger where he lay. But if Jim made any except the tiniest movement, the tiger would hear it. By leaning to his left and looking down, he could see most of the tiger's tail and part of one back leg – and he realised that if he fired a shot straight down, he could put a bullet through its back. Yet he found the idea repugnant.

The thought of disabling an animal, and a sleeping one at that, simply because he occasionally liked a change of diet, was hateful. Sentiment, however, where a man-eater was concerned, was out of place. I had been trying for days to shoot this tiger, to save further loss of human life, and now that I had a chance of doing so, the fact that I would have to break his back before killing him would not justify my throwing away that chance. So the killing

210

would have to be done, no matter how unpleasant the method might be, and the sooner it was done, the better.

Keeping my body perfectly rigid, I gradually released my hold on the trellis, got both hands on the rifle and fired a shot behind and under me, which I have no desire ever to repeat. When I pressed the trigger of the 450/400 high-velocity rifle, the butt was pointing to heaven, and I was looking under, not over, the sights. The recoil injured but did not break either my fingers or my wrist, as I had feared it would, and as the tiger threw the upper part of his body round and started to slide down the hill on his back, I swung round on my seat and fired the second barrel into his chest. I should have felt less a murderer if, at my first shot, the tiger had stormed and raved, but – being the big-hearted animal that he was – he never opened his mouth, and died at my second shot without having made a sound.

He was a fine big male in the prime of life and in perfect condition, and would have measured – if we had had anything to measure him with – nine feet six inches between pegs, or nine feet ten over curves. And the right canine tooth in his lower jaw was broken. Later I found several pellets of buckshot embedded in different parts of his body.

The tiger was too heavy for the four of us to carry back to camp, so we left him where he lay, after covering him up with grass, branches and deadwood, heaped over with big stones, to protect him from bears. Word travelled round that night that the man-eating tiger was dead, and when we carried him to the foot of the ficus tree in the village next morning to skin him, more than a hundred men and boys crowded round to see him. Among the latter was the ten-year-old brother of the Chuka man-eater's last human victim.

CHAPTER EIGHTEEN

The Thak Man-eater

1938

In September 1938 a report reached Nainital that a tiger had killed a twelve-year-old girl while she was collecting windfall mangoes in full view of the village of Kot Kindri, close to where Jim had killed the Chuka man-eater the year before. Further pressure to take action was put on him by the fact that the Forest Department had marked all the trees in the area for felling, and if a man-eater was still at large when the work was due to begin, the contractors would cancel their agreements.

Jim agreed to take action 'more in the interests of the local inhabitants than in the interest of the contractors,' and as he was preparing for the long march up-country, another report of a death –this time of an elderly woman – came in from Sem, a small village on the river Ladhya about half a mile from Chuka. Once again he set out reinforced by William and Jean Ibbotson; their route took them up the Nandhour river, in which they fished with no little success, catching 120 fish on light trout rods in a single day. The river wound back and forth between rock cliffs, so that they had to cross it every quarter of a mile or so, and at one of the fords Jim's cook, who stood five feet in his boots, was nearly washed away, saved only by the prompt assistance of the man carrying the lunch basket,

On the 11th day of their trek they reached Sem and made camp in a deserted field 200 yards from where the woman had been killed. Jim, soon in action, found tracks which he took to be those of a young tigress, an average-sized animal in the prime of life, which had crossed and re-crossed the river, leaving prints in the sand on the banks. Could this be the killer? It was possible, but unlikely, as the prints showed no sign of injury.

Two days later, a man went missing from Thak, a village two miles away. The news was brought by Tewari, brother of the village Headman, and Jim, in company with the Ibbotsons, set out to investigate. They soon found the white loin-cloth of the missing man, and started to follow the trail left by the tigress as she carried him off, but because the undergrowth was so thick, and visibility extended only to a few yards, it took them two hours to cover half a mile. At last they reached a ridge, above the valley in which, six months before, they had killed the Chuka man-eater.

On this ridge was a great slab of rock, which sloped upwards and away from the direction in which we had come. The tigress's tracks went down to the right of the rock, and I felt sure she was lying up under the overhanging portion of it, or in the close vicinity. Both Ibbotson and I had on light, rubber-soled shoes – Terawi was bare-footed – and we had reached the rock without making a sound.

Signing to my two companions to stand still and keep a careful watch all round, I got a foothold on the rock, and inch by inch went forward. Beyond the rock was a short stretch of flat ground, and as more of this ground came into view, I felt certain my suspicion that the tigress was lying under the projection was correct.

I still had a foot or two to go before I could look over, when I saw a movement to my left front. A goldenrod that had been pressed down had sprung erect, and a second later there was a slight movement in the bushes beyond, and a monkey in a tree on the far side of the bushes started calling. The tigress had chosen the spot for her after-dinner sleep with great care, but unfortunately for us she was not asleep, and when she saw the top of my head – I had removed my hat – appearing over the rock, she had risen, and, taking a step forward, had disappeared under a tangle of blackberry bushes. Our so-carefully-carried-out stalk had failed at the very last moment, and there was nothing to be done now but find the kill and see if there was sufficient left of it, for us to sit up over.

The tigress had eaten her meal close to where she had been lying, and as this spot was open to the sky and to the keen eyes of vultures she had removed the kill to a place of safety where it would not be visible from the air. Tracking now was easy, for there was a blood trail to follow. The trail led over a ridge of great rocks, and fifty yards beyond these rocks we found the kill.

I am not going to harrow your feelings by attempting to describe that poor torn and mangled thing, stripped of every stitch of clothing and atom of dignity, which only a few hours previously had been a Man, the father of two children and the bread-winner of the wailing woman who was facing – without any illusions – the fate of a widow in India.

I have seen many similar sights, each more terrible than the one preceding it, in the thirty-two years I have been hunting man-eaters, and on each occasion I have felt that it would have been better to leave the victim to the slayer than to recover a mangled mass of flesh, to be a nightmare ever after to those who saw it. And yet the cry of blood for blood, and the burning desire to rid a countryside of a menace than which there is none more terrible, is irresistible; and then there is always the hope, no matter how absurd one knows it to be, that the victim by some miracle may still be alive and in need of succour.

215

While Ibbotson and Tewari went back to the village for ropes with which to construct a *machan*, Jim wedged himself in the fork of a small tree and kept guard over the remains of the kill. After a few minutes he heard a rock tilt forward and back as the tigress crept up to within twenty yards of him; he never saw her, but, as he wrote, 'she had come, seen me, stayed some time watching me and then gone away without my having seen a leaf or a blade of grass move.' Determined to miss no chance of getting a shot at her, he wrapped himself in a blanket and spent the whole of the night on his perch – but his only nocturnal visitors were two porcupines and a bear. In the morning tracks showed that Ibbotson and his companion had had a lucky escape, for the tigress had followed them all the way back to camp.

Over the next few days the tigress killed two buffaloes, and the *shikaris* made repeated attempts to come to terms with her. Several times they were within a few yards, but she continued to elude them. Then on 7 November the Ibbotsons had to leave, and set out on a twelve-day walk to the small town of Askot.

Two days later Jim also broke camp and prepared to start his trek to catch the train at Tanakpur; a contingent of men from the surrounding villages begged him not to leave, but all he could do was promise that he would return as soon as possible. Having walked twenty miles in the day, he caught the train next morning, and was back in Nainital on 9 November, after almost a month's absence.

He had just moved down to his winter home in Kaladhungi when news arrived that the tigress had killed a man in Thak. Even though he was already sixty-two, the challenge was too great for him to resist – but he promised Maggie that this would be his last expedition after man-eaters. Years of exposure and strain, and long absences from home, were beginning to tell as much on his own constitution as on the nerves of his family, and he promised to be back in ten days.

By means of a series of what he called 'forced marches' he was back in the man-eater's territory a little after sunrise on November 24 . It had been his intention to camp in the village, but in the neighbouring hamlet of Chuka he learnt that every man, woman and child had left Thak immediately after the man had been killed, and that there was nobody there to protect his own men. He therefore decided to stay in Chuka, where he would have some privacy from the thousands of wood-cutters who were arriving to fell the forest, and when he walked over to Thak, taking a buffalo as bait, he found the place deserted.

Silence reigned over it. Every one of the hundred or more inhabitants had fled, taking their livestock with them. The only animal I saw in the village was a cat, which gave me a warm welcome. So hurried had the evacuation been that many of the doors of the houses had been left wide open. On every path in the village, in the courtyards of the houses and in the dust before all the doors I found the tigress's pug marks. The open doorways were a menace, for the path as it wound through the village passed close to them, and in any of the houses the tigress might have been lurking.

Having tied up his buffalo, Jim set off on his return to camp at Chuka. When he paused for a drink at a spring which he had visited on his way out, he found the tigress's pugmarks superimposed on his own footprints. More tracks showed that she had followed him all the way up from camp that morning, and from her close attendance he reckoned she was eager to secure another human victim. His time would soon run out. When leaving home on 22 November, he had promised to be back in ten days. It was already the night of the 24th – so that he had only six clear days and nights in which to accomplish his mission – and his task had been made all the more difficult by the arrival of an enormous Government work force.

Several thousand men – the contractors put the figure at 5,000 – had now concentrated at Chuka and Kumaya Chak to fell and saw up the timber and carry it down to the motor road that was being constructed, and all the time this considerable labour force was working they shouted at the tops of their voices to keep up their courage. The noise in the valley resulting from axe and saw, the crashing of giant trees down the steep hillside, the breaking of rocks with sledgehammers, and combined with it all the shouting of thousands of men, can be better imagined than described. That there were many and frequent alarms in this nervous community was only natural, and during the next few days I covered much ground and lost much valuable time in investigating false rumours of attacks and kills by the man-eater.

That a single animal should terrorise a labour force of these dimensions, in addition to the residents of the surrounding villages and the hundreds of men who were bringing foodstuffs for the labourers or passing through the valley with hill produce in the way of oranges (purchasable at twelve annas a hundred), walnuts and chillies to the market at Tanakpur, is incredible, and would be unbelievable were it not for the historical, and nearly parallel, case of the man-eaters of Tsavo, where a pair of lions, operating only at night, held up work for long periods on the Uganda railway.

On the morning of the 25th Jim staked out three fat buffaloes at strategic points, hoping that the tigress would kill at least one of them, and that he would get a chance to shoot her over it. But when, next morning, he went round the baits, he found that she had not touched any of them. Her tracks

showed that she had walked up and down the path to Thak
– so he got his men to build a rope *machan* from which he
could cover it.

*It was now quite evident that the tigress had no fancy for my fat
buffaloes, and as in three days I had seen her tracks five times
on the path leading to Thak, I decided to sit up over the path
and try to get a shot at her that way. To give me warning of the
tigress's approach I tied a goat with a bell round its neck on the
path, and at 4pm I climbed into the tree. I told my men to return
at 8am the following morning, and began my watch.*

*At sunset a cold wind started blowing, and while I was
attempting to pull a coat over my shoulders, the ropes on one side of
the machan slipped, rendering my seat very uncomfortable. An hour
later a storm came on, and though it did not rain for long, it wet
me to the skin, greatly adding to my discomfort. During the sixteen
hours I sat in the tree I did not see or hear anything. The men turned
up at 8 am.. I returned to camp for a hot bath and a good meal, and
then, accompanied by six of my men, set out for Thak.*

*The overnight rain had washed all the tracks off the path,
but about two hundred yards above the tree I had sat in I found
the fresh pugmarks of the tigress, where she had come out of
the jungle and gone up the path in the direction of Thak. Very
cautiously I stalked the first buffalo, only to find it lying asleep
on the path; the tigress had skirted round it, rejoined the path
a few yards further on, and continued up the hill. Following on
her tracks, I approached the second buffalo, and as I got near the
place where it had been tied, two blue Himalayan magpies rose
off the ground and went screaming up the hill.*

*The presence of these birds indicated (a) that the buffalo
was dead, (b) that it had been partly eaten and not carried away,
and (c) that the tigress was not in the close vicinity. On arrival at
the stump to which it had been tied, I saw that the buffalo had
been dragged off the path and partly eaten; and on examining the*

animal I found that it had not been killed by the tigress but in all probability had died of snakebite (there were many hamadryads in the surrounding jungle), and that, finding it lying dead on the path, the tigress had taken a meal of it and then tried to drag it away. When she found she could not break the rope, she had partly covered the kill over with dry leaves and brushwood, and continued on her way up to Thak.

That night Jim sat up again, this time in an almond tree. When the moon rose out of the dusk over the Nepalese hills behind him and flooded the hillside with brilliant light, there was still enough daylight to shoot by. The illumination was so good that he could see a *sambar* and her young one feeding in a wheat field 150 yards away.

The moon had been up two hours, and the sambar had approached to within fifty yards of my tree, when a kakar started barking on the hill just above the village. The kakar had been barking for some minutes when suddenly a scream, which I can only very inadequately describe as Ar-ar-arr, dying away on a long-drawn-out note, came from the direction of the village. So sudden and so unexpected had the scream been that I involuntarily stood up, with the intention of slipping down from the tree and dashing up to the village, for the thought flashed through my mind that the man-eater was killing one of my men. Then in a second flash of thought I remembered I had counted them one by one as they had passed my tree, and that I had watched them out of sight on their way back to camp to see if they were obeying my instructions to keep close together.

The scream had been the despairing cry of a human being in mortal agony, and reason questioned how such a sound could have come from a deserted village. It was not a thing of my imagination, for the kakar had heard it and had abruptly stopped barking, and the sambar had dashed away across the fields closely followed by her young one. Two days previously, when I had escorted the men to the village, I had remarked that they appeared to be very confident to leave their property behind doors that were not even shut or latched, and the Headman had answered that even if their village remained untenanted for years, their property would be quite safe, for they were priests of Purnagiri, and no one would dream of robbing them. He added that as long as the tigress lived she was a better guard of their property – if guard were needed – than any hundred men could be, for no one in all that countryside would dare to approach the village for any purpose, through the dense forests that surrounded it, unless escorted by me, as they had been.

The screams were not repeated, and as there appeared to be nothing else that I could do, I settled down again on my rope seat. At 10pm a kakar that was feeding on the young wheat crop at the lower end of the fields dashed away barking, and a minute later the tigress called twice. She had now left the village and was on the move, and even if she did not fancy another meal of the buffalo, there was every hope of her coming along the path. With finger on the trigger and eyes straining I sat hour after hour until daylight succeeded moonlight, and when the sun had been up an hour, my men returned. Very thoughtfully they had brought a bundle of dry wood with them, and in a surprisingly short time I was sitting down to a hot cup of tea.

When Jim questioned the Headman of Thak closely about the most recent death, he learned that the man had cried out as he was seized. Did he cry out once? Jim asked. 'No,' came the answer, 'three times.' At Jim's request the Headman then gave an imitation of the cry.

It was the same – but a very modified rendering – of the screams I had heard the previous night. When I asked if he could give any explanation of the screams having come from a village in which there could not – according to him – have been any human beings, his answer was that he could not. And as I could do no better than the Headman, it were best to assume that neither the kakar, the sambar nor I heard those very real screams – the screams of a human being in mortal agony.

Jim gave no further explanation of this mystery. But when he got back to his camp, before he could enjoy the cup of tea and hot bath that his servant had prepared for him, he had to get rid of an excited throng of people clamouring to tell him their experiences of the night before.

It appeared that shortly after moonrise the tigress had started calling close to Chuka, and after calling at intervals for a couple of hours had gone off in the direction of the labour camps at Kumaya Chak. The men in these camps, hearing her coming, started shouting to try to drive her away, but so far from having this effect the shouting only infuriated her the more, and she demonstrated in front of the camps until she had cowed the men into silence. Having accomplished this, she spent the rest of the night between the labour camps and Chuka, daring all and sundry to shout at her. Towards morning she had gone away in the direction of Thak, and my informants were surprised and very disappointed that I had not met her.

The crowd round the tent included many sawyers from Delhi, but included the petty contractors, agents, clerks, timekeepers and gangmen of the financier who had taken up the timber and road construction contracts in the Ladhya valley. They told Jim that many of the hillmen carrying timber and working on the road had left for their homes that morning, and that if he left – as they had heard he intended doing – they too would depart at once, for they were too frightened to eat or sleep, and no one would dare remain in the valley after he had gone.

Jim's time was running out, and though he was badly in need of rest and sleep, he was determined to make one last attempt to get in touch with the tigress. Local people were urging him to sit up over a goat, and as he had already bought two goats for baits, he agreed to stake them out on the path from Chuka to Thak. About a hundred yards from the tree in which he had sat two nights earlier there was a giant almond tree, and he reckoned that if he climbed about half-way up it, he would be able to see both goats, on separate stations, and also the remains of the dead buffalo. He armed himself for any encounter with 'an accurate .275 rifle', and with a 450/400 which he took along 'for an emergency'.

I found the climb up from Chuka on this last day very trying, and I had just reached the spot where the path leaves the ridge for the flat ground when the tigress called about 150 yards to my left. The ground here was covered with dense undergrowth and trees interlaced with creepers, and was cut up by narrow and deep ravines, and strewn with enormous boulders – a very unsuitable place in which to stalk a man-eater. However, before deciding on what action I should take, it was necessary to know whether the tigress was lying down, as she very well might be, for it was then 1pm, or whether she was on the move, and if so, in what direction. So, making the men sit down behind me, I listened, and presently the call was repeated; she had moved some fifty yards, and appeared to be going up the main ravine in the direction of Thak.

This was very encouraging, for the tree I had selected to sit in was only fifty yards from the ravine. After enjoining silence on the men and telling them to keep close behind me, we hurried along the path. We had about two hundred yards to go to reach the tree, and had covered half the distance when, as we approached a spot where the path was bordered on both sides by dense brushwood, a covey of kalege pheasants rose out of the brushwood and went screaming away. I knelt down and covered the path for a few minutes, but as nothing happened we went cautiously forward and reached the tree without further incident.

As quickly and silently as possible one goat was tied at the edge of the ravine, while the other was tied at the foot of the hill to the right. Then I took the men to the edge of the cultivated land and told them to stay in the upper verandah of the Headman's house until I fetched them, and ran back to the tree. I climbed to a height of forty feet and pulled the rifle up after me with a cord I had bought for the purpose. Not only were the two goats visible from my seat, one at a range of seventy and the other at a range of sixty yards, but I could also see part of the buffalo, and as the .275 rifle was accurate, I felt sure I could kill the tigress if she showed up anywhere on the ground I was overlooking.

The goats had lived together ever since I had purchased them on my previous visit, and, being separated now, were calling lustily to each other. Even if the tigress had moved after I had heard her, it was impossible for her not to hear them. If she was hungry, as I had every reason to believe she was, there was a very good chance of my getting a shot.

My seat was not uncomfortable, and the sun was pleasingly warm, so for the next three hours I remained in the tree without any discomfort. At 4pm the sun went down behind the high hill above Thak, and thereafter the wind became unbearably cold. For an hour I stood the discomfort, and then decided to give up, for the cold had brought on an attack of ague, and if the tigress came now it would not be possible for me to hit her. I retied the cord to the rifle and let it down, climbed down myself and walked to the edge of the cultivated land to call up my men.

There are few people, I imagine, who have not experienced that feeling of depression that follows failure to accomplish anything they have set out to do. Excluding the time spent on journeys from and to home, I had been on the heels of the man-eater from 23 October to 7 November, and again from 24 to 30

November, and it is only those of you who have walked in fear of having the teeth of a tiger meet in your throat who will have any idea of the effect on one's nerves of days and weeks of such anticipation.

Then again my quarry was a man-eater, and my failure to shoot it would very gravely affect everyone who was working in, or whose homes were in, that area. Already work in the forests had been stopped, and the entire population of the largest village in the district had abandoned their homes. Bad as the conditions were, they would undoubtedly get worse if the man-eater was not killed, for the entire labour force could not afford to stop work indefinitely, nor could the population of the surrounding villages afford to abandon their homes and their cultivation, as the more prosperous people of Thak had been able to do.

The tigress had long since lost her natural fear of human beings, as was abundantly evident from her having carried away a girl picking up mangoes in a field close to where several men were working, killing a woman near the door of her home, dragging a man off a tree in the heart of a village, and, the previous night, cowing a few thousand men into silence.

And here was I, who knew full well what the presence of a man-eater meant to the permanent and to the temporary inhabitants and to all the people who passed through the district on their way to the markets in the foothills or the temples at Punagiri, plodding down to camp on what I had promised others would be my last day of man-eater hunting; reason enough for a depression of soul which I felt would remain with me for the rest of my days. Gladly at that moment would I have bartered the success that had attended thirty-two years of man-eater hunting for one unhurried shot at the tigress.

I knew that I was being watched and followed, and every time I went through the two miles of jungle between my camp and Thak, I tried every trick I have learnt in a lifetime spent in the jungles to outwit the tigress. Bitter though my disappointment was, I felt that my failure was not in any way due to anything I had done or left undone.

As there was nothing further I could do, I set off on my weary tramp to camp. The path, as I have already mentioned, joins the ridge that runs down to Chuka a quarter of a mile from Thak, and when I now got to this spot, where the ridge is only a few feet wide, I heard the tigress call once and again across the valley on my left. She was a little above and to the left of Kumaya Chak, and a few hundred yards below the Kot Kindri ridge on which the men working in that area had built themselves grass shelters.

Here was an opportunity, admittedly forlorn and unquestionably desperate, of getting a shot; still, it was an opportunity, and the last I should ever have, and the question was, whether or not I was justified in taking it.

I had one hour in which to get back to camp before dark. Calling up the men, hearing what they had to say, collecting the goats and walking to the ridge had taken about thirty minutes, and judging from the position of the sun, which was now casting a red glow on the peaks of the Nepal hills, I calculated I had roughly half an hour's daylight in hand. The time factor, or perhaps it would be more correct to say the light factor, was all-important, for if I took the opportunity that offered, on it would depend the lives of five men.

The tigress was a mile away, and the intervening ground was densely wooded, strewn over with great rocks and cut up by a number of deep nullahs — but she could cover the distance well within the half-hour if she wanted to.

The question I had to decide was, whether or not I should try to call her up. If I called and she heard me, and came while it was still daylight and gave me a shot, all would be well; on the other hand, if she came and did not give me a shot, some of us would not reach camp, for we had nearly two miles to go and the path the whole way ran through heavy jungle, and was bordered *in some places by big rocks, and in others by dense brushwood.*

Handing my rifle over to one of the men, I waited until the tigress called again and, cupping my hands round my mouth, and filling my lungs to their utmost limit, sent an answering call over the valley. Back came her call, and thereafter, for several minutes, call answered call. She would come, had in fact already started, and if she arrived while there was still light to shoot by, all the advantages would be on my side, for I had the selecting of the ground on which it would best suit me to meet her. November is the mating season for tigers, and it was evident that for the past forty-eight hours she had been rampaging through the jungles in search of a mate, and that now, on hearing what she thought was a tiger answering her mating call, she would lose no time in joining him.

Four hundred yards down the ridge the path coming down from Thak runs for fifty yards across a flat, rectangular bit of ground forty yards wide and eighty yards long, ending in a more or less perpendicular rock face. After continuing down the centre for twenty-five yards the path bends to the right and leaves the rectangle on its long or east side. At the point where the path leaves the flat ground there is a rock about four feet high. From a little beyond where the path bends to the right, a ridge of rock, three or four feet high, rises and extends to the north side of the rectangle, where the ground falls away in a perpendicular rock face. On the near side of this low ridge there is a dense line of bushes approaching to within ten feet of the four-foot-high rock. The rest of the rectangle is grown over with trees, scattered bushes and short grass.

It was my intention to lie on the path by the side of the rock and shoot the tigress as she approached me; but when I tried this position I found it would not be possible for me to see her until she was within two or three yards, and further, that she could get at me either round the rock or through the scattered bushes on my left without my seeing her at all. Projecting out of the rock,

227

from the side opposite to that from which I expected the tigress to approach, there was a narrow ledge. By sitting sideways I found I could get a little of my bottom on the ledge, and by putting my left hand flat on top of the rounded rock and stretching out my right leg to its full extent and touching the ground with my toes, retain my position on it. The men and goats I placed immediately behind and ten to twelve feet below me.

The stage was now set for the reception of the tigress, who, while these preparations were being made, had approached to within three hundred yards. Sending out one final call to give her direction, I looked round to see if my men were all right.

The spectacle these men presented would under other circumstances have been ludicrous, but here was tragic. Sitting in a tight little circle with their knees drawn up and their heads together, with the goats burrowing in under them, they had that look of intense expectancy on their screwed-up features that one sees on the faces of spectators waiting for a big gun to go off.

From the time we had first heard the tigress from the ridge, neither the men nor the goats had made a sound, beyond one suppressed cough. They were probably by now frozen with fear – as well they might be – and even if they were, I take my hat off to those four men who had the courage to do what I, had I been in their shoes, would not have dreamt of doing. For seven days they had been hearing the most exaggerated and blood-curdling tales of this fearsome beast that had kept them awake the past two nights, and now, while darkness was coming on, and sitting unarmed in a position where they could see nothing, they were listening to the man-eater drawing nearer and nearer. Greater courage, and greater faith, it is not possible to conceive.

The fact that I could not hold my rifle, a DB .400/500, with my left hand (which I was using to maintain my precarious seat on the ledge) was causing me some uneasiness, for apart from the fear of the rifle's slipping on the rounded top of the rock – I had folded my handkerchief and placed the rifle on it to try to prevent this – I did not know what would be the effect of the recoil of a high-velocity rifle fired in this position. The rifle was pointing along the path, in which there was a hump, and it was my intention to fire into the tigress's face immediately it appeared over the hump, which was twenty feet from the rock,

The tigress, however, did not keep to the contour of the hill, which would have brought her out on the path a little beyond the hump, but crossed a deep ravine and came straight towards where she had heard my last call, at an angle which I can best describe as one o'clock. This manoeuvre put the ridge of rock, over which I could not see, between us. She had located the direction of my last call with great accuracy but had misjudged the distance, and not finding her prospective mate at the spot she expected him to be, she was now working herself up into a perfect fury – and you will have some idea of what the fury of a tigress in her condition can be when I tell you that not many miles from my home, a tigress on one occasion closed a public road for a whole week, attacking everything that attempted to go along it, including a string of camels, until she was finally joined by a mate.

I know of no sound more liable to fret one's nerves than the calling of a tiger at close range. What effect this appalling sound was having on my men I was frightened to think; and if they had gone screaming down the hill, I should not have been at all surprised, for even though I had the heel of a good rifle to my shoulder and the stock against my cheek, I felt like screaming myself.

But even more frightening than the continuous calling was the fading-out of the light. Another few seconds, ten or fifteen at the most, and it would be too dark to see my sights, and we should then be at the mercy of a man-eater, plus a tigress wanting a mate. Something would have to be done, and done in a hurry, if we were not to be massacred, and the only thing I could think of was to call.

The tigress was now so close that I could hear the intake of her breath each time before she called, and as she again filled her lungs, I did the same with mine, and we called simultaneously. The effect was startlingly instantaneous. Without a second's hesitation she came tramping with quick steps through the dead leaves, over the low ridge and into the bushes a little to my right front, and just as I was expecting her to walk right on top of me, she stopped, and the next moment the full blast of her deep-throated call struck me in the face and would have carried the hat off my head, had I been wearing one. A second's pause, then again quick steps, a glimpse of her as she passed between two bushes, and then she stepped right out into the open, and, looking into my face, stopped dead.

By great and unexpected good luck the half-dozen steps the tigress took to her right front carried her almost to the exact spot at which my rifle was pointing. Had she continued in the direction in which she was coming before her last call, my story – if written – would have had a different ending, for it would have been as impossible to slew the rifle on the rounded top of the rock as it would have been to lift and fire it with one hand.

Owing to the nearness of the tigress, and the fading light, all that I could see of her was her head. My first bullet caught her under the right eye, and the second, fired more by accident than with intent, took her in the throat, and she came to rest with her nose against the rock. The recoil from the right barrel loosened my hold on the rock and knocked me off the ledge, and the recoil from the left barrel, fired while I was in the air, brought the rifle up in violent contact with my jaw and sent me heels over head right on top of the men and goats. Once again I take my hat off to those four men for, not knowing but what the tigress was going to land on them next, they caught me as I fell and saved me from injury and my rifle from being broken.

When I had freed myself from the tangle of human and goat legs, I took the .275 rifle from the man who was holding it, rammed a clip of cartridges into the magazine and sent a stream of five bullets singing over the valley and across the Sarda into

Nepal. Two shots, to the thousands of men in the valley and in the surrounding villages who were anxiously listening for the sound of my rifle, might mean anything, but two shots, followed by five more, spaced at regular intervals of five seconds, could only be interpreted as conveying one message, and that was, that the man-eater was dead.

I had not spoken to my men from the time we had first heard the tigress from the ridge. On my telling them now that she was dead, and that there was no longer any reason for us to be afraid, they did not appear to be able to take in what I was saying, so I told them to go up and have a look while I found and lit a cigarette. Very cautiously they climbed up to the rock, but went no further, for the tigress was touching the other side of it.

In camp that night, while sitting round a camp fire and relating their experiences to relays of eager listeners, their narrative ended up with, 'And then the tiger whose roaring had turned our livers into water hit the sahib on the head and knocked him down on top of us – and if you don't believe us, go and look at his face.' A mirror is superfluous in camp, and even if I had had one, it could not have made the swelling on my jaw, which put me on milk diet for several days, look as large and as painful as it felt.

By the time a sapling had been felled and the tigress lashed to it, lights were beginning to show in the Ladhya valley and in all the surrounding camps and villages. The four men were very anxious to have the honour of carrying the tigress to camp, but the task was beyond them; so I left them and set off for help.

If the greatest happiness one can experience is the sudden cessation of great pain, then the second greatest happiness is undoubtedly the sudden cessation of great fear. One short hour previously it would have taken wild elephants to have dragged from their homes and camps the men who now, singing and shouting, were converging from every direction, singly and in groups, on the path to Thak. Some of the men of this rapidly-growing crowd went up the path to help carry in the tigress, while *others accompanied me on my way to camp, and would have carried me had I permitted them.*

Progress was slow, for frequent halts had to be made to allow each new group of arrivals to express their gratitude in their own particular way. This gave the party carrying the tiger time to catch us up, and we entered the village together. I will not attempt to describe the welcome my men and I received, or the scenes I witnessed at Chuka that night, for, having lived the greater part of my life in the jungles, I have not the ability to paint word pictures.

A hayrick was dismantled and the tigress laid on it, and an enormous bonfire made from driftwood close at hand, to light up the scene and for warmth, for the night was dark and cold, with a north wind blowing. Round about midnight my servant, assisted by the Headman of Thak and Kunwar Singh, near whose house I was camped, persuaded the crowd to return to their respective villages and labour camps, telling them they would have ample opportunity of feasting their eyes on the tigress the following day. Before leaving himself, the Headman of Thak told me he would send word in the morning to the people of Thak to return to their village. This he did, and two days later the entire population returned to their homes, and have lived in peace ever since.

After my midnight dinner I sent for Kunwar Singh and told him that in order to reach home on the promised date I should have to start in a few hours, and that he would have to explain to the people in the morning why I had gone. This he promised to do, and I then started to skin the tigress. Skinning a tiger with a pocket knife is a long job, but it gives one an opportunity of examining the animal that one would otherwise not get, and in the case of man-eaters enables one to ascertain, more or less accurately, the reason for the animal's having become a man-eater.

The tigress was a comparatively young animal, and in the perfect condition one would expect her to be at the beginning of the mating season. Her dark winter coat was without a blemish, and in spite of having so persistently refused the meals I had provided for her, she was encased in fat. She had two old gunshot wounds, neither of which showed on her skin. The one in her left shoulder, caused by several pellets of home-made buckshot, had become septic, and when healing the skin over quite a large surface had adhered permanently to the flesh.

To what extent this wound had incapacitated her, it would have been difficult to say, but it had evidently taken a very long time to heal, and could quite reasonably have been the cause of her having become a man-eater. The second wound, which was in her right shoulder, had also been caused by a charge of buckshot, but it had healed over without becoming septic. These two wounds, received over kills in the days before she became a man-eater, were quite sufficient reason for her not having returned to the human and other kills I had sat over.

After having skinned the tigress, I bathed and dressed, and though my face was swollen and painful and I had twenty miles of rough going before me, I left Chuka walking on air, while the thousands of men in and around the valley were peacefully sleeping.

I have come to the end of the jungle stories I set out to tell you, and I have also come near the end of my man-eater hunting career. I have had a long spell, and count myself fortunate in having walked out on my own feet and not been carried out on a cradle in the manner and condition of the man of Thak. There have been occasions when life has hung by a thread, and others when a light purse and disease resulting from exposure and strain have made the going difficult; but for all these occasions I am amply rewarded if my hunting has resulted in saving one human life.

CHAPTER NINETEEN

At War Again

1939-45

At the beginning of 1939 Jim was shaken up by another serious accident – as he reported in a letter.

My Dear Lord Hailey,
Kaladhungi,
2 Feb 39

I have been confined to this house for four weeks. A tiger was calling one day in the jungle above the canal and I went off to try and get a picture. After sitting up for three hours I decided to go home and for some reason that I cannot account for, I dived head-foremost off the branch on which I had been sitting. I had got up high to overlook the surrounding jungle, and it was a miracle I was not killed. I have not broken any bones, and hope to be on my feet again in a few weeks.

The accident obliged him to refuse a generous invitation from Hailey to go fishing in Ireland. This was something he had dreamed of for years, but now, to his great regret, he was not fit enough to travel so far. 'The trip would have done me a world of good,' he wrote, 'and would in fact have set me on my feet again.'

In June he told Hailey that he had just been to the new national park, and reported– without comment – that the Viceroy (Linlithgow) had shot one tiger 'in a block across the river,' and then had concentrated on fishing. 'Although he is a very expert fisherman, he did not kill in ten days as many fish as you and I used to kill in a single morning.'

In the three years since the park's inception, Jim reported, things had changed greatly.

Now that all Forest Officials use cars, the roads in the Park have been greatly improved and by next winter it will be possible to motor into the Park one way, and out another way, passing right through the area in which game is most plentiful. It would be very gratifying to you to see how the animals in the Park have increased, and how tame they are. Motoring of an evening, along the new road that skirts the edge of the Dhakala maidan, one can see 500 head of game, at a range of ten yards onwards. On several occasions when motoring in the middle of the day we saw tigers and bear right out in the open.

Anticipating the outbreak of war by one week, Jim falsified his age by lopping ten years off his sixty-four, and applied to Command Headquarters for a job. In January 1940 he suggested to Hailey that he might try 'in a very small way, to entertain the troops in billets and in hospitals at home, and behind the lines in France. I would, of course, pay all my own expenses, and all my shows would be free.' In August he wrote to Hailey again:

I am older in years but very little older in body since you left. For the second time in twenty-six years the raising of the age limit and a sound constitution have enabled me to join the Army. I am joining up again as a 2/Lieutenant with local field rank.

As a member of the District Soldiers' Board he set about recruiting for the Army, and in Kumaon he raised 1,400 men for the Civil Pioneer Corps, many of them grandsons of the men he had taken to France during the First World War. Jim was too old to return to service in Europe – and in 1942 he was struck down by tick typhus; he spent three months in hospital at Agra and was then moved to the Ramsay hospital in Nainital, becoming so ill that his weight went from twelve stone to eight. Recovering, in February 1944 he was commissioned Lieutenant Colonel and appointed Senior Instructor in jungle warfare at a new army training centre near Chhindwara, in what was then the Central Provinces (now Madhya Pradesh).

Having spent a month learning about the flora and fauna of Burma , he started teaching young troops how to deal with the environment. Most of his pupils were about twenty years old, and when a new class arrived, he would go round them asking about their fears. Always they were most afraid of darkness, silence and jungle sounds, in that order. Jim's training had three main objects:

A   To banish fear of the unknown.
B   To avoid getting lost.
C   To live on the jungle.

If there was a tiger kill in the vicinity, he would take the young men up to it – and once, when he led four of them in for a close-up look at two tigers, one of them passed out, from fear or excitement – and for a few moments Jim thought he had killed him.

Another day, while instructing a fresh draft of fifty British troops, he heard a serpent eagle screaming as it circled 'high in the heavens' above them. Even through binoculars it was no more than a dot in the sky; so, telling his companions to stand still, he brought out a three-inch reed, split at one end and blocked at the other, and blew a note. The call, which sounded like a natural product of the forest, and would not attract any human enemy, reproduced the cry of a young deer in distress. Jim knew it would attract the eagle, which lived principally on snakes, but was not averse to other flesh. Sure enough, the bird folded its wings, dropped a few hundred feet and resumed its soaring. A few more calls, and it was passing just above the tree-tops. Jim's pupils' only disappointment was that he could not induce it to land in a tree, so that they could take photographs.

Another skill which he taught was that of tracking enemy. From his own perambulations he knew that it was possible to glean useful information from human footprints left on roads and paths, and by studying heel-marks left in mud or dust he could tell roughly how many men had passed in a group.

There are other interesting things you can learn from the footprints, and one of the most important of these is the speed at which the party was travelling. When a human being is moving at a normal pace his weight is distributed evenly over his footprint, and his stride is from thirty to thirty-two inches, according to his height. As the speed is increased, less weight falls on the heel and more on the toes, the imprint of the heel gets less and the imprint of the toes greater, and the length of the stride gets longer. This process of less heel and more toes tends to get more apparent until when running at full speed little more than the ball of the foot and the toes come in contact with the ground. If the party was a small one, ten or a dozen in all, it will be possible to see if any were limping, and blood on the track will indicate that one or more were wounded.

In general, he taught newcomers that the jungle was a perfectly habitable place: he showed them which fruits, flowers and roots were edible, which plants made effective medicines, which yielded dye for camouflage, which creepers were good for ropes. He showed them how to create fire, and find dry fuel in a wet forest. He also trained the men to pin-point sounds, as well as to maintain a full, 180-degree field of vision when moving from place to place, recalling how on one occasion 'the darting-in-and-out of the forked tongue of a cobra in a hollow tree, and on another occasion the moving of the tip of the tail of a wounded leopard lying behind a bush, warned me just in time that the cobra was on the point of striking and the leopard on the point of springing.' In general, he taught the novices 'to live at peace with all wildlife,' and to realise that 'the book of nature has no end, as it has no beginning.'

To ordinary soldiers, most of them probably from urban backgrounds, Jim's skills must have seemed magical, almost supernatural – and no one can say how many lives his instruction may have saved when the men reached the battleground in Burma. He himself did not escape unscathed: exposure to frequent monsoon deluges left him with a severe form of malaria, which plagued him intermittently for years. But in recognition of his services, in 1946 he was made a Companion of the Indian Empire.

Even in the middle of the war his fame as a hunter pursued him. One day in 1942, at a lavish garden party in Meerut, he and Maggie were invited to entertain wounded men who were about to be sent home. With fifty or sixty of them sitting on chairs round the edges of a tennis court, he and his sister went opposite ways, talking to each in turn – and Jim was profoundly moved by one of his encounters.

Half-way round the circle he came to a seriously-wounded young man sitting in a low chair. At Jim's approach the youth painfully slid off the chair and tried to put his head on the visitor's feet. Jim picked him up and made him comfortable. 'He was woefully light,' he remembered, but the lad said:

'I was a small boy when you shot the man-eater, and as our village is far from Rudraprayag, I was not able to walk there, and my father not being strong was unable to carry me, so I had to stay at home. When my father returned, he told me he had seen the man-eater, and that with his own eyes he had seen the sahib who had shot it. He also told me of the sweets that had been distributed that day, and of the great crowds he had seen. And now, Sahib, I will go back to my home with great joy in my heart, for I shall be able to tell my father that with my own eyes I have seen you, and, maybe, if I can get anyone to carry me to the great fair that is held every year at Rudraprayag to commemorate the death of the man-eater, I shall tell all the people I meet there that I have seen and had speech with you.'

A typical son of Garhwal [Jim concluded] *of that simple and hardy hill-folk, and of that greater India, whose sons only those few who live among them are privileged to know. It is these big-hearted sons of the soil, no matter what their caste or creed, who will one day weld the contending factions into a composite whole, and make of India a great nation.*

CHAPTER TWENTY

AUTHOR

1943

When Jim became an author, people often asked him how he could recall so much detail of long-gone encounters – for he claimed never to have kept a diary, never to have made notes. 'I do not possess a note-book,' he once wrote, 'and I have never made a note in my life. If one uses one's senses as it was intended they should be used, there is no need to make notes, for everything one sees or hears is photographed on one's memory, and is there for all time... All I had to do was turn up the photograph selected and make a verbal copy of it.' For him, this seems to have been true. Nevertheless, the precision with which he remembered places, incidents, distances and timings remains astonishing.

He was goaded into writing by an aggressive woman who heard him telling jungle stories one evening during a dinner at Government House in Nainital, and made him promise that he would put some of them on paper so that other people could enjoy them. Exasperated by her persistence, he agreed to make some notes. Another enthusiast was Colonel Archie White, a British officer on leave in Nainital whom he met in the 1930s. One evening they watched Jim's film of the leopard attacking the goat, and White was so struck by the camera-man's knowledge that he walked with him down to Kaladhungi. There Jim took him into the jungle and gave the call of a chital stag: within seconds a hind appeared, only to vanish when Jim gave the call of a leopard. White, immensely impressed, suggested that he should write up some of his experiences and send the results to *Blackwood's,* the Scottish monthly magazine popular throughout the Empire. Jim revealed that he had already done so, but that his offerings had been rejected – and when the Colonel read them, he saw why: the narratives were so disorganised, and so badly presented in school exercise books or on tattered typing paper, as to be barely comprehensible.

Back in Nainital a year later, White gave Jim some coaching in grammar and syntax – and perhaps this encouraged the budding author. Perhaps Maggie also had a hand in shaping the stories. The creation of the text involved no small amount of work, for the author typed it – as he later typed all his books – using only one finger. As Maggie remembered, 'He was always very neat, and if there was even one mistake on a page, he would scrap it and start another. He always wanted a sentence to read "smoothly", and would take infinite pains in making it do so.'

The first collection was put together by a friend, editor of the local newspaper, the *Lake Zephyr,* who had a small printing press – but his equipment was so primitive that he could produce only one page at a time, after which the type had to be broken up so that the letters could be used again. With these handicaps, it took him four months to print the book, which the Corbetts entitled *Jungle Stories.* Bound in brown paper covers, but embellished with gold type on the front, and stitched with twine on the spine, it ran to 104 pages. Jim sent out seventy-five copies to friends, many of whom later reported that the book had been 'read to death.' The response was so enthusiastic that he started planning a larger edition; but he had not got far before Hitler (as he put it) 'began his land-collecting tour.'

When he went down with typhus, he had been told he would have to spend the rest of his life in a bath chair. Refusing to accept this dismal prediction, he exercised vigorously and got down to revising the manuscript of his book. When he sought advice from a friend who had brought out a book of his own, he was told that no publishing house would accept his typescript unless he indemnified the firm against all possible loss.

Having talked the matter over, he and Maggie decided that there could be no harm in asking a publisher's opinion; so, early in 1943, they sent a new version of the manuscript – again entitled *Jungle Stories* – to the Bombay branch of the Oxford University Press, bolstered by recommendations from Linlithgow, the Viceroy, and Sir Malcolm Hailey.

Hailey remembered that Jim had no idea of the value of his work. 'He did not realise how enthralling were the stories he had to tell, nor how greatly their interest would be enhanced by his manner of telling them. Yet... he possessed that supreme art of narrative which owes nothing to conscious artistry.' Roy Hawkins, known as 'Hawk', the editor in Bombay who came to handle most of Jim's writing, was certain from the first that the book would be a huge success – especially when an American war correspondent, to whom he sent proofs for an opinion, returned them saying he had been so entranced that he had read the stories three times. So the O.U.P. accepted the book for publication, insisting only that its title be changed from *Jungle Stories* (which meant practically nothing) to *Man-Eaters of Kumaon*. Jim dedicated the book to 'the gallant soldiers, sailors and airmen of the United Nations who during this war have lost their sight in the service of their country', and specified that all royalties from the first Indian edition should go to St. Dunstan's, the training school for Indian soldiers blinded in the war, which had opened in 1943.

The first edition was published by the O.U.P. in Bombay in August 1944, and immediately attracted the attention of the new Viceroy, General Sir Archibald Wavell:

The Viceroy's House,
New Delhi

My Dear Corbett,
I have just finished reading your book, and have hardly ever enjoyed one more. They are thrilling stories, and you have told them extraordinarily well. I have already ordered several copies for friends.

Another edition appeared from the branch of the same publisher in Madras in 1945. In the West, the book came out simultaneously on both sides of the Atlantic in March 1946, with an introduction by Hailey and a preface by Linlithgow. As in India, it took off like a rocket. 'It would be fair a fair guess that *Man-Eaters of Kumaon* is the most beguiling book about big game hunting ever written,' said James Hilton in the *New York Herald Tribune*.

Jim had been invited to a large publication party at the O.U.P.'s headquarters on Fifth Avenue, but he had felt obliged to decline. According to the firm's publicity chief, Virginia B. Carrick, 'Colonel Corbett was greatly missed. He sent me a wonderful cable which I had photostatted and blown up so that it could be hung on the wall and read by the guests at the party.' Henry Z. Walck, President of the firm in New York, took a hand in the publicity campaign, and organised the printing of posters which depicted tigers with eyes that glowed with luminous ink.

Luckily a suggestion that tiger skins should be exhibited in shop windows was never taken up. Reviews were enthusiastic, the sole dissenter being the spiky author and critic Edmund Wilson, who described Jim's style as being

Author

'like ruptured Kipling' (he later called J.R.R. Tolkien's *Lord of the Rings* 'juvenile trash').

The American Book of the Month Club printed 250,000 copies, and two tiger cubs, flown to New York in a private plane from a zoo in Florida, autographed copies with their pug-marks at a reception in the Hotel Pierre. Complaints about the number of 'gruesome tales' the book contained left the author unmoved: 'I can't help this, for if I did not paint the whole picture as I saw it, there would be no point in trying to paint it at all.'

He was much annoyed when a rumour got around in New York that he was a professional hunter: 'The thought is hateful to me, for it makes me feel so cheap.' In August 1946 a postal strike somehow gave credence to the rumour that he had been killed by a man-eater. 'I did think of asking you and your people in New York to deny the rumour,' he wrote to the publisher, 'but on second thoughts I refrained, fearing that it might look like an attempt at cheap advertisement.'

In England, the Readers' Union also made the book the club's monthly choice, and reviewers were equally enthusiastic. 'Often my heart almost stopped, and I had to lay down the book, it was so exciting,' wrote J.W. Turner in the *Spectator*. In February Jim told a correspondent that the two Indian editions had already sold out, and that 'by the end of this year a million copies will be in circulation in half a dozen countries.'

Praise flowed in from all directions. 'It is certainly the best adventure book that I have read since Patterson's *Man-Eaters of Tsavo**, which was such a success forty years

---

**The Man-Eaters of Tsavo* by Lieutenant Colonel J.H. Patterson was set in Africa in 1898, when a pair of lions severely harassed the men building the railway line from the coast to Nairobi, killing 135 workers.

ago,' wrote Leo Amery, the Secretary of State for India and Burma. Seventy-five years, on Jim's book has been translated into fifteen European and eleven Indian languages, as well as into Afrikaans and Japanese. One enthusiast claimed to have read it a hundred times, another that he could repeat the entire text word for word.

At about the time of first publication, a visitor to Kaladhungi, the American Red Cross officer Marjorie Clough, stayed with the Corbetts for four days in the winter, and left a charming account of Jim and his sister. 'Jim stands an erect six feet tall,' she reported. 'He has a ruddy complexion, blue eyes that laugh and are sad all at once.' When she asked him why he had never married, he side-stepped the question by answering, 'It's been my privilege – no. I have had the honour – to make a home for the best mother and sisters in the world. Maggie has spent her life spoiling me.'
As for Maggie, Clough wrote:

> *She is small, has white, bobbed hair, is very blue of eye, and fragile-looking as a piece of Dresden china. But any sense of delicacy this sight might impose on the visitor is belied by the vigour with which she strides out behind Jim on their walks through the jungle. Because of cool nights and chilly days, Maggie dresses in smartly-tailored tweeds and slacks. Jim's felt hat that accompanies him through the jungles is worn at a rakish angle that becomes his twinkling Irish eyes, but Maggie's hat is 'put on properly', and she looks at you shyly from under its brim.*

She might have added that Maggie wore heavy shoes, made for her by a Chinese cobbler, and cooked on a charcoal brazier, even after electricity had arrived in Nainital. She and Jim, Marjorie wrote, 'sit together night after night before their wood fire, he at his typewriter, she brewing the after-dinner cup of tea. They ponder over words to describe to the outside world something of the innermost secrets of the jungle they love and know so well.'

Jim shot his last tiger in 1945, soon after he got home from the war. This was no man-eater, but a persistent killer of farm animals, which took up residence in the jungle close to Kaladhungi: among its victims were a calf, two bullocks and a horse. By then Jim was so debilitated by fever that Maggie doubted his ability to hold a rifle steady: nevertheless, he called the tiger up and shot it through the eye from a range of a few feet. 'It was murder, of course,' he remembered, 'but justifiable murder, for though I was willing to let the tiger live in the dense patch of lantana it had selected for its home – two hundred yards from the village – and pay compensation for all the animals it killed, it was difficult to replace these animals owing to the country-wide shortage brought about by the war. And, as I have said, the tiger resisted all my attempts to drive it away.'

Sudden fame made Jim's life no easier. 'My book has brought me in contact with many other people in all parts of the world whom I had never even heard of,' he wrote from Kaladhungi to a friend on 25 February 1946.

If I was to set out to visit all the countries I have been invited to, it would take me a year to complete the journey. America is offering me free passage by air, and a Good Will lecturing and broadcasting tour. I am wanted in New York on 4th April, and I have to make up my mind today whether to accept or refuse

*the offer. I find the decision very hard. India is in turmoil, and
I don't want to leave Maggie alone. I know Maggie will be safe,
and I need only be away two or three weeks, even so I am finding
it hard to make up my mind.*

He never went to America. Even without the interruption
of a long trip, he was struggling to keep up with his
correspondence. Letters from readers poured in, and at one
time he was writing a thousand replies a month. At first he
tried to do this by hand, but soon writer's cramp forced him
to use his old machine.

In writing that first best-seller, he had by no means
expended all his ammunition. The book contained accounts
of only seven man-eaters, and he had a large number of
other hunting exploits stored in his mind, not least one of
his most enthralling narratives – the story of the man-eating
leopard of Rudraprayag. After months of effort, and many
disappointments, he had killed the villain in May 1926, but
he did not finish his account of the hunt until November
1946 – and he explained to a friend why the tale had taken
so long to appear in print:

*Ibbotson undertook to write up the story, and after ten years
he abandoned the attempt, and I am glad that he did. Being a
Senior Wrangler, his brain works on too high a plane for him
to be able to tell a simple story in simple words. And another
thing, I had a suspicion that his object in writing the story was
to say more than I wanted him to say – so I am glad he gave
up the attempt.*

He now had a new mentor in London – Geoffrey Cumberlege,
generally known as 'Jock', who had served with distinction
during the First World War, winning a DSO, an MC,
three Mentions in Dispatches and a *Croce di Guerra*. He was
naturally sympathetic to Indian projects, as he had spent eight

years as manager of the Press in Bombay, where the O.U.P. often trained young executives. He had also worked for six years as Manager and Vice-President of the firm in New York, before becoming become Publisher to the O.U.P. at the firm's headquarters in London in 1945.

He quickly established a cordial relationship with Jim, who wrote to him on 5 September 1946:

> *I finished the Rudraprayag story last evening and took the last chapter to a friend's house to try it out. I had an audience of three, a man, his wife and their daughter of twenty. After I had finished reading, the man blew his nose and said in a husky voice, 'Splendid.' The girl said, 'Mother and I are crying too much to be able to say anything.' I did not write the book with the intention of making people cry. I am not clever enough to paint a word picture with any but the words at my command, nor have I the art of creating imaginary scenes. So when I tell a story I try and tell it as I actually saw it, and if I were to leave out all the tragic scenes, the resulting story would be flat and meaningless.*

Unlike his first book, which was a collection of different stories, *The Man-Eater of Rudraprayag* was one sustained narrative, full of close encounters and disappointments, but no less absorbing.

Jim was still active in the *shikar* field, and in January 1947 he ran a high-powered shoot near Dehra Dun, at which he greatly impressed Wavell with his knowledge. 'His talk on tigers and jungle life is of extraordinary interest,' the Viceroy wrote in his journal, 'and I wish I could have had more of it.'

> *He has rather pessimistic views on the future of tigers; he put the present tiger population of India at 3,000-4,000 (I was rather surprised at the smallness of this estimate) and thinks that in many parts of India tigers will become almost extinct in the next ten or fifteen years; his chief reason is that 'Indian politicians are*

no sportsmen, and tigers have no votes, while the right to hold a gun licence will go with a vote.'

For years Jim had grown increasingly worried by the approach of Partition – the political division of the country into two, India and Pakistan, which (as he accurately foresaw) would give rise to widespread disorder and conflict between Hindus and Muslims. As far back as February 1940 he had written to Hailey saying 'As control weakens, due in a large measure to Indianisation, the communal question becomes more acute, and here in our province the police force is having to be increased by 800 men, to keep the peace.'

Now, after the war, anti-British feeling was on the increase. For families like the Corbetts who had been caught up in the mutiny of 1857, the change in atmosphere raised uncomfortable memories.

On a personal level, Jim convinced himself that, once the British had handed over to native administrators, he would no longer be welcome in the land he had always known as home, and that the only sensible course would be to go and live in Africa.

On a national level, he foresaw terrible atrocities as hundreds of thousands of people were uprooted from their homes and forced to seek new lives in alien territory. In fact his private worries were unfounded: in Kumaon, far from being resented, he was loved and revered and regarded as a hero. On the wider front, however, he accurately foresaw disaster – as he showed in a cynical letter to an executive of the O.U.P. in New York.

21 February 1947
Gurney House

My Dear Brander,
Attlee [the British Prime Minister] has made his unconditional
offer of a sub-continent to anyone who is willing to accept it. I
take the offer as implying: here for the family is a basket of eggs.
If the family do not want them, give them to the servants, and
if they do not want them, throw them into the dustbin, for they
are bad anyway, and I am fed up with carrying them round from
door to door.

By the autumn, his worst fears were being realised, as he
showed in another agitated letter, undated, but written about
a month after Independence had been declared on 15 August.

Gurney House,
Nainital
1947

My dear Brander,
If the leaders at your end and mine co-opted the devil when
drawing up their plan for the rivers in India to run with blood,
they can today congratulate themselves on having planned with
great success, for never in any part of the world has there been
greater slaughter, with as much brutality, as India is witnessing
today. And the end is not yet, for disease and famine have to take
their toll, as have the frontier tribes, who in their turn will be
followed by the Russians. And all this misery has been brought
about by the leaders at your end trying to earn a little cheap
publicity for themselves, and by the leaders at my end being vain
enough to think that they could break a dam and stop the rush of
water by merely raising a hand.
When all the pent-up water, fouled with blood has seeped
into the land, the Russians will quietly walk in, and no one in

this stricken land will raise a protest. Yes – the leaders and the devil can indeed congratulate themselves on having done a very thorough job.

Millions of people old and young are on the move by road and rail, and yesterday we were told over the wireless that between the 18th and 23rd of September seven refugee trains had been attacked, and that out of one train alone a thousand dead bodies had been removed. And this is not war, it's India, who for 200 years has lived in peace and happiness under the rule of a handful of men, enjoying the freedom that has been thrust upon her by a parcel of fools. The India that you and I loved has been sacrificed on the altars of ambition and greed, and has gone for ever.

It was my intention to try and regain my health in Kenya, and then come back and try and better the lot of the people among whom I have spent so many happy years – the whole of my life, in fact – but that intention must now be abandoned, for it is too distressing to stand by and see my friends flying at each other's throats for no reason other than they wear different headgear.

CHAPTER TWENTY-ONE

AFRICA

On 30 November 1947 – a glorious morning – Jim and Maggie left home. As Maggie told a friend later, 'Our servants did not make our departure any easier, as they stood with tears trickling down their cheeks as we moved down the hill from the house we knew we should never see again.' Gurney House had been sold a few days earlier, but their home in Choti Haldwani remained on the market, and, as Jim had kept the date secret from the villagers, they did not know when he and his sister were leaving.

For the first stage of their journey they were accompanied by their faithful bearer Ram Singh, who had begged to be taken to Africa, or, if that was impossible, at least to stay with them as far as Bombay. In the event, they felt they had to leave him at Lucknow, where he stood crying on the station platform as the train pulled out. Their ship, the *Aronda*, docked at Mombasa on 15 December, and they went first to stay with the Ibbotsons at Karen, near Nairobi (Ibby had by then retired to Kenya). Soon they moved on to a guest-house built for them by Jim's nephew Ray Nestor at Kipkaren, near Eldoret, some 200 miles north-west of the capital. This proved a disappointment: the house was primitive, with no running water, and Maggie took against it at once, so Jim decided to move to another nephew, Tom Corbett, who was farming at Mweiga, closer to the capital.

There they had an elaborate plan for building a replica of Gurney House. They began, but never realised their dream. Again Maggie decided that the site was too remote, and the couple moved once more, eventually settling in the cottage known as Paxtu, in the garden of the Outspan Hotel in Nyeri, some sixty miles north of Nairobi. There at last they found a comfortable refuge, renting the little house built in 1938 for Lord Baden-Powell as part of a silver wedding gift from the Boy Scout movement, which he had founded. Set in a beautiful garden alive with birds, some 200 yards from the hotel, Paxtu had two bedrooms, each with a bathroom, and between them a large sitting-room with glass doors opening onto a verandah, which made a perfect spot for breakfast on fine mornings.

Soon Jim was appointed an honorary game warden, and a reserve police officer. But by then he was 72, and not as robust as he had been. A recent bout of pneumonia had exacerbated the damage caused by recurrent malaria, the war-time tick typhus and his incessant smoking, and he walked slowly, racked by an intermittent cough, exacerbated by the fact that Paxtu was 6,000 feet above sea level. 'I never thought the time would come when I would have to consider heights,' he told to a friend, 'but considering that I nearly died three times during the last war, I have very little to complain of.'

In any case, he remained active. Driving his Citroen, which he had bought on the second day after arrival, he travelled far afield to film animals and birds, and went with Maggie for holidays to Malindi, on the Indian Ocean. He also took a share in Safariland, an American company which promoted films of wild life, sending over large parties of camera-men and technicians. For a while he was enthusiastic about their activities, since they encouraged shooting with cameras rather than with rifles; but when they asked him to make animal calls for the films, he declined on the grounds that his throat was too old, and lost interest in the enterprise.

In writing to friends in other countries he was inclined to gloss over the reasons for his exile. Thus, in a letter to a contact in Madras, sent in August 1949, he wrote not about the political and social upheaval in India, but about his own health: 'I was fit and well until this last war came, when in training Indian troops in Jungle Warfare in the jungles of U.P., Central Provinces and Burma, I lost my health and came to Kenya to try and regain it, as the doctors said I could not be cured in India.' The extent to which his fitness had declined was borne out by E.A.Temple-Perkins, a hunter who claimed to be a conservationist but shot lions, elephants, crocodiles and buffalos with enthusiasm. One day, as he was leading a photographic safari, they got too close to a group of seven bull elephants, which took fright and stampeded. By then Jim was unable to move quickly, and when the elephants stormed across a road only forty or fifty yards from where he was sitting, he continued to film imperturbably, with his camera steadied on his knees.

On 1 May 1950 he wrote to 'My Dear Lord Hailey':

We are very comfortable and very happy in our little cottage, and all the people who have ever been in India, and who come to Nyeri, come and see us. On an average 150 a month have morning coffee with us on our verandah, so we are never dull, and in our spare time we write to friends and in addition I write books and Maggie corrects my spelling.

And yet, in spite of the comfort of their surroundings, and in spite of – or perhaps because of – this stream of visitors, Jim's thoughts were constantly turning to his former haunts. He had retained the legal rights over the land at Kaladhungi by paying annual rent to the Government, and still took a keen interest in developments there.

As he told Hailey,

The last rumour, that I had been killed, reached Kaladhungi, and when a few days later Bahadur received a letter from me, thanksgiving prayers were offered up in the mosques and temples, and the children were fed with sweets. The loyalty of the Indian, that you and I know, to the white man, brings tears to one's eyes.

I am now writing my last-ever book, Jungle Stories. I have a lot to put into this book, for it goes back to my catapult days, and the publishers want it to be long enough to run to two volumes, for they say they are fed up with the complaints they have received that my books are too short, and that I do not produce them as fast as they are wanted. They forget, as I have pleasure in pointing out to them, that I am not a professional writer of books, and that they would not have known of my existence if I had not set out to make a little money for St. Dunstan's.

We long to get back to India and our home in the Himalayas. When you read my next book, which I have called My India, you will have some idea of my affection for the people of India. My family has been in India for 200 years now; for the time being that connection has been broken. I listen to the Indian broadcast twice a day and am very distressed to learn of the unrest in the country, and of the attempts that have been made on the lives of those who are trying to hold India together.

In 1951 he went again to England – but flying, in those days tended to be unpredictable. 'The Hermes I travelled in developed engine trouble at Khartoum and again at Cairo,' he told Geoffrey Cumberlege. 'Instead of arriving in London at 11am on 7 May, I did not get there until 2am on 10 May.'

CHAPTER TWENTY-TWO

ROYAL ASSIGNMENT
1952

The high point of Jim's time in Africa came in February 1952, when Princess Elizabeth, elder daughter of King George VI of England, asked to meet him as she came out from England with her husband Prince Philip, Duke of Edinburgh, on the first stage of a grand Commonwealth tour. The rendezvous was at Tree Tops, a rickety, primitive, tree-house-cum-hotel perched on stilts in the branches of a giant ficus tree, some ten miles from Nyeri, built in 1932 by Eric Sherbrooke Walker. An eccentric early settler in Kenya, he had had a remarkably varied career: he had been captured as a pilot in the Royal Flying Corps during the First World War, and then had fought for the White Russians in the south of Russia, before becoming a bootlegger, smuggling whisky in America. Settling in Africa, he had founded the Outspan Hotel in 1928.

Jim had often been to Tree Tops, and regarded it as an enchanted spot. The tree-house was by no means luxurious: three bedrooms, a dining-room with a wood-burning stove, a chemical lavatory, a cubby hole for the resident guard, and an open balcony, reached by a thirty-foot ladder. The structure looked down on an oval-shaped clearing in the forest, 200 yards long and 100 wide, with a lake and a salt-lick in the middle. The salt-lick extended to within a few feet of the ficus tree, so that people on the viewing platform often found themselves perched right above the animals. Many species were wont to gather in the clearing, not least a herd of almost fifty elephants, which at the time of the royal visit were in a fractious mood, as three of the bulls were in musth, the season when sexual activity is at its highest.

Jim was nervous on two counts. One was that the terrorist movement known as Mau Mau was gathering strength. A state of emergency was not declared until October 1952, but the rebels were already established in the forests surrounding Tree Tops and had begun sallying forth to commit murder and arson. The other danger was that in approaching the hotel the royal visitors would have to walk the final six hundred yards along a path that ran through dense cover, and might suddenly find themselves in the middle of an elephant altercation.

On the afternoon before the visit Jim and Maggie absented themselves from a polo match near Nyeri, in which the Duke of Edinburgh was playing. They had been invited to watch, but instead drove out to monitor a ravine which ran through thick jungle and afforded an easy, covered approach to the playing field. Reverting to old habits, Jim parked his Citroen on a bridge over the gully and walked down into it to inspect stretches of sand for human footprints. He was relieved to find none, but he and his sister spent most of the afternoon in their car, on the lookout.

By 2pm next day he was on the platform of the hotel, poised for the arrival of the royal party, and growing increasingly anxious because the elephants were crowded together on the salt-lick, and a big bull was feuding with two youngsters which were trying to gain access to one of the cows. At the critical moment the master bull charged the other two, and all three hurtled into the forest, trumpeting with rage.

Minutes later Jim saw the royal party approaching, led by a man carrying a rifle. Close behind him came 'a small, trim figure', clearly Princess Elizabeth. Hastily slipping down the ladder to greet her, Jim was amazed by the way she walked fearlessly towards the elephants, which by then were crowded together at the end of the salt-lick, and by the composure with which she passed only ten yards from them as she made for the bottom of the ladder.

Up on the viewing platform, he quickly fell for his attractive young visitor, as she did for him. Throughout the afternoon and evening he admired the intense interest she showed in the animals, and the equanimity with which she watched one waterbuck kill another with a savage jab of its horns. When dinner-time came, she invited Jim to sit between herself and Prince Philip, with whom he talked about the Abominable Snowman. Then, after what he called 'a sumptuous repast' the guests went out again onto the platform to watch a herd of nine rhinos enjoying the salt-lick in the moonlight. Jim's key moment had come.

Taking my old British warm, which had served me well during the war years, I went down and made myself comfortable on the top step of the thirty-foot ladder. I had spent so many long nights on the branches of trees that a few hours on the step of a ladder were no hardship... The moon set, and in the heart of the forest the night was intensely dark. Visibility was nil, but that did not matter, for with the exception of a snake nothing could climb the ladder without my feeling the vibration.

Within a few inches of my face, and visible against the sky through a break in the foliage of the ficus tree, was hanging a manila rope which went over a pulley and was used for hauling up luggage and provisions from the ground to the room above. Presently, and without my having heard a sound, this rope was agitated. Something moving on soft feet had laid a hand on it, or had brushed against it. A few tense moments passed, but there was no vibration on the ladder – and then the rope was agitated again for the second time. Possibly one of the leopards whose pug marks I had seen on the path had come to the ladder and on finding it occupied had gone away. The ladder, though steep, would have offered no obstacle to an animal with the climbing ability of a leopard... In contrast with an Indian jungle the African forest is disappointingly silent at night, and, except for an occasional quarrel among the rhinos, all I heard throughout the night was the mournful call of a hyena, the bark of a bushbuck, and the cry of a tree hyrax.

After a few hours' sleep Princess Elizabeth started the next day (in Jim's view) 'with eyes sparkling and a face as fresh as a flower'. For once he reported what the party had for breakfast: scrambled eggs and bacon, toast, marmalade and coffee. Then, as she set out to walk back to the cars, the 'radiantly happy' Princess waved her hand and called out 'I will come again' – only to hear, an hour later, the shattering news that her father had died in the night, and that she had become Queen. The Commonwealth tour was abandoned, and the royal couple flew back to England.

In the Visitors' Book at Tree Tops Jim wrote:

For the first time in the history of the world a young girl climbed into a tree one day a Princess, and after having what she described as her most thrilling experience, she climbed down again from the tree the next day a Queen – God bless her.

At the time of the royal visit, Jim was still writing. *The Man-Eating Leopard of Rudraprayag* had come out in 1948, and now, in his third book, *My India*, published later in 1952, he recalled many incidents of his life in and around Kaladhungi, and characters with whom he had shared them. The short chapters were infused with his love of the hill people – and a typical anecdote concerned Sher Singh, whom he described as 'the happiest child in the village', and 'fearless as the animal whose name he bore'. The boy's special task was to look after his family's herd of cattle, which he took out to graze in the jungle, singing as he went; but he also acted as a beater on Jim's bird shoots, and whenever a bird was put up, he would yell, 'It's coming, Sahib! It's coming!' He was never happier than when, at the end of the day, he made for home with a peacock in full plumage proudly draped over his shoulders.

As the lad grew older, Jim planned to apprentice him to a friend who had a garage nearby, then to employ him as a driver, and as a caretaker, to look after the house and garden when he and Maggie were away at Nainital.

Sher Singh was speechless with delight when I told him of the plans I had made for him, plans which ensured his continued residence in the village, and within sight and calling distance of the home he had never left from the day of his birth.

Plans a-many we make in life, and I am not sure there is cause for regret when some go wrong. Sher Singh was to have started his apprenticeship when we returned to Kaladhungi in November. In October he contracted malignant malaria which led to pneumonia, and a few days before we arrived, he died. During his boyhood years he had sung through life happy as the day was long, and, had he lived, who can say that his life in a changing world would have been as happy, and as carefree, as those first few years?

Jim also wrote lyrically about his beloved forests and their denizens:

While walking through the Kumaon jungles in the half-light between day and night, or night and day, a bird will flit by on silent wings pouring out a stream of golden song which, once heard, will never be forgotten. The songster is the whistling thrush, also known as the whistling schoolboy, bidding the closing day good night or welcoming the new-born day. Morning and evening he pours out his song while in flight, and during the day he sits for hours in a leafy tree, whistling in a soft, sweet minor key a song that has no beginning and no end.

Next to greet the coming light is the racket-tailed drongo, and a minute later he is followed by the peafowl. No one may sleep after the peafowl has given his piercing call from the topmost branch of the giant samal tree, and now, as night dies and daylight comes, a thousand throbbing throats in nature's orchestra fill the jungle with an ever-growing volume of melody.

In a letter to Hailey he confessed, 'Writing is like a drug, and once you fall victim to it, you cannot give it up.' But as he recalled people and incidents from his past, the fate of one special weapon was much on his mind. 'My dear Cumberlege,' he wrote from Nyeri in October 1953,

One of our most valued possessions is the .275 rifle that Sir John Hewett, Governor of the United Provinces, presented to me when I shot the Champawat man-eater. This rifle has accounted for many man-eaters, and its exploits are mentioned a hundred times in my book. My shooting days are now over, and I am wondering if you could find a corner in Amen House [then the O.U.P.'s head office in London] where this faithful old friend, who has saved my life on many occasions, could pass his well-earned retirement in peace and comfort. He would not feel lonely at Amen House, for he would know that he was among friends.

Cumberlege agreed to take in the battered survivor, and for more than twenty years it remained tucked away in a cupboard in Amen House, unlicensed, to the slight unease of the firm's directors, who felt they should not be harbouring such a weapon . Their problem was eventually resolved in 1977, when the O.U.P.'s head office moved to Oxford, and the local constabulary confiscated the rifle and took it into custody.

In 1953 O.U.P. published Jim's fourth book, *Jungle Lore,* in which he returned lovingly to his childhood – his first experiments with weapons (catapult, pellet bow, bow-and-arrow), his progression to guns, his attempt with Percy Wyndham to catch a giant python. Among many other stories he told of the immense excitement of bagging his first leopard, and the extraordinary occasion when a tiger had ridden on the back of a stampeding buffalo, tearing great chunks out of it as it went.

During the early 1950s increasing Mau Mau activity had begun to make life in Kenya less comfortable. 'Nyeri, with all its distractions of bombing, shelling, machine-gun fire and troops dashing about from here to there, is not a suitable place in which to do any writing,' Jim complained to Cumberlege in a letter of November 1954.

We can still see well enough to do a little reading and writing. I have had to give up photography, but hope to be able to take it up again after my eyes have been operated on in London.

In spite of the difficulties, he completed his last book, a slender volume entitled *Tree Tops,* which told the story of the royal visit, and ended by saying that the hotel had 'gone for ever. All that now remains of the ficus tree and the hut... is a dead and blackened stump standing in a bed of ashes.' What he did not say was that the whole structure, which had attracted world-wide publicity as a result of the royal visit, had been burned to the ground by Mau Mau terrorists on 27 May 1954.

Early in 1955 he sent a typewritten version of the text, via Hailey, to the Queen, for her approval. On 21

June Edward Ford, then an Assistant Private Secretary at Buckingham Palace, wrote back:

> The Queen has read the typewritten copy of Jim Corbett's account of her visit to Tree Tops and was much interested by it. Her Majesty would have no objection to publication, but I am to ask if some of Her Majesty's own remarks, particularly about her father, could be put into oratio obliqua [reported speech].

Some very small changes were made. Among the marked passages was the line 'Oh, Daddy is like that. He never thinks of himself.' In the published version of the book this came out as 'she said that he was like that; he never thought of himself.' Jim considered dedicating the book to the Queen, but in the end refrained. Hailey contributed a substantial introduction, and the first printing of *Tree Tops* was 25,000 copies. In due course two beautifully bound copies found their way to the Queen at Buckingham Palace.

Jim still dreamed of a return to India, but his longing was never fulfilled. His health was failing – as was Maggie's – and neither had the energy for a long trek back. His eyes were deteriorating further, and Maggie's were even worse: she could no longer negotiate steps without help. They were both well aware that the past was another country, and that even if they made the effort to go, they might be disappointed to find how life in Kumaon had changed.

In April 1955 he wrote again to Cumberlege, about plans to fly to England at the end of May: 'When we have got our sight back, there are a hundred things we want to do, and I hope you will not think me a nuisance if you see me too often at Amen House'.

Within days of sending that letter, on 19 April he was stricken with severe chest pains and rushed into the Mount Kenya hospital in Nyeri; but he died of a heart attack that same evening, aged 77, and was buried in the small cemetery of St Peter's Anglican church, only a mile from Paxtu. In a letter to an old friend, Jagat Singh Negi, a month later, Maggie wrote:

Life seems to be very empty without the Sahib, but he told me I must be brave and cheerful and help to make the world a happier place to live in. His thoughts were always for other people, never for himself. He was busy with his writing up to the last.

Of the numerous obituaries and memorial notices which appeared in the world's press, none was more heart-felt than a letter sent anonymously to *The Times* in London. Its self-effacing author was John Glendevon (formerly Lord John Hope):

He was a great man. Not only was he a genius in the ways of the jungle, as millions who have read his books can tell, but he also had in him the depth and the gentleness that go with the best sort of greatness. With it all went, too, the quietest and softest of voices, which was a joy to listen to, whether it was telling you a story about a tiger in the past or instructing you how to deal with one in a few minutes. His sense of duty and unselfishness were paramount, alike to his country in war as to the villagers of his Kumaon hills in peace. How these adored him, and how they must miss him.

In a private letter Hope wrote:

My Dear Maggie,

I find it difficult to say all I want to say to you, my heart is full to overflowing. So many perfect memories of Jim's friendship, and of unforgettable days with him in his beloved jungles come welling up. In all the forty-three years I have lived so far, those days were the happiest I've spent, and their magic and beauty under Jim's guidance and companionship are as alive and vivid to me today as they were eighteen years ago.

Hailey wrote of 'the regard in which he came to be held by the people of Kumaon. As kindly and generous as he was fearless. He gave freely of himself, and asked nothing in return... In the olden days he would have been one of the small band of Europeans whose memory has been worshipped by Indians as that of men who were in some measures also gods.'

Maggie outlived her brother by eight years, occupying the same room in Paxtu, and remaining as quiet, self-effacing and generous as ever. In 1957 she sent a large amount of money to Jagat Singh – 1,000 rupees for himself, and 50 for each of the 40 tenants at Choti Haldwani. Five hundred rupees went to the Hindu temple and to the Moslem mosque, and 1,000 each to the temples at Almora and Rudraprayag. A year later she gave the land on which Arundel had stood for the site of a new high school, which was completed and named after Jim in 1961.

In 1957 she dictated thirteen pages of notes about Jim to a friend, Ruby Beyts, the wife of a brigadier in the Indian Army, with instructions to write them up after her death. These included many valuable reminiscences. She died at Nyeri on Boxing Day 1963, aged eighty-nine; her body was cremated, and her ashes were interred in Jim's grave – a perfect end to their lifelong partnership.

CHAPTER TWENTY-THREE

THE LEGACY

His books continued to sell by the thousand, especially in India, and five years after his death the Indian Government accorded him the signal honour of re-naming the Hailey National Park after him, 'in memory of one who had dedicated his life to the service of the simple hill folk of Kumaon'. Already once re-named the Ramganga National Park, on 2 July 1957, by a U.P. Government notification, it became the Corbett National Park – and it remains, to this day, his most remarkable memorial. In 1974 the park lost forty-six square kilometres of land when its fast-flowing river was dammed at Kalagarh to form a large lake, to generate electricity and conserve water for agriculture below; but the sanctuary was later extended to a total area of 529 square kilometres.

From small beginnings, in which Jim had a hand, the campaign to preserve India's tigers has gradually gathered strength. In 1970 all forms of hunting were banned. The biggest single step forward was the launch, in April 1973, of Project Tiger, the national attempt to save the species, championed by the Prime Minister, Indira Gandhi, and partly financed by the World Wildlife Fund. At that date it was thought that only 1,200 tigers remained in the whole of India, and it seemed that the species was heading for extinction. But active and increasingly skilful management gradually halted the decline and raised the number to 1,411 in 2006, to 2,226 in 2014, and to 2,967 in 2018-19. In that year the population of Corbett was reckoned at 250.

Drastic measures were needed to give tigers more living-space; more and more areas were declared reserves, until Project Tiger had control of 73,000 square kilometres. Whole villages were removed from forest areas, and the inhabitants were settled elsewhere. Thenceforth core areas in the centre of each park were kept free of human activities. Wood-collecting and the grazing of animals were banned. Another vital element has been the war on poachers bent on fuelling the incessant demands from China and elsewhere for tiger skins, bones, claws and skulls, all misguidedly thought to be of medical value. Better training of wildlife guards, better radios and other improved equipment such as surveillance cameras and 4 x 4 vehicles, have made the poachers' lives more difficult.

If Jim were alive today, he would be astonished, and probably dismayed, by the number of tourists visiting the park named after him – at least 100,000 a year in 2021. But he would also be thrilled by scale and ingenuity of the attempts to encourage its unique wildlife, manifest in the work of The Corbett Foundation (TCF, for short), established in 1994 by Dilip Khatau, a leading industrialist and businessman with a passion for conservation, as a tribute to the legendary hunter/conservationist. The foundation is now active not only in Corbett, but also in several other reserves, and it has fostered many imaginative projects, among them the campaign to save the Great Indian Bustard from extinction.

One major aim of TCF is to mitigate the conflict between wildlife and humans. If a tiger kills a cow, local people, fuelled by deep-seated resentment towards the Forest Department, often resort to revenge killing, putting poison or a home-made bomb in the remains of the carcass. To alleviate this animosity, in 1995 TCF introduced a Cattle Compensation Scheme, whereby anyone who loses an animal receives financial or medical help – an innovation that has substantially reduced antagonism towards the park. Another successful initiative has been the scheme to deter crop-raiders like *sambar, chital* and wild boar, by planting areas of camomile, an aromatic plant unpalatable to herbivores. In the first experiment a camera trap watched a herd of deer approach the trial area, intent on grazing, but then turn away, leaving the crop untouched.

Other important innovations include the introduction of primary health care through mobile clinics, the provision of veterinary care, the digging of wells, the installation of energy-efficient stoves and solar lighting in villages, as well as instruction in kitchen gardening, poultry-keeping and carpentry, and the provision of rainwear and winter jackets for forest staff.

Gurney House, Jim's home in Nainital, is now a museum dedicated to his memory, as his home in Kaladhungi. But it is in his books that his reputation mainly lives on. By 1980 world-wide sales had reached two million copies, and today they have gone far beyond that. An omnibus edition, containing his first book and two later ones, published by the O.U.P. in India, in 1991, reached its 43rd impression by 2017, and a collection of other writings was in its 35th impression. In Canada, in 1994, the Jim Corbett Foundation was established in Edmonton, Alberta, by the author and enthusiast Jerry Jaleel, who has travelled widely on his subject's trail in India and Africa, and has restored Jim's grave in Nyeri - all with the aim of keeping his memory alive for future generations. His book *Under the Shadow of Man Eaters,* containing a wealth of information about its hero, was first published in 1979 and is still in print. A Facebook page, the

Jim Corbett Group, was started in 2008 and now has 4,900 members world-wide. Dedicated enthusiasts revisit the scenes of Jim's encounters with killer cats, determined to find the exact spot on which he ended each of his most spectacular hunts. American academics write learned analyses of Jim's mentality.

One potent survivor is the Rigby Mauser .275 rifle, presented to him in 1907 as a reward for killing the Champawat man-eater, and used frequently by him thereafter. In April 2016 Marc Newton, who had recently resuscitated the firm John Rigby in London and become its Managing Director, took the famous weapon on a tour of Kumaon, where its appearance evoked immense enthusiasm and excitement. As he remarked afterwards, getting an unlicenced rifle into India was no easy task, but once bureaucratic obstacles had been overcome, 'it was almost as if we had brought the Holy Grail – people were so thrilled to see the gun that had released their families from terror.' One high point of the tour came at Chota Haldwani, where Trilok Singh Negi, a silk farmer, brought out an ancient muzzle-loader which Jim had given his father a century ago. Another key stop was Rudraprayag, where a head-and-shoulders bust of Jim, and a notice commemorating his feat, are mounted on the trunk of the mango tree from which he despatched the killer leopard. In a ceremony at the Ramnagar headquarters of the Corbett National Park, Rigby's presented the park with a brand-new 4 x 4 pick-up, ideal for the hounding of poachers.

So the flame of Jim's renown burns on, as much in his home territory as in the minds of the several million readers whom his books have captivated.

SOURCES

There is an unclassified collection of documents relating to Jim Corbett in the archive of the Oxford University Press in Great Clarendon Street., Oxford. I am most grateful to Martin Maw, the O.U.P.'s Archivist, for making these easily available.

I should like to thank Dilip Khatau for his hospitality, and for much information about The Corbett Foundation, which he inaugurated.

I am much indebted to Jerry A. Jaleel, for his enthusiasm, for his help in correspondence, and for permission to quote from his book *Under the Shadow of Maneaters*.

Otherwise, I have drawn on published accounts, and on visits to Uttarakhand.

Books consulted:

Baylis, Audrey, *And then Garhwal*. British Association for Cemeteries in South Africa, Putney, London, 1981

Booth, Martin, *Carpet Sahib*. Constable & Co., 1986.

Brayne, F.L., *The Remaking of Village India*. H. Milford, Oxford University Press, 1929

Champion, F.W., *The Jungle in Sunlight and Shadow*. Chatto & Windus, 1933

Corbett, Jim, *Man-Eaters of Kumaon*. Oxford University Press, New York & Bombay, 1946

Corbett, Jim, *The Man-Eating Leopard of Rudraprayag*. Oxford University Press, 1948

Corbett, Jim, *My India*. Oxford University Press, 1952

Corbett, Jim, *Jungle Lore*. Oxford University Press, 1955

Ghadvi, Priyvrat *et al*, *Behind Jim Corbett's Stories*. Logos, 2016

Glendevon, John, *The Viceroy at Bay*. Collins, 1971

Kala, D.C., *Jim Corbett of Kumaon*.
Penguin Books India, 2009

Jaleel, Jerry A., *Under the Shadow of Man Eaters*. The Jim
Corbett Foundation, Edmonton, Alberta, Canada, 1997.

Johnsingh, A.J.T., On Jim Corbett's Trail. Natraj Publishers,
New Delhi, 2018

Moon, Penderel (Editor), *Wavell: the Viceroy's Journal*.
Oxford University Press, 1973

Temple-Perkins, E.A., *Kingdom of the Elephant*.
Andrew Melrose, 1955

You might also enjoy from Merlin Unwin Books

Man-Eaters of Kumaon Jim Corbett

Ascension *The Story of an Atlantic Island* Duff Hart-Davis

The Yellow Earl *Almost an Emperor, not Quite a Gentleman*
Douglas Sutherland

Ovington's Bank Stanley Weyman

Right Royal John Masefield with Cecil Aldin illustrations

Full details of these and all our countryside books

www.merlinunwin.co.uk